ATLANTIS COMPUTATIONAL INTELLIGENCE SYSTEMS
VOLUME 4

SERIES EDITOR: DA RUAN

Atlantis Computational Intelligence Systems

Series Editor:

Da Ruan, Belgian Nuclear Research Centre (SCK • CEN)
Mol & Ghent University, Gent, Belgium

(ISSN: 1875-7650)

Aims and scope of the series

The series 'Atlantis Computational Intelligence Systems' aims at covering state-of-the-art research and development in all fields where computational intelligence is investigated and applied. The series seeks to publish monographs and edited volumes on foundations and new developments in the field of computational intelligence, including fundamental and applied research as well as work describing new, emerging technologies originating from computational intelligence research. Applied CI research may range from CI applications in the industry to research projects in the life sciences, including research in biology, physics, chemistry and the neurosciences.

All books in this series are co-published with Springer.

For more information on this series and our other book series, please visit our website at:

www.atlantis-press.com/publications/books

ATLANTIS
PRESS

AMSTERDAM – PARIS

© **ATLANTIS PRESS**

Trust Networks for Recommender Systems

Patricia Victor, Chris Cornelis, Martine De Cock

Ghent University,

Dept. of Applied Mathematics and Computer Science (WE02),

Krijgslaan 281 (S9),

9000 Gent, Belgium

ATLANTIS
PRESS

AMSTERDAM – PARIS

Atlantis Press
8, square des Bouleaux
75019 Paris, France

For information on all Atlantis Press publications, visit our website at:

www.atlantis-press.com

Atlantis Computational Intelligence Systems

Volume 1: Linguistic Values Based Intelligent Information Processing: Theory, Methods, and Applications – Zheng Pei, Da Ruan, Jun Liu, Yang Xu
Volume 2: Computational Intelligence in Complex Decision Systems – Da Ruan (Editor)
Volume 3: Intelligence for Nonlinear Dynamics and Synchronisation – K. Kyamakya, A. Bouchachia, J.C. Chedjou

ISBN 978-94-91216-07-7
ISBN 978-94-91216-08-4 (eBook)
ISSN: 1875-7650

Foreword

Recommendation Systems are gaining tremendous prominence in the digital society, and are fast becoming the bastions of electronic commerce. "Will I like this book?", "Is this a movie I can see with my kids?', 'Which hotel will suit me the best?": we increasingly rely on the social aspects of the world wide web (WWW) to help us navigate through such questions in our everyday life. We are quick to judge, and even quicker to just imitate our friends and do what they did. The magic potion that casts a spell on us to imitate and even at times make irrational decisions is trust. Trust enhanced recommender systems are designed to help us to form an opinion on matters that are not entirely known to us, or even not known at all.

The social web allows people to express their views to other users of the system. We call the resulting network a social network. There are social networks in which the users can explicitly express their opinion as trust and distrust statements. We refer to these kinds of social networks as trust networks.

The particular focus of this book, infusion of the theory of how online trust networks can be modeled and the utility of these models to enhance the quality of recommendations generated in the online recommendation systems arena is not only groundbreaking and innovative; it is likely to be the central pivot for the next generation of research in social network analysis. Think of any system where humans need subjective judgments from their peers and seers. As you start to read the book, it will be quickly evident that issues explored in this book are the backbone of any such system. Some of these broad issues are: who you know, who you don't know, who you trust, why you trust them, how does this trust translate, aggregate, and propagate; and how to efficiently and correctly identify key trust figures to enhance the quality of generated recommendations.

As the book notes in its introduction, the year was early 2006, the stage was set with the majority of the developed world focusing on the tremendous excitement that online communication and collaboration tools on the internet had started to foster. At the same time, the developing world was catching up very fast with the number of people getting access to communication technologies through cell-phones and low-cost internet access points. Electronic commerce was outpacing the brick-and-mortar business in every retail sector and sites such as Epinions.com and Amazon.com were becoming the e-bazaars of the post 9/11 tumulus world where it was safer and easier to shop from home than to face the uncertainty of the physical world. The internet was enabling those that never had a voice to express their opinions freely and without the need for filters enforced by traditional media. YouTube and MySpace were redefining individual reputations and authority in real-life more than someone's social standing in the physical world. The key question on everyone's mind then was: can this online world of inter-human communication be trusted? Can trust be used to infuse confidence in getting the most accurate, relevant and unbiased information about commodities (amazon, ebay), news (twitter), relationships (facebook), etc. Being there is only half the work. Keeping your eyes open to address these needs is the other half. The authors of this book were not only there, they also had their eyes open to see the need for addressing these issues about online trust computation to facilitate online commerce.

Considering the extraordinary ability of this book to make you think, reflect, and to likely influence future research directions in enhancing our understanding of how online social networks behave, I wish you, the reader, a most wondrous journey through the folds of Trust Networks for Recommender Systems. Welcome aboard!

Prof. Ankur M. Teredesai, Ph.D.

Institute of Technology

University of Washington, Tacoma,

USA

Web 2.0 is a massive social experiment, and like any experiment worth trying, it could fail. There's no road map for how an organism that's not a bacterium lives and works together on this planet in numbers of excess of 6 billion. But 2006 gave us some ideas. This is an opportunity to build a new kind of international understanding, not politician to politician, great man to great man, but citizen to citizen, person to person.

Cover story TIME Magazine Dec 25th, 2006. Lev Grossman

Preface

'Person of the Year' is an annual issue of the American news magazine Time, featuring someone or something that "has done the most to influence the events of the year" [135]. The list of the last decade contains famous names such as Barack Obama, Vladimir Putin, Bono, and Bill Gates, just to name a few. However, in 2006, the honor went to 'You' [46]. Yes, indeed. You. If you did not invent a life-saving vaccine, or won the lottery that year and let everyone share in your gains, you are probably wondering what it is exactly that you did to deserve this...

The answer to this question lies with the 'Web 2.0', the umbrella term used most often to refer to the current generation of social web applications. The driving forces behind these applications are collaboration, interaction and information sharing; the key factor to their success being the users themselves, in other words: you and me. Without our enthusiasm and curiosity, the social networking site Facebook[1] would not be so popular; without our movie ratings, the e-commerce giant Amazon.com[1] or the movie rental system Netflix[1] would not be able to recommend us a movie that we are very likely to enjoy; without our hotel reviews, only a few would think of consulting the travel guide TripAdvisor[1] for their next holiday, and so on. The following quotation about the Web 2.0 sums it up nicely:

> It's a story about community and collaboration on a scale never seen before. It's about the cosmic compendium of knowledge Wikipedia and the million-channel people's network YouTube and the online metropolis MySpace. It's about the many wresting power from the few and helping one another for nothing and how that will not only change the world, but also change the way the world changes.

---

[1]See www.facebook.com, www.amazon.com, www.netflix.com, www.tripadvisor.com

The source of the quote is the cover article for the Time issue of December 2006. The authors decided that we had a great influence on that year's events. You and me. Because we "control the Information Age": thanks to our input, millions of users can freely look up information on the online encyclopedia Wikipedia[2], MySpace[2] can make people wonder about other lives, YouTube[2] becomes a way for common people to publish and distribute content online, etc.

But these are only a few examples. In fact, while looking up the Time article in preparation for this book, we came across several of the Web 2.0's success stories: typing '2006 time magazine person of the year' yielded over 18 million results on Google; the fourth and fifth hit were two influential blogs (online journals that are frequently updated) and the second one was a Wikipedia page, the textbook example of a wiki (a website where users can easily add or change content). The first hit was the magazine's web page. On that page you could indicate if you wanted to share the article with your friends (on Facebook), if you wanted to 'retweet' it (via the micro-blogging service Twitter[3]) or 'digg' the article (an application[3] to discover and share content on the web). Clearly, the Web 2.0 experiment has not failed so far. On the contrary, four years after the publication of the Time article, social web applications are alive and very kicking.

Of course, not everything stemming from the Web 2.0 wave is wonderful and useful, and consequently the 2006 nomination caused some controversy. We, too, are skeptical about all these hip and shiny applications/toys/gadgets, but we are also convinced that it has brought us a lot of social applications that we can truly benefit from. In this book, we will focus on one such set of applications, namely social recommender systems. In particular, we will show how trust networks, a specific type of social networks, can enhance the recommendation experience.

This book originated from the doctoral thesis of the first author, which was successfully defended in June 2010. Encouraged by the enthusiastic reports of the committee members, we have decided to publish this book, and make the obtained results available to a larger audience. We are grateful to Etienne Kerre, Paulo Pinheiro da Silva, and Steven Schockaert for their comments and suggestions which have clearly influenced the results in this work. We also would like to thank the external members of the reading committee, Bart D'Hoedt, Enrique Herrera-Viedma and Ankur Teredesai, for their useful suggestions on the first version of the thesis, and Da Ruan for his help with the publication of this book. Thanks also

---

[2] See wikipedia.org, www.myspace.com, www.youtube.com
[3] See twitter.com and digg.com

to Epinions.com and CouchSurfing.org for making their social network data available. Finally, we would like to thank the Institute for the Promotion of Innovation through Science and Technology in Flanders (IWT-Vlaanderen) for the financial support.

Contents

*It's not what you know but who you
know that makes the difference.*

Anonymous

Chapter 1

Introduction

Although the saying above is an old one, it is surprisingly applicable to the Information Age we are living in now. We are flooded with social networking sites on which we can manage our friends, relatives, or business relations. Some of them are merely used to keep track of our acquaintances, but others can be quite convenient for other purposes too, think e.g. of the business oriented social networking tool LinkedIn or the image hosting website and online community Flickr. Many other useful applications will follow in the next sections.

As will become clear throughout this book, the proverb at the top of this page is especially true for the application that we will focus on. Trust-enhanced recommender systems are designed to help us to form an opinion on matters that are not entirely known to us, or even not at all: 'will I like this book?', 'is this a movie that I can see with my kids?', 'which hotel will suit me the best?', ... Trust-based recommender systems can provide us with personalized answers (or 'recommendations') because they use information that is coming from a social network consisting of people we (may) trust.

1.1 Trust Networks

Social web applications often allow people to express their view on other users of the system. We call the resulting network a *social network*. The relations and/or evaluations between the users come in many flavors: users can add their connections as 'friends' in Facebook, bookmark 'interesting people' in Amazon.com, allow 'followers' in Twitter and 'fans' in Yahoo!Answers[1] (which, as the name suggests, gives users the opportunity to ask and answer questions), etc. Apart from these positive labels, in a large group of users, each with their own intentions, tastes and opinions, it is only natural that also negative evaluation

---

[1]See answers.yahoo.com

1

concepts are needed. For example, the technology news web site Slashdot[2] lets its users tag each other as 'friends', 'fans', 'foes' or 'freaks', and the political forum Essembly[2] as 'friends', 'allies' or 'nemeses'. A lot of the social web applications rely heavily on the relations between their users, and frequently mine the underlying social network to offer new services. Users of Last.fm[2], e.g., are able to listen to personalized radio stations which are based on the music tastes of their friends. As another example, users of the social bookmarking system Delicious[2] can discover the web pages that their friends like.

In this book, we focus on one type of social networks, namely social networks in which the users explicitly express their opinion as trust and distrust statements. We refer to this kind of social networks as *trust networks*. A popular example is the trust network of the consumer review site Epinions.com[3], a large American e-commerce site where users can write reviews about consumer products and assign a rating to the products and the reviews. The main novelty of Epinions, however, is that users can also evaluate other users, by adding them to their personal web of trust or block list (indicating distrust), based on their quality as a reviewer. Another interesting application is CouchSurfing[3], a large world-wide hospitality exchange network. Users can create a profile and indicate if they are offering sleeping accomodation; other users looking for a couch can then browse through the profiles and try to determine which users are trustworthy enough to be their host (and vice versa). To this aim, CouchSurfing provides several evaluation possibilities, such as leaving references or creating friendship relations. After a couch experience, users can also indicate how much they trust or distrust each other, which constitutes a large trust network among the CouchSurfers.

Forming your own opinion on the users might have been easy when the network was still rather small, but nowadays CouchSurfing contains over one million users, making it increasingly difficult to find the hosts/guests that you would get along with well, let alone the ones that are trustworthy. In the same respect, in Epinions, users may find it overwhelming to form an opinion on a particular reviewer: if there are –very often conflicting– opinions of hundreds of users available, how do you find the users that reflect your tastes the most?

As many trust networks are large, it is very unlikely that all users know each other directly. In other words, the network is unlikely to be fully connected. This means that, if a user a wants to form a trust opinion about an unknown user x, a has to inquire about x with one of its own trust relations, say b, who in turn might consult a trust connection, etc., until

---

[2] See `slashdot.org`, `www.essembly.com`, `www.last.fm`, `delicious.com`
[3] See `www.epinions.com` and `www.couchsurfing.org`

a user connected to x is reached. The process of predicting the trust score along the thus constructed path from a to x is called trust propagation. Since it often happens that a has not one, but several trust connections that it can consult for an opinion on x, we also require a mechanism for combining several trust scores originating from different sources. This process is called trust aggregation. Propagation and aggregation are the two key building blocks of *trust metrics*, a set of techniques which aim to estimate the trust between two unknown users in the network. Note that the word metric has a different meaning here than the traditional mathematical notion of metric as distance measure in a metric space.

So far, we have not mentioned context and/or goal, although this is an important factor in computing trust estimations and taking decisions based on them: for example, your neighbor might be very good at fixing bicycles, so naturally you would trust him with your flat tire, but that does not imply that you would trust him to baby-sit your six months old daughter. A lot of trust frameworks take into account the trust context, especially when they are general models to be used in several kinds of applications/networks, see e.g. [1, 61]. In this book, we omit the context factor for the sake of simplicity (chapters 2-4) and because we focus on recommendation systems for one type of items only; in other words, we work on recommendations and trust statements that belong to the same domain/context (chapters 6-7).

Omitting the context factor does not harm generality: while an agent in a simplified trust model without context can choose between one or more trust statement types (e.g. trust and distrust in a binary application such as Epinions, or 6 gradual trust levels in CouchSurfing), in a trust application that takes into account context, each one of these possible statements must be accompanied by a context statement. In this respect, we can see a trust connection between two agents as a couple (trust statement,context statement). The operators of chapters 3 and 4 can then easily be applied in context-aware trust applications as well, since propagation and aggregation can only be performed sensibly on trust estimations within the same context.

Obviously, context and goal are also present when defining trust. For example, Gambetta defines trust as a subjective probability that an agent will perform a particular action which affects his own actions [31], and Jøsang *et al.* as the extent to which one is willing to depend on somebody in a given situation [63]. As trust is used in a wide range of application domains, plenty of trust definitions exist. Many of them focus on a different aspect of trust, or stem from a different background (e.g. social sciences versus agent theory): Mui *et al.* see trust as a subjective expectation about an agent's future behavior based on the history of encounters between the agents [99], while Castelfranchi and Falcone augment Gambetta's definition with a competence dimension [17]. These examples illustrate that there is no consensus on how to define trust. In this book, in which we focus on trust that is explicitly given by the users of a recommender application domain, we adopt the general definition of Jøsang *et al.* We will define trust more precisely when needed to grasp the rationale behind trust operators and their properties.

1.2   Recommender Systems

In the previous pages, we mentioned a lot of Web 2.0 applications: Facebook, MySpace, Twitter, Last.fm, blogs, wikis,... For the remainder of this work, however, we will focus on one specific type of applications, namely *social recommender systems*. Social recommender systems use information about their user's profiles and/or relationships to suggest items that might be of interest to them [121]. Such suggestions (recommendations) can come in many forms: top 10 lists, promotions, 'people who liked movie x also liked movie y', '80% of all people found the following review helpful', etc. And it is certainly not all about movies, cds or books only; also other fields might benefit from a good recommendation system; think for example of research papers, travel packages, courses, and so on.

Good and accurate recommender applications that guide users through the vast amounts of online information are gaining tremendous importance, as the wealth of information makes it increasingly difficult to find exactly what you want or need; all the more because every person has his own preferences. Suppose that you want to go to the movies, but have no idea what to choose: you can surely find a lot of opinions and reviews online, but how do you know which ones are the closest to your tastes and likes? This is where personalized recommendation systems come into play.

From an e-commerce perspective too, the value of a good recommender system cannot be underestimated: Cinematch, the recommender of the American online movie rental system Netflix[4], delivers two third of Netflix's rented movies, Google News[4] recommendations generate 38% click-throughs, and Amazon.com claims that 35% of their sales results from recommendations [72]. Their importance is even more illustrated by the Netflix prize competition, which offered a $ 1 000 000 reward for any recommendation algorithm that is 10%

---

[4]See www.netflix.com and news.google.com

more accurate than their own Cinematch[5].

Most widely used recommendation systems are either content-based or collaborative filtering methods. Content-based systems tend to have their recommendation scope limited to the immediate neighborhood of a user's past purchase or rating record. For instance, if you have highly rated a romantic movie with Keanu Reeves, your next recommendation might be a romantic movie or a movie featuring Keanu. The system will continue to recommend related items only, and not explore your other interests. In this sense, recommender systems can be improved significantly by (additionally) using collaborative filtering, which typically identifies users whose tastes are similar to yours (we call them 'neighbors') and recommends items that they have liked. This technique allows for more serendipitous recommendations: you might receive recommendations for movies in a genre that you are not familiar with but that are appreciated by your neighbors, so that there is a good chance that you will like them too.

The advanced recommendation techniques that we will discuss in this book adhere to the collaborative filtering paradigm, in the sense that a recommendation for an item is based on ratings by other users for that item, rather than on an analysis of the item's content. In this sense, as with collaborative filtering systems, they also belong to the class of social recommender systems. More specifically, we will focus on one present-day set of social recommenders, namely *trust-enhanced recommender systems*. The social dimension reaches a whole new level, since trust-enhanced recommenders mine the trust network among their users to offer their services. Such systems incorporate a trust network in which the users are connected by scores indicating how much they trust and/or distrust each other, and use that knowledge to generate recommendations: users can receive recommendations for items rated highly by people in their web of trust (WOT), or even by people who are trusted by these WOT members (through trust propagation and aggregation) etc., yielding more, more accurate, and more personalized recommendations.

1.3   Overview

Trust metrics and recommendation technologies constitute the two pillars of trust-enhanced recommender systems. Trust metrics are covered in detail in chapters 2-4, while chapter 5 deals with the basics of recommender systems. In chapters 6-7 we focus on the intersection of the two fields, viz. trust-enhanced recommender systems.

---

[5]See http://www.netflixprize.com

In chapter 2 we give an overview of existing trust and distrust models and explain their shortcomings. Current models are either not capable of properly handling inconsistency, or cannot differentiate unknown agents from malicious agents. These shortcomings can possibly have a large effect on the (ranking) of trust estimations, recommendations, etc. Therefore, to meet the needs for a framework that can help agents to make better informed (trust) opinions, we propose a new bilattice-based model that preserves valuable provenance information including partial trust, partial distrust, ignorance and inconsistency.

The following two chapters focus on the mechanisms that are needed to predict trust and distrust values in this framework. Chapter 3 covers the propagation problem. Whereas there is a general consensus on how trust can be propagated, the picture gets much more complicated when also distrust is involved. We describe the state of the art of trust propagation, and embark upon the problem of distrust propagation, a research area that has not received much attention so far. We discuss possible distrust propagation strategies, propose and examine a set of propagation operators that exhibit the desired behavior, and illustrate them by investigating propagation patterns in real-world data sets from Epinions and CouchSurfing.

Chapter 4 concentrates on aggregation techniques for trust and distrust values. This field, too, is still in its very infancy. To help in reaching a better understanding of the problem, we propose a set of properties that aggregation operators should fulfill in a (dis)trust context. We demonstrate that the classical aggregation operators for bilattice elements are not always suitable, and therefore propose new families of aggregation operators for trust-enhanced applications. We examine their behavior and show their applicability on data sets from CouchSurfing and Epinions.

The second part of the book deals with the application of trust metrics and their operators in the field of recommender systems. In chapter 5 we cover the recommender basics which are vital for a good understanding of the subsequent chapters. We explain the collaborative filtering mechanism and discuss common evaluation methods and measures (related to coverage and accuracy). We examine the problems of classical recommendation systems — transparency, sparsity, malicious users, cold start users, controversial items — and propose a new detection measure for the latter, which is more suited for evaluation of the corresponding shortcoming.

In chapter 6, we focus on trust- and distrust-enhanced recommendation systems, and show how they can alleviate the problems pointed out in the previous chapter. We provide a comparative coverage and accuracy analysis of the performance of collaborative filtering and trust-enhanced algorithms for controversial and random items, conducted on data sets from Epinions, and introduce a new algorithm that maximizes the synergy between collaborative filtering and its trust-based variants. Furthermore, to the best of our knowledge, we also provide the first attempt to experimentally evaluate the potential of utilizing distrust in the recommendation process; we investigate the use of distrust as debugger, filter and as an indication to reverse deviations, and its role in the aggregation process for trust-enhanced recommendations.

In chapter 7, we give special attention to the user cold start problem, one of the main difficulties faced by collaborative filtering and trust-enhanced recommender systems. The users of such systems are highly encouraged to connect to other users to expand the trust network, but choosing whom to connect to is often a difficult task. Given the impact this choice has on the delivered recommendations, it is critical to guide newcomers through this early stage connection process. To this aim, we identify several classes of key figures in a trust network, and introduce measures to evaluate the influence of these users on the coverage and accuracy of the recommendation algorithm. Experiments on a dataset from Epinions support the claim that generated recommendations for new users are more beneficial if they connect to an identified key figure compared to a random user; it is indeed who you know that makes the difference.

Chapter 2

Trust Models

Multi-agent systems consist of a large number of intelligent, interactive and (partially) autonomous agents that must cooperate to complete a certain task, often too difficult to solve for an individual agent. Such systems are used in a wide range of applications, ranging from mobile environments [73], over the creation of crowd-related effects for movies[1], to online trading [57]. Multi-agent systems can often benefit from a trust system, especially when the circumstances do not allow for perfect information about the interaction partners' behavior and intentions [117]. They may for example incorporate a trust network to monitor and control the behavior of the agents that participate in a process, think e.g. of an online market place such as eBay. Another nice illustration can be found in [66], in which a trust network is used to alleviate the problem of corrupt sources in peer-to-peer file-sharing networks by keeping track of the peers' trustworthiness. With the advent of the Semantic Web [12], even more applications and systems will need solid trust mechanisms. The Semantic Web is an extension of the current web where content is annotated (see RDF[2] and OWL[3]) such that machines and computers are able to understand its meaning and reason with it. Hence, since more and more intelligent agents will take over human tasks in the future, they also require an automated way of inferring trust in each other, see for instance [123].

Nowadays, effective models already play an important role in many Web 2.0 applications. Question answering systems can compute trust indications along with the answers based on how much trust the user puts into certain sources [153], recommender systems can produce suggestions more tailored to the users' tastes (chap-

---

[1] Massive Software, see www.massivesoftware.com
[2] Resource Description Framework, see www.w3.org/TR/rdf-primer
[3] Web Ontology Language, see www.w3.org/TR/owl-features

ter 6), consumer review sites can show personalized orderings of reviews based on which people the user trusts (think of Epinions), etc.

In the first part of this book (chapters 2-4) we will focus on the most general use of trust models; trust in social networks will be discussed in detail in the second part. Therefore, in the remainder of this chapter, we will use the term 'agent' to refer to the people/machines that participate in a certain process, and only use the term 'user' in the specific context of social network applications.

A lot of agent and social applications (will) use, in one way or another, a web of trust that allows agents to express trust in other agents. Trust recommendations derived from these networks are supposed to help them to develop their own opinions about how much they may trust other agents and sources. However, despite recent developments in the area, most of the trust models and metrics proposed so far tend to lose potentially important trust-related knowledge.

In the following sections, we give an overview of existing trust models (Sec. 2.1) and explain their shortcomings with regard to preserving trust provenance information (Sec. 2.2). These are serious drawbacks in large networks where many users are unknown to each other and might provide contradictory information. Therefore, to meet the needs for a framework that can help agents to make better informed (trust) decisions, we propose a new trust model in which trust values are derived from a bilattice that preserves valuable trust provenance information including partial trust, partial distrust, ignorance and inconsistency (Sec. 2.3 and 2.4).

2.1 Classification of Trust Models

Trust and trust models have been used in many fields of computer science, and also in a wide range of applications; a nice overview can be found in [7] in which Artz and Gil classify trust research in four major areas: models that use policies to establish trust (enforcing access policies, managing credentials, etc.), general trust models such as [26] and [158], models for trust in information sources such as [153], and reputation-based trust models. The first category deals with 'hard' trust, which involves identity verification and authorization. However, it is not because an agent is who he claims to be, that everyone automatically should trust his actions, statements or intentions; some agents might trust a particular agent while others do not. In this book, we will not handle the 'security side' of trust, but focus on 'soft', interpersonal trust; trust that can be computed among two individuals in a network. In particular, we will mainly discuss trust models and metrics that belong to Artz and Gil's last category. This category includes, among others, research that uses the history of an agent's actions or behavior (see e.g. [66, 104]), and work that computes trust over social networks, such as [50, 86]. The trust-enhanced recommender techniques that we will describe in Chap. 6 all belong to this class.

Trust models come in many flavors and can be classified in several ways. We focus on two such classifications, namely probabilistic versus gradual approaches, and representations of trust versus representations of both trust and distrust. Table 2.1 shows some representative references for each class.

A *probabilistic* approach deals with a single trust value in a black or white fashion — an agent or source can either be trusted or not — and computes a probability that the agent can be trusted. In such a setting, a higher suggested trust value corresponds to a higher probability that an agent can be trusted. Examples can, among others, be found in [153] in which Zaihrayeu *et al.* present an extension of an inference infrastructure that takes into account the trust between users and between users and provenance elements in the system, in [123] where the focus is on computing trust for applications containing semantic information such as a bibliography server, or in contributions like [78] in which a trust system is designed to make community blogs more attack-resistant.

Trust is also often based on the number of positive and negative transactions between agents in a virtual network, such as in Kamvar *et al.*'s Eigentrust for peer-to-peer (P2P) networks [66], or Noh's formal model based on feedbacks in a social network [102]. Both [62] and [113] use a subjective logic framework (discussed later on in this section) to represent trust values; the former for quantifying and reasoning about trust in IT equipment, and the latter for determining the trustworthiness of agents in a peer-to-peer system.

On the other hand, a *gradual* approach is concerned with the estimation of trust values when the outcome of an action can be positive to some extent, e.g. when provided information can be right or wrong to some degree, as opposed to being either right or wrong (e.g. [1, 23, 38, 50, 82, 88, 134, 158]). In a gradual setting, trust values are not interpreted as probabilities: a higher trust value corresponds to a higher trust in an agent, which makes the ordering of trust values a very important factor in such scenarios. Note that in real life, too, trust is often interpreted as a gradual phenomenon: humans do not merely reason in terms of 'trusting' and 'not trusting', but rather trusting someone 'very much' or 'more or less'. Fuzzy logic [69, 152] is very well-suited to represent such natural language labels which represent vague intervals rather than exact values. For instance, in [134] and [76], fuzzy

Table 2.1   Classification of trust models

	trust only	*trust and distrust*
probabilistic	Kamvar *et al.* [66] Richardson *et al.* [123] Zaihrayeu *et al.* [153]	Jøsang *et al.* [62]
gradual	Abdul-Rahman and Hailes [1] Falcone *et al.* [26] Golbeck [38] Massa *et al.* [88]	De Cock *et al.* [23] Guha *et al.* [50]

linguistic terms are used to specify the trust in agents in a P2P network, and in a social network, respectively. A classical example of trust as a gradual notion can be found in [1], in which a four-value scale is used to determine the trustworthiness of agents, viz. very trustworthy – trustworthy – untrustworthy – very untrustworthy.

The last years have witnessed a rapid increase of gradual trust approaches, ranging from socio-cognitive models (for example implemented by fuzzy cognitive maps in [26]), over management mechanisms for selecting good interaction partners on the web [134] or for open and dynamic environments (e.g. [119] or Almenárez *et al.*'s PTM [4]), to representations for use in mobile environments [82] or recommender systems [38, 86], and general models tailored to Semantic Web applications [156].

While trust is increasingly getting established, the use and modeling of *distrust* remains relatively unexplored. Although recent publications [27, 40, 129] show an emerging interest in modeling the notion of distrust, models that take into account both trust and distrust are still scarce. Most approaches completely ignore distrust (see for example [76, 78, 80, 99, 123, 153]), or consider trust and distrust as opposite ends of the same continuous scale (see e.g. [1, 42, 134]). However, in agent network theory there is a growing body of opinion that distrust cannot be seen as the equivalent of lack of trust [19, 32, 85]. Moreover, work in the psychology area has repeatedly asked for a re-examination of the assumption that positive- and negative-valent feelings are not separable [16, 112, 116], and some researchers even claim that trust and distrust are not opposite, but related dimensions that can occur simultaneously [20, 79, 94].

To the best of our knowledge, there is only one probabilistic model that considers trust and distrust simultaneously: in Jøsang's subjective logic [60, 62], an opinion includes a belief b that an agent is to be trusted, a disbelief d corresponding to a belief that an agent is not to be trusted, and an uncertainty u. The uncertainty factor leaves room for ignorance, but the requirement that the belief b, the disbelief d and the uncertainty u sum up to 1, rules out options for inconsistency even though this might arise quite naturally in large networks with contradictory sources.

Examples of gradual models that represent trust and distrust as two separate values can be found in [23, 50, 115]. De Cock and Pinheiro Da Silva [23] propose to model the trust network as an intuitionistic fuzzy relation [9], but the same remark w.r.t. inconsistency applies to their model too: the sum of the membership degree (trust t, in $[0, 1]$) and the non-membership degree (distrust d, in $[0, 1]$) must be less or equal than 1. The pair can then be represented as an interval $[t, 1 - d]$. This approach is somewhat similar to Prade's work [115] where trust evaluations are represented as an interval in a bipolar trust scale. However, the interval is seen as an imprecise evaluation of the degree of trust [115], rather than an evaluation of trust and distrust independently (like in [23] and [60]). The latter is also the approach taken by Guha et $al.$, who use a couple (t, d) with a trust degree t and a distrust degree d, both in $[0, 1]$. To obtain the final suggested trust value, they subtract d from t [50]. As we explain later on, potentially important information is lost when the trust and distrust scales are merged into one.

In the next section, we point out the importance of a provenance-preserving trust model. It will become clear that current models (only taking into account trust or both trust and distrust) are either not capable of properly handling inconsistency, or cannot differentiate unknown agents from malicious agents, although these problems can possibly have a large effect on the (ranking of) trust estimation, recommendations, etc.

2.2 Trust Provenance

The main aim in using trust networks is to allow agents to form trust opinions on unknown agents or sources by asking for a trust opinion from acquainted agents. Existing trust network models usually apply suitable trust propagation and aggregation operators to compute the resulting trust estimation. But in passing on this trust value to the inquiring agent, often valuable information on how this value is obtained is lost.

Agent opinions, however, may be affected by provenance information exposing how trust values have been computed. For example, a trust opinion in a source from a fully informed agent is quite different from a trust estimation from an agent who does not know the sources too well but has no evidence to distrust it. Unfortunately, in current models, agents cannot really exercise their right to interpret how trust is computed since most models do not preserve trust provenance.

Trust networks are typically challenged by two important problems influencing trust opinions. Firstly, in large networks it is likely that many agents do not know each other, hence there is an abundance of ignorance. Secondly, because of the lack of a central authority, different agents might provide different and even contradictory information, hence inconsistency may occur. Below we explain how ignorance and inconsistency may affect trust estimations. The first two examples illustrate the need for a provenance-preserving trust model in agent networks and on the Semantic Web, while the last example focuses on its application in the recommender system area.

Example 2.1 (Ignorance without provenance). Agent a needs to establish an opinion about both agents c and d to find an efficient web service. To this end, agent a calls upon agent b for trust opinions on agents c and d. Agent b completely distrusts agent c, hence agent b trusts agent c to degree 0 in the range $[0, 1]$, where 0 is full absence of trust and 1 full presence of trust. On the other hand, agent b does not know agent d, hence b trusts d to the degree 0. As a result, agent b returns the same trust opinion to a for both agents c and d, namely 0, but the meaning of this value is clearly different in both cases.

With agent c, the lack of trust is caused by a presence of distrust, while with agent d, the absence of trust is caused by a lack of knowledge. This provenance information is vital for agent a to make a well informed decision. For example, if agent a has a high trust in b, a will not consider agent c anymore, but might ask for other opinions on agent d. Models working with only one value cannot cope with this kind of situations. A trust model that takes into account both trust and distrust (i.e., two values) could be a possible solution. However, as the examples below illustrate, the existing approaches fall short in other scenarios.

Example 2.2 (Ignorance without provenance). Agent a needs to establish an opinion about agent c in order to complete an important bank transaction. Agent a may ask agent b for an opinion of c because agent a does not know anything about c. In this case, b is an agent that knows how to compute a trust value of c from its web of trust. Assume that b has evidence for both trusting and distrusting c. For instance, let us say that b trusts c to degree 0.5 in the range $[0, 1]$ where 0 is absence of trust and 1 is full presence of trust; and that b distrusts c to the degree 0.2 in the range $[0, 1]$ where 0 is full absence of distrust and 1 is full presence of distrust. Another way of saying this is that b trusts c at least to the extent 0.5, but also not more than 0.8. The length of the interval [0.5,0.8] indicates how much b lacks information about c.

In this scenario, by getting the trust value 0.5 from b, agent a is losing information indicating that b has some evidence to distrust c too. Models working with only one value cannot correctly represent this kind of situations. The problem can be solved by the models that take into account two values, and in particular Guha *et al.*'s [50]. However, their approach has one main disadvantage: agent b will pass on a value of $0.5 - 0.2 = 0.3$ to a. Again, agent a is losing valuable trust provenance information indicating, for example, how much b lacks information about agent c.

Example 2.3 (Contradictory information). A stranger tells you that a particular movie was very bad. Because you do not know anything about this person, you make inquiries with two of your friends who are acquainted with him. One of them tells you to trust him, while the other tells you to distrust that same person. In this case, there are two equally trusted friends that tell you the exact opposite thing. In other words, you have to deal with inconsistent information.

This example illustrates how inconsistencies may arise: when an agent in the trust network inquires for a trust estimation about another agent, it often happens that he does not ask one agent's opinion, but several. Then these information pieces, coming from different sources and propagated through different propagation chains, must be combined together into one new trust value representing the opinion of all the agents, which is not always an easy task when conflicting evidence has been gathered. Nevertheless, this information must be represented unambiguously as it may indicate that it is not possible to take decisions based on the obtained trust value.

Note that models that work only with trust and not with distrust are again not expressive enough to represent these cases adequately. Taking e.g. 0.5 (the average) as an aggregated trust value is not a good solution for Ex. 2.3, because then we cannot differentiate this case from the partial trust situation in which both of your friends trust the movie recommender to the extent 0.5, which indicates that the recommender is somewhat reliable. Furthermore, what would you answer if someone asks you if the stranger can be trusted? A plausible answer is: "I don't really know, because I have contradictory information about him". Note that this is fundamentally different from "I don't know, because I have no information about him". Hence, an aggregated trust value of 0 is not a suitable option either, as it could imply both inconsistency and ignorance.

Previous models considering both trust and distrust degrees do not offer the option of representing (partial) inconsistency, even though this might arise quite naturally in large networks with contradictory sources. Jøsang's subjective logic [60] for example cannot cope with this scenario because the belief and disbelief have to sum up to 1. A similar remark applies to De Cock and Pinheiro da Silva's intuitionistic fuzzy model [23]. Guha *et al.* [50] do not impose a restriction on the trust and distrust degrees but their approach suffers from another kind of shortcoming, as Ex. 2.2 illustrated.

2.3   Trust Score Space

The examples in the previous section indicate the need for a model that preserves information on whether a 'trust problem' is caused by presence of distrust or rather by lack of knowledge, as well as whether a 'knowledge problem' is caused by having too little or too much, i.e. contradictory, information. In other words, we need a model that, on one hand, is able to represent the trust an agent may have in another agent, and on the other hand, can evaluate the contribution of each aspect of trust to the overall trust opinion. As a result, such a model will be able to distinguish between different cases of trust provenance.

To this end, we propose a new framework in which trust values are derived from a bilattice [35]. Since their introduction by Ginsberg in 1988, much attention has been paid to bilattices and their applications. It has for instance been shown that bilattices are useful for providing semantics to logic programs (see e.g. [28]), and as underlying algebraic structures of formalisms for reasoning with imprecise information (see e.g. [21, 33]). The use of these bilattices results in a gradual model for (trust,distrust)-couples. We call such couples trust scores.

Definition 2.1 (Trust Score). A trust score (t,d) is an element of $[0,1]^2$, in which t is called the trust degree, and d the distrust degree.

Trust scores will be used to compare the degree of trust and distrust an agent may have in other agents in the network, or to compare the uncertainty that is contained in the trust scores. This information can e.g. be used in the ranking mechanisms of a recommender system, a file-sharing system, and so on; for example by giving preference to recommendations/files from sources that are trusted more, or to opinions that are better informed. To this aim, we introduce the trust score space as a model that allows to compare and preserve information about the provenance of trust scores.

Definition 2.2 (Trust score space, Trust-Distrust and Knowledge ordering). The trust score space

$$\mathscr{BL}^{\square} = ([0,1]^2, \leqslant_{td}, \leqslant_k, \neg)$$

consists of the set $[0,1]^2$ of trust scores, a trust-distrust ordering $\leqslant_{td}$, a knowledge ordering $\leqslant_k$, and a negation $\neg$ defined by

$$(t_1, d_1) \leqslant_{td} (t_2, d_2) \text{ iff } t_1 \leqslant t_2 \text{ and } d_1 \geqslant d_2$$
$$(t_1, d_1) \leqslant_k (t_2, d_2) \text{ iff } t_1 \leqslant t_2 \text{ and } d_1 \leqslant d_2$$
$$\neg(t_1, d_1) = (d_1, t_1)$$

for all (t_1, d_1) and (t_2, d_2) in $[0,1]^2$. while d_1 is the distrust degree.

One can verify that the structure $\mathscr{BL}^{\square}$ is a bilattice in the sense of Ginsberg [35], that is $([0,1]^2, \leqslant_{td})$ and $([0,1]^2, \leqslant_k)$ are both lattices and the negation $\neg$ serves to impose a relationship between them:

$$(t_1, d_1) \leqslant_{td} (t_2, d_2) \Rightarrow \neg(t_1, d_1) \geqslant_{td} \neg(t_2, d_2)$$
$$(t_1, d_1) \leqslant_k (t_2, d_2) \Rightarrow \neg(t_1, d_1) \leqslant_k \neg(t_2, d_2),$$

such that $\neg\neg(t_1, d_1) = (t_1, d_1)$. In other words, $\neg$ is an involution that reverses the $\leqslant_{td}$-order and preserves the $\leqslant_k$-order.

Note that Ginsberg's bilattice is a generalization of $FOUR$, the logic introduced by Belnap in [10, 11], in which he advocated the use of four truth values ('true', 'false', 'unknown' and 'contradiction').

Figure 2.1 shows $\mathscr{BL}^{\square}$, along with some examples of trust scores. These scores are interpreted as epistemic values: compared to Jøsang's subjective logic, the trust and distrust degrees are not complementary, but they reflect the imperfect knowledge we have about the actual trust and distrust values (which are complementary). The lattice $([0,1]^2, \leqslant_{td})$ orders the trust scores going from complete distrust $(0,1)$ to complete trust $(1,0)$. The lattice $([0,1]^2, \leqslant_k)$ evaluates the amount of available trust evidence, ranging from a "shortage of evidence", $t_1 + d_1 < 1$, to an "excess of evidence", viz. $t_1 + d_1 > 1$.

The boundary values of the $\leqslant_k$ ordering, $(0,0)$ and $(1,1)$, reflect ignorance, resp. contradiction. We call trust scores (t,d) with $t + d < 1$ incomplete, while those with $t + d > 1$ are called inconsistent . In both cases, there is a knowledge defect, which can be quantified by the following $[0,1]$-valued measure:

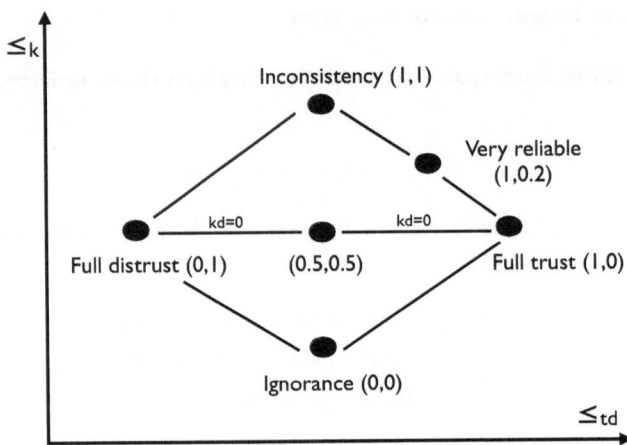

Fig. 2.1   The trust score space $\mathscr{BL}^{\square}$, a bilattice-based trust model that enables us to compare trust scores according to the available trust-distrust content ($\leqslant_{td}$) and to evaluate the uncertainty that is involved ($\leqslant_{k}$).

Definition 2.3 (Knowledge defect, Knowledge defective trust score). We   define   the knowledge defect of a trust score (t,d) as $kd(t,d) = |1-t-d|$. We say that trust scores (t,d) for which $kd(t,d) = 0$, i.e., $t+d=1$, have perfect knowledge (i.e., there is no uncertainty about the trust value), while all others are called knowledge defective.

Definition 2.4 (Consistent, Inconsistent trust score). We call a trust score (t,d) consistent iff $t+d \leqslant 1$, and inconsistent otherwise.

The bottom part of the bilattice (or lower triangle, under the $kd(t,d) = 0$ line) contains the trust scores for which there is some doubt (uncertainty) about the trust degree. The information contained in such a trust score (t,d) can be represented as an interval $[t, 1-d]$, denoting that the agent should be trusted at least to the degree t, but not more than $1-d$; note the similarities with De Cock *et al.*'s [23] and Prade's [115] approaches. In such an interval representation, complete ignorance is represented as $[0,1]$.

We call agents that issue consistent trust scores consistent agents. In this work, we assume that every agent is consistent. However, although we start from consistent agents, modelling inconsistent information is still needed when we want to accurately represent the result of a trust score aggregation process. This is illustrated by Ex. 2.3; we will elaborate upon this in Chap. 4. The upper part of the bilattice (higher triangle, above the $kd(t,d) = 0$ line) contains such inconsistent trust scores denoting conflicting information, i.e., trust scores with $t+d > 1$. Note that trust scores in the higher triangle cannot be represented as intervals, since they contain too much information instead of a lack.

The trust scores in $\mathscr{BL}^\square = ([0,1]^2, \leqslant_{td}, \leqslant_k, \neg)$ can also be considered within the alternative space $([0,1]^2, \leqslant_t, \leqslant_d, \neg)$, with $\neg$ defined in Def. 2.2, and $\leqslant_t$ and $\leqslant_d$ as in Def. 2.5. Note that $\leqslant_t$ and $\leqslant_d$ are quasi-orderings, since they are not antisymmetric.

Definition 2.5 (Trust ordering, Distrust ordering). The trust ordering $\leqslant_t$ and distrust ordering $\leqslant_d$ are defined by

$$(t_1, d_1) \leqslant_t (t_2, d_2) \text{ iff } t_1 \leqslant t_2$$
$$(t_1, d_1) \leqslant_d (t_2, d_2) \text{ iff } d_1 \leqslant d_2$$

The trust and distrust orderings can also be seen as two extra orderings on $\mathscr{BL}^\square$, which separately evaluate the amount of trust and distrust information respectively. The negation $\neg$ serves to impose a relationship between them:

$$(t_1, d_1) \leqslant_t (t_2, d_2) \Leftrightarrow \neg(t_1, d_1) \leqslant_d \neg(t_2, d_2).$$

Proposition 2.1. *The orderings from Definitions 2.2 and 2.5 are related to each other by* $(t_1, d_1) \leqslant_k (t_2, d_2) \Leftrightarrow (t_1, d_1) \leqslant_t (t_2, d_2) \wedge (t_1, d_1) \leqslant_d (t_2, d_2)$*, and* $(t_1, d_1) \leqslant_{td} (t_2, d_2) \Leftrightarrow (t_1, d_1) \leqslant_t (t_2, d_2) \wedge (t_1, d_1) \geqslant_d (t_2, d_2)$*.*

Proof. By definition of $\leqslant_k$ it holds that $(t_1, d_1) \leqslant_k (t_2, d_2) \Leftrightarrow t_1 \leqslant t_2 \wedge d_1 \leqslant d_2$, and hence by definition of $\leqslant_t$ and $\leqslant_d$ that $t_1 \leqslant t_2 \wedge d_1 \leqslant d_2 \Leftrightarrow (t_1, d_1) \leqslant_t (t_2, d_2) \wedge (t_1, d_1) \leqslant_d (t_2, d_2)$. Analogously for $\leqslant_{td}$. $\square$

The mapping is illustrated in Fig. 2.2. The dotted line denotes the trust scores (t, d) with perfect knowledge, i.e., $kd(t, d) = 0$. The triangles underneath (in the gray area) contain the consistent trust scores; inconsistent trust scores reside in the upper triangles.

The trust score space allows for a widely applicable lightweight trust model that is nevertheless able to preserve a lot of provenance information by simultaneously representing partial trust, partial distrust, partial ignorance and partial inconsistency, and treating them as different, related concepts. Moreover, by using a bilattice model the aforementioned problems disappear:

(1) By using trust scores we can now distinguish full distrust $(0, 1)$ from ignorance $(0, 0)$ and analogously, full trust $(1, 0)$ from inconsistency $(1, 1)$. This is an improvement of, among others, [1, 153].

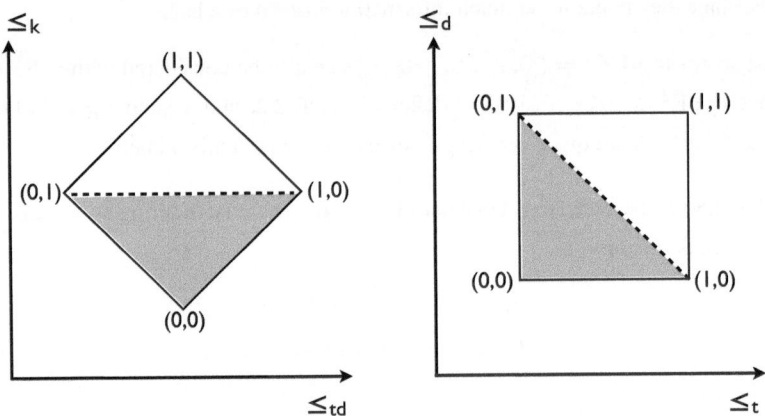

Fig. 2.2   The four orderings on $\mathscr{BL}^{\square}$: trust-distrust ordering $\leqslant_{td}$, knowledge ordering $\leqslant_k$, trust $\leqslant_t$ and distrust $\leqslant_d$ ordering.

(2) We can deal with both incomplete information and inconsistency (improvement of [23, 60]).

(3) We do not lose important information (improvement of [50]), because, as will become clear in the next chapters, we keep the trust and distrust degree separated throughout the whole trust process (propagation and aggregation).

2.4   Trust Networks

A trust network is a network in which every couple of agents is connected through a trust statement. This statement can denote full trust, partial trust, complete distrust, ..., or ignorance (when two agents do not know each other at all). In other words, the trust relationship between every agent couple can be represented by a trust score. Remark that trust statements are not necessarily reciprocal; think e.g. of a trust network between teachers and students: students may highly trust their math professor for statistical problems, but this certainly does not imply that the teacher will trust every single pupil to the same degree. It is easy to see that a trust network can be modeled as a directed, fully connected graph. The agents in the trust network can then be represented by nodes in the graph, the relations between the agents by directed edges, and the corresponding levels of trust (trust scores) as weights on the edges.

As has become clear throughout this chapter, we do not work in a binary setting where agents are either trusted or distrusted, but in an environment where agents can express partial and gradual trust, distrust and ignorance. This brings us to the domain of fuzzy set theory [69, 152], an extension of the classical set theory. In the latter, an element either completely belongs to a set, or not at all. Fuzzy sets, however, allow elements to partially belong to a set, and consequently also to belong to several sets at the same time. As a simple example, consider the concept of age: a baby certainly fully belongs to the set of 'young people', whereas everyone will agree that an elderly man does not. We say that the baby belongs to the young people set with a membership degree of 1 (on a scale from 0 to 1), while the elderly man has an associated membership degree of 0. On the other hand, what can we say about a teenager? Obviously, a teenager is still a young person, but not as young as a baby; hence, the membership degree will be somewhere in between 0 and 1. Just like 'young' and 'old', 'trust' and 'distrust' are also clearly gradual phenomena; hence, fuzzy sets are the pre-eminent tools for modeling trust networks.

Our formal definition of a trust network relies on the notion of a fuzzy relation. A fuzzy relation is characterized by the same two items as a fuzzy set, i.e., its elements and associated membership degrees. This time however, the elements of a fuzzy relation are couples. In our setting, the trust relation between agents in the trust network can be defined by the set of agent couples (a,b) where a trusts b to a certain degree (which we call the 'trust set'). E.g., if a completely trusts b, then the membership degree of (a,b) in the trust set is 1, and if c and d do not know each other, the membership degree of (c,d) in the trust set is 0. Analogously, (c,d)'s membership degree in the set of agents who distrust each other (the distrust set) is 0, and for (a,b) as well. In other words, the trust relation is a fuzzy mapping from the set of couples of agents into $[0,1]$, and the same definition holds for the distrust relation as well.

However, as we have argued in the previous sections, it is not wise to consider trust and distrust as separate concepts. Hence, it is better to replace the two fuzzy relations (denoting trust and distrust) by one bilattice-fuzzy relation, a mapping from the set of agent into $[0,1]^2$. This brings us to our final definition of a trust network:

Definition 2.6 (Trust Network). A trust network is a couple (A,R) in which A is the set of agents and R is an $A \times A \rightarrow [0,1]^2$ mapping that associates with each couple (a,b) of agents in A a trust score $R(a,b) = (R^+(a,b), R^-(a,b))$ in $[0,1]^2$, in which $R^+(a,b)$ and $R^-(a,b)$ denote resp. the trust and distrust degree of a in b.

In other words, the available trust information is modeled as a $\mathscr{BL}^{\square}$-fuzzy relation in the set of agents that associates a score drawn from the trust score space with each ordered pair of agents. It should be thought of as a snapshot taken at a certain moment, since trust scores can be updated.

2.5 Conclusions

Seldom, very seldom, we have just enough information to make a perfect assessment of someone's character, tastes or intentions. Instead, we often have too little information or too much information for a good estimation. This is certainly the case in large agent networks where (partial) ignorance and conflicting opinions are the rule rather than the exception. The trust models that had been proposed so far could not cope with such knowledge defects, since they do not preserve vital trust provenance information. Representing trust estimations as elements of a bilattice as we have proposed in this chapter resolves these issues and enables agents to accurately describe their own or computed (via propagation and aggregation) opinions, so that the requiring agents can safely act upon them. The ability to handle ignorance and inconsistency becomes extremely meaningful in an agent network where the trustworthiness of many agents is initially unknown to an agent, which does not imply that he distrusts all of them, but that he may eventually gather evidence to trust or distrust some agents and still ignore others.

*Eh! madame, qui sait? reprit Athos. Il y a un proverbe
populaire qui dit qu'il n'y a que les montagnes qui ne
se rencontrent pas, et les proverbes populaires sont
quelquefois d'une justesse incroyable.*

Vingt Ans après, 1845. Alexandre Dumas

Chapter 3

Trust Propagation

How often do you not hear someone exclaiming "it's a small world", astonished at bumping into somebody he/she thought almost impossible to meet, or at discovering they have a mutual acquaintance. This 'small world' idea dates back ages, and has ever since found its way into our daily lives and even our popular culture; think for example of the movies[1] and the song lyrics[2]. And it is not only an established expression in the English language: the Spanish compare the world to a handkerchief[3], and the Namibians have an old, even more poetic proverb saying that it is only the mountains that never meet[4]. Despite their old age, these sayings are still remarkably up-to-date and widely applicable; not only in our everyday life, but also online.

The scientific research about small worlds started with a letter experiment in the sixties, initiated by the American social psychologist Stanley Milgram. Although he was not the first scientist investigating whether there was an element of truth in the popular proverb, it was his experiment that became well-known thanks to the publication in Psychology Today [97]. Milgram asked several random people to contact (via traceable letters) other people that were selected from a random set of residents from distant American cities. If the starting person did not know the target person directly, he was asked to send the letter to one of his acquaintances who he thought would be most likely to know the target person. The goal of the experiment was to find out if there truly existed such a thing as 'a small world', and if so, how many links were needed to reach the target users. His study showed that people could indeed be linked to each other in only a few steps, yielding connection

---

[1] See www.imdb.com/find?q=small+world for a list of movies.
[2] One of the most well-known examples is featured in Disney's The Lion King.
[3] El mundo es un pañuelo, according to [100].
[4] See www.worldofquotes.com/author/Proverb/185 and www.proverbatim.com/namibian

chains with a mean of somewhat more than 5 intermediaries [97, 137]. This result gave rise to the term 'small-world phenomenon', later also known as 'six degrees of separation', made popular by an American play [48] and its film adaptation.

Thirty years later, the mathematicians Duncan Watts and Steven Strogatz introduced the small-network theory [143]. Traditionally, most networks are either modeled as completely random or as completely regular (nodes are only connected with their k nearest nodes, with k fixed). However, a great deal of real-world networks fall somewhere in between, such as the social network in Milgram's experiment. Watts and Strogatz introduced a new method to model and study this kind of intermediate networks, and focussed on two of their statistics, namely the clustering coefficient that measures to which degree nodes in a graph are interrelated to each other, and the average shortest path length between any two agents in the network. They demonstrated that, starting from a regular network, replacing a few of the edges between the nearest neighbors by longer random edges (i.e., to nodes that are not as near) leads to a drastic decrease in the average shortest path length (i.e., the agents in the network are separated less far from each other), while the clustering coefficient remains almost unchanged. The resulting networks are highly clustered (as in regular networks) and have a small shortest path length (as in random networks); hence, in such networks, agent pairs are connected through a small number of intermediate agents. They called the resulting networks small-world networks, by analogy with Milgram's small world phenomenon.

It turns out that the small-world network theory can be applied to many real-world networks, from biological (for instance protein interaction networks or neural networks of worms) to technological networks (w.r.t. memory storage or power grids), the research collaboration network between mathematicians [37], and also other social networks. A nice example of the latter category is the Kevin Bacon Oracle[5], which determines how far any actor is separated from the American movie star Kevin Bacon, based on the social network formed by actors and the movies they featured in (the maximum distance is 8; more than 4 hops away is considered a rarity). Another illustrations is a Facebook group[6] with over five million users, which revealed that the average separation between its users is a bit less than 6.

Watts and Strogatz's findings can be applied to a lot of trust networks as well, since these are a specific set of social networks, see e.g. [45]. Recently it has been demonstrated

---

[5] See oracleofbacon.org . Even the young Belgian actor Kenneth Vanbaeden, who only played in one movie so far according to their database, has a Bacon number of 3!

[6] See www.facebook.com/group.php?gid=14436512661

that several real-life trust networks are indeed small-world networks: the trust graph of Epinions is investigated in [155], while Yuan *et al.* give an overview of the characteristics of the Advogato, Robots, SqueakFoundation, Kaitiaki and Epinions trust networks[7] [151]. So now that we know that many trust networks exhibit the small-world property, we can assume that most of its agents can be connected to each other in only a few steps. However, the fact that agents can be connected does not mean that they should fully trust each other automatically. Hence, the next question is how to determine the amount of trust an agent should place in another agent. And this is where trust metrics come into play: their task is to compute a trust estimate, based on the existing trust relations/links between other agents in the network. The key building blocks in this procedure are trust propagation and aggregation mechanisms. The latter will be discussed in detail in chapter 4; in this chapter, trust propagation operators are at the centre stage. As will become clear in the following sections, trust propagation operators cleverly take advantage of Milgram's and Watts & Strogatz's small-world findings.

In agent networks, most other agents are typically unknown to a specific agent. Still there are cases in which it is useful to be able to derive some information on whether or not an unknown agent can be trusted, and if so, to what degree. In the context of recommender systems e.g., this is important if none of the users the agent knows has rated a specific item that the user is interested in, but there are some ratings available by unknown users (who are a member of the trust network). E.g., the number of people that users have in their personal web of trust (i.e., the people that are directly trusted by a particular user) in Epinions is estimated to be around 1.7 on average. The total number of users on the other hand well exceeds 100 000 [50]. In other words, a user's web of trust only contains a very tiny fraction of the user community. Hence, it would be very useful to be able to tap into the knowledge of a larger subset of the user population to generate recommendations. A first step in that direction is propagation.

When only dealing with trust, it is reasonable to assume that, if agent a trusts agent b and b trusts agent x, a can trust x to some degree. However, when we also have to take into account distrust, the picture gets more complicated. In Sec. 3.1 we describe the state of the art of trust propagation, while in the following sections we embark upon the problem of distrust propagation, a topic that has received almost no attention so far. We discuss desirable propagation properties and possible distrust propagation strategies in Sec. 3.2,

---

[7]See www.trustlet.org/wiki/Trust_network_datasets for further references and information on these trust data sets.

and propose and examine a set of propagation operators that exhibit the intended behaviors in Sec. 3.3. Their applicability on real-world data sets from Epinions and CouchSurfing is tested in Sec. 3.4.

3.1   Setting the Scene

Propagation operators are an important part of many trust metrics. Various types of trust metrics exist in the literature; we refer to [158] for a good overview. In that paper, Ziegler and Lausen classify trust metrics along three dimensions: group versus scalar metrics, centralized versus distributed approaches, and global versus local metrics. The first dimension refers to the way trust relations are evaluated, while the second classification is based on the place where the trust estimations are computed. The last dimension refers to the network perspective: trust metrics can take into account all agents and trust relationships between them when computing a trust estimation (see e.g. [66, 102, 123]), or only rely on a part of the trust network, hence taking into account personal bias (for example [38, 50, 87]). The methods that we will discuss in Sec. 3.3 belong to the latter type.

Trust metrics usually incorporate techniques that are based on the assumption that trust is somehow transitive. We call these techniques trust propagation strategies. Let us illustrate this with Fig. 3.1: if agent a trusts agent b (whom we call a trusted third party, or TTP for short), and TTP b trusts agent x, then it is reasonable to assume that a should trust x to a certain degree. This basic propagation strategy is known as atomic direct propagation, atomic because the propagation chain only contains one intermediate agent. Besides direct propagation, also other strategies exist: one might e.g. believe that x's trust in a should give rise to a trusting x (transpose trust, see Fig. 3.2). One can also argue that a should trust x since both b and x are trusted by the same agent c (cocitation, see Fig. 3.3) or because b and x share the same trust relations (trust coupling, see Fig. 3.4). For a discussion of the latter strategies, we refer to [50]. In the remainder of this chapter, and throughout the book, we only focus on direct propagation, the strategy which is most agreed upon.

Trust is of course not always transitive, think of our discussion in chapter about goal and context. For example, if Jane trusts Alice to give her a good-looking haircut and Alice trusts John to fix her bicycle, this does not imply that Jane trusts John to fix bicycles, nor to give a nice haircut. But, in the same context/scope, and under certain conditions, trust can be transitive [61]. Suppose e.g. that Jane is new in town and wants to have a haircut. Jane trusts that Alice can find a good hairdresser, while Alice trusts Mariah to be

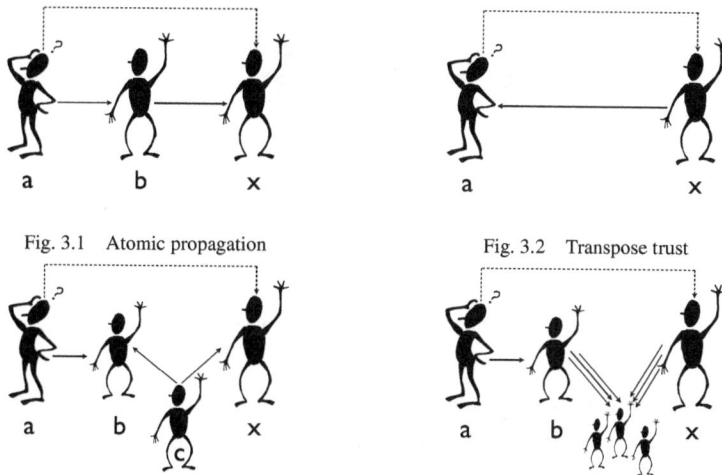

Fig. 3.1   Atomic propagation   Fig. 3.2   Transpose trust

Fig. 3.3   Cocitation   Fig. 3.4   Trust coupling

a good hairdresser. Hence, Jane can trust Mariah to be a good hairdresser. This example also shows us that a distinction must be made between trust in a agent's competence to assess the trustworthiness of a agent (functional trust, Alice trusting Mariah), or trust in a agent's competence to recommend/evaluate a good recommender agent (referral trust, Jane trusting Alice) [1, 61]. As explained in [61], it is the referral part that allows trust to become transitive. A propagation path can then be seen as a transitive chain of referral trust parts, which ends with one functional trust scope.

When dealing with trust only, in a probabilistic setting, multiplication is very often used as the standard propagation operator, see for instance [123]. This is also the case in gradual settings [4, 38, 50], but there is a wider spectrum of propagation operators available, dependent on the goal or the spirit of the application, which we will further illustrate in Sec. 3.3. Other trust propagation work includes techniques based on fuzzy if-then rules [76, 134], on the theory of spreading activation models (Ziegler and Lausen's Appleseed [158]), or on the semantic distance between a trusted third party's trust and an agent's perception of the TTP's trust [1].

The small-network theory taught us that almost all agents can be reached in only a few propagation steps, so that we do not have to propagate for all eternity. But of course, not all propagation paths will have the same length. In Fig. 3.5 e.g., there are two paths leading from agent a to agent x. If we suppose that all trust links in the network denote complete

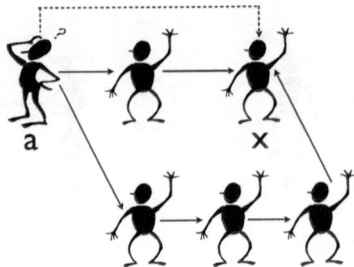

Fig. 3.5   Propagation example

trust, then intuitively we feel that the estimated trust of the second propagation path should
be lower than that of the first path (or that the trust score should contain less knowledge),
since we are heading further away from the source user. This idea of 'trust decay' [49]
is often implemented in propagation strategies. For instance, in Ziegler's approach this is
incorporated through a spreading factor [158], Golbeck only takes into account shortest
paths and ignores all others [38], and in applications that only work with bivalent trust
(instead of gradual), Massa determines the propagated trust based on an agent's distance
from a fixed propagation horizon [88].

3.2   Propagation Properties and Strategies

The rationale behind direct trust propagation says that, if agent a trusts agent b and b trusts
agent x, a can trust x. In the same way, it is reasonable to assume that, if a trusts b and b
distrusts agent y, a will also distrust y. Now, let us consider the reverse case. If a distrusts
b and b trusts y, there are several possibilities: a possible reaction for a is to do the exact
opposite of what b recommends, in other words, to distrust y. But another interpretation
is to ignore everything that b says. This example reveals part of the complex problem of
choosing an appropriate propagation scheme.

Our aim in this chapter is not to provide the holy grail solution, but rather to provide
some propagation operators that can be used in different schemes (that are applicable in
several agent and social applications), as well as to discuss some of their properties. The
example indicates that there are likely to be multiple possible propagation operators for
trust and distrust. We expect that the choice will depend on the application and the context,
but might also differ from person to person. Thus, the need for provenance-preserving trust
models becomes more evident, and hence also for propagation operators that are able to

preserve the provenance information as much as possible.

In this section, we first approach the problem from a theoretical point of view and discuss useful properties for trust score propagation operators. Subsequently, we will test our intuitions on a more practical basis; we describe which recurring propagation patterns have arisen from a small user study.

3.2.1 Desirable Propagation Properties

Let $\mathscr{BL}^\square = ([0,1]^2, \leqslant_{td}, \leqslant_k, \neg)$ be the trust score space introduced in the previous chapter. In this space, we look for a trust score propagation operator $P : [0,1]^2 \times [0,1]^2 \to [0,1]^2$ satisfying as many of the following requirements pinned down in Def. 3.1–3.5 as possible.

Definition 3.1 (Knowledge monotonicity). We say that a propagation operator P is knowledge monotonic iff for all (t_1,d_1), (t_2,d_2), (t_3,d_3) and (t_4,d_4) in $[0,1]^2$, $(t_1,d_1) \leqslant_k (t_2,d_2)$ and $(t_3,d_3) \leqslant_k (t_4,d_4)$ implies $P((t_1,d_1),(t_3,d_3)) \leqslant_k P((t_2,d_2),(t_4,d_4))$.

We call a propagation operator P knowledge monotonic if the arguments can be replaced by higher trust scores w.r.t. the knowledge ordering $\leqslant_k$ without decreasing the resulting propagated trust score. Knowledge monotonicity reflects that the better agent a knows agent b with whom it is inquiring about agent x and the better b knows x, the more informed a will be about how well to (dis)trust agent x.

Knowledge monotonicity is not only useful to provide more insight in the propagation operators but it can also be used to establish a lower bound w.r.t. $\leqslant_k$ for the actual propagated trust score without immediate recalculation. This might be useful in a situation where one of the agents has gained more knowledge about another agent and there is not enough time to recalculate the whole propagation chain immediately, as will for instance be the case in many trust-enhanced recommender systems.

The analogue for the trust-distrust ordering $\leqslant_{td}$ is not a useful property, because it counteracts normal real-life behavior as we illustrate next.

Example 3.1. If a new colleague tells you to distrust someone, you might decide not to take into account his opinion because you do not know him sufficiently. This comes down to

$$P((0,0),(0,1)) = (0,0) \tag{3.1}$$

However, over time this colleague might become a trusted friend, i.e. your trust in your colleague increases, and you will start distrusting others because your colleague tells you to (think of our example in the introduction of this section). In this case the trust score in one of the links of the chain goes up from (0,0) to (1,0) while the overall trust score of the chain drops from (0,0) to (0,1).

Analogously to knowledge monotonicity, we can define an extra monotonicity condition w.r.t. $\leqslant_t$ for the trust score space, which ensures that the more trust is involved in a propagation chain, the more trust the final trust estimation should contain:

Definition 3.2 (Trust monotonicity). We say that a propagation operator P is trust monotonic iff for all (t_1,d_1), (t_2,d_2), (t_3,d_3) and (t_4,d_4) in $[0,1]^2$, $(t_1,d_1) \leqslant_t (t_2,d_2)$ and $(t_3,d_3) \leqslant_t (t_4,d_4)$ implies $P((t_1,d_1),(t_3,d_3)) \leqslant_t P((t_2,d_2),(t_4,d_4))$.

The analogue for the distrust ordering $\leqslant_d$ would counteract normal behavior:

Example 3.2. In the previous example we explained that propagation of ignorance and distrust leads to ignorance, see (3.1). Suppose that after a while the colleague becomes someone you trust, then

$$P((1,0),(0,1)) = (0,1), \tag{3.2}$$

as discussed in the previous example. Note that $(1,0)$ in (3.2) $\leqslant_d (0,0)$ in (3.1), and trivially, $(0,1) \leqslant_d (0,1)$, but that the propagated result $(0,1)$ in (3.2) contains more distrust than $(0,0)$ in (3.1).

Besides atomic propagation, we need to be able to consider longer propagation chains, so TTPs can in turn consult their own TTPs and so on. For an associative propagation operator, this extension can be defined unambiguously. In particular, with an associative propagation operator, the overall trust score computed from a longer propagation chain is independent of the choice of which two subsequent trust scores to combine first.

Definition 3.3 (Associativity). A propagation operator P is said to be associative iff for all (t_1,d_1), (t_2,d_2) and (t_3,d_3) in $[0,1]^2$,

$$P(P((t_1,d_1),(t_2,d_2)),(t_3,d_3)) = P((t_1,d_1),P((t_2,d_2),(t_3,d_3)))$$

If an operator is not associative, this means that we need to fix a particular evaluation order to propagate trust scores over paths with more than two edges. In a network with a central authority that maintains all trust information, one can choose which order to use. On the other hand, if there is no central authority, and each agent has access only to the trust scores it has issued, it is necessary to perform the propagation in a right-to-left direction (i.e., right associative). With this order, at each node in the propagation path, an agent combines its trust score in its successor, with the propagated trust score it receives from this successor. This is illustrated below for a path containing three edges, and a propagation operator P:

$$P((t_1,d_1),(t_2,d_2),(t_3,d_3)) = P((t_1,d_1),P((t_2,d_2),(t_3,d_3)))$$

The issue of central authority versus privacy-preserving environments, and their effect on the propagation and aggregation calculations, will be discussed in more detail in Sec. 4.1.

Even for non associative propagation operators, instead of calculating a whole chain, sometimes it is sufficient to look at only one agent to determine the overall trust score in a longer propagation chain.

Definition 3.4 (Knowledge absorption). We say that a propagation operator P is knowledge absorbing iff for all (t_1,d_1) and (t_2,d_2) in $[0,1]^2$,

$$P((0,0),(t_2,d_2)) = P((t_1,d_1),(0,0)) = (0,0)$$

Hence, as soon as one of the agents is ignorant, we can dismiss the entire chain. As such, for an operator with this property, precious calculation time can possibly be saved.

Since we assume all users to be consistent, i.e., to issue consistent trust scores, it is desirable that a trust score propagation operator preserves the consistency. In this way, we can also ensure that all inputs (either direct trust scores or the result of propagations) for the aggregation process will be consistent (see chapter 4).

Definition 3.5 (Consistency preserving propagation). We say that a propagation operator P preserves the consistency iff, when all inputs are consistent, the propagated result is consistent too. In other words, if for all (t_1,d_1) and (t_2,d_2) in $[0,1]^2$, $t_1 + d_1 \leqslant 1$ and $t_2 + d_2 \leqslant 1$ implies $P((t_1,d_1),(t_2,d_2)) = (p,q)$, with $p+q \leqslant 1$.

3.2.2 Propagation Patterns in Practice

A lot of trust score operators can be found that satisfy one or more of the above properties; however, not all of them may behave logically in real-life trust networks. Therefore, in this section, we investigate which propagation patterns occur in practice. We start the discussion with some intuitive examples.

Example 3.3. If a friend (i.e., b) whom you (a) fully trust tells you to distrust someone (x), and you have no other information about this person, you likely will choose to distrust him. In other words, using the trust network notation from Def. 2.6, from $R(a,b) = (1,0)$ and $R(b,x) = (0,1)$ is derived that $R(a,x) = (0,1)$, or:

$$P((1,0),(0,1)) = (0,1) \tag{3.3}$$

Example 3.4. If a colleague whom you distrust tells you to trust someone, you might decide this is too little information to act on. Indeed, if you distrust your colleague, it is reasonable not to take into account whatever he is telling you. Hence, from $R(a,b) = (0,1)$ and $R(b,x) = (1,0)$ is derived that $R(a,x) = (0,0)$. This means that, if no additional information is available, x remains unknown to you. This comes down to

$$P((0,1),(1,0)) = (0,0) \tag{3.4}$$

On the other hand, you might think that the colleague you distrust is giving you wrong information on purpose, or you might conclude that trusted friends of your distrusted colleague are best also to be distrusted. In this case, from $R(a,b) = (0,1)$ and $R(b,x) = (1,0)$ is derived that $R(a,x) = (0,1)$, hence we are confronted with a propagation operator which is clearly different from the one in (3.4) since

$$P((0,1),(1,0)) = (0,1) \tag{3.5}$$

The examples above serve two purposes: first, Eq. (3.3) and (3.4) illustrate that a trust score propagation operator is not necessarily commutative because the ordering of the arguments matters. Note how this is different from the traditional case (i.e., only trust) where the commutative multiplication seems sufficient to do the job. Secondly, Eq. (3.4) and (3.5) illustrate that different operators yielding different results are possible depending on the interpretation.

To our knowledge, so far, not much practical research on real-world data sets has been done to find out whether useful information can be derived from propagating distrust as the first link in a propagation chain or not [50, 56, 70] (see page 49 for more information). Therefore, we have set up a small questionnaire to gather evidence in favor of the scenarios depicted by Eq. (3.4) and (3.5), or evidence that dismisses our arguments about multiple distrust propagation possibilities.

In the experiment, we focus on propagation paths with one intermediate agent, i.e., a chain in which agent a is in a trust relation with agent b, who is in a relation with agent x. The goal is to find out how the participant (agent a) feels about x, or, in other words, how he/she propagates trust information via agent b. As it may be hard for the subjects to express their trust opinions explicitly, we instead asked to which degree they would follow x's advice. Following Jøsang's definition of trust (see the end of Sec. 1.1), this will give us an indication of $R(a,x)$. Since trust and the willingness to depend on someone is closely related to context and goal, we have designed the experimental setup according to a movie recommender context; see Fig. 3.6.

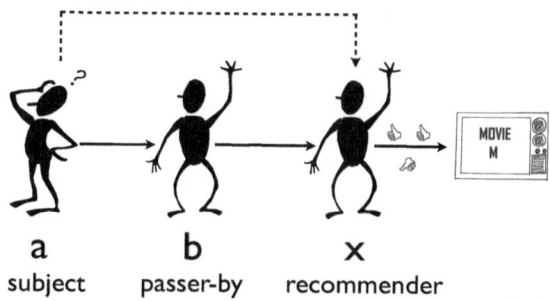

Fig. 3.6   Movie recommender scenario for the experimental setup.

Each subject a was asked to imagine himself in a movie theatre, having no clue on which movie to see. A passer-by (or TTP) b tells him he knows someone (x, the recommender) who has seen movie M and liked it a lot. We distinguish three basic types of passers-by b: someone who is completely trusted by a when it comes to movies $(1,0)$, a person a fully distrusts for movie advice $(0,1)$, and a stranger, someone a has never seen before $(0,0)$. The relation between b and the recommender x also belongs to one of these types. The subjects were then asked how they would handle x's positive advice about watching movie M. We provided six possible answers, with each of the choices/actions accompanied by their intended meaning, in order to exclude as much misunderstanding as possible. An example of such a question is given in Fig. 3.7. Note that, since we also include unknown and distrusted passers-by, we are able to investigate the role of ignorance and distrust as first link in the propagation chain.

Twenty four people took part in the experiment. Although this was a very small user study, it did yield some interesting observations. Firstly, atomic trust propagation as described in the previous pages turns out to be a recurring pattern indeed: all subjects follow the opinion of a trusted agent. If the TTP b distrusts the recommender x, the subjects would not see the movie, despite the fact that x gave a positive recommendation (hence distrusting x, as $R(b,x)$ suggested). We call this the basic trust profile, which consists of fully relying on a completely trusted third party.

Secondly, with regard to distrust as the first propagation link, the answers showed that half of the subjects present a coherent behavior. Two distrust profiles came to the fore, each of them followed by the same amount of people. The subjects of the first distrust profile reverse the opinion of a distrusted passer-by b; the subject would still see the movie if b distrusts the recommender x (hence trusting x) and not see it when b trusts x (distrust). This attitude can informally be described as 'the enemy of your enemy is your friend' and 'the friend of your enemy is your enemy too', friend and enemy denoting a person that is trusted and distrusted respectively. Subjects with the second distrust profile also reverse b's opinion when $R(b,x)$ denotes trust, but ignore the advice of the recommender when b distrusts x (i.e., ignorance is inferred). In other words, these people do not consider the enemy of their enemy as their friend.

A last observation that can be made is with respect to the role of ignorance. A quarter of the subjects showed a coherent behavior when ignorance is involved. They ignore everything that is coming from a stranger b: irrespective of $R(b,x)$, the subjects decide not to pay any attention to the recommendation (i.e., inferring $R(a,x)$=ignorance). We call this the basic ignorance profile.

Question 1/20: You hear a *complete stranger* talking to his friend: `Personally, I do not know anything about movie M, but I have just asked *some guy I do not know* if he had seen the movie, and he said he liked M a lot, and greatly recommended it to me'.

What do you do with this advice?

○ Fully accept. You accept the advice wholeheartedly. Unless an even better recommendation comes along, you'll choose M.
○ Rather accept. You accept the recommendation as mild (non-compelling) evidence in favour of M. In case this is the only information (about any movie) you obtained, you'd probably go for M.
○ Ignore. It doesn't have an influence on your decision whether to watch M or not.
○ Rather reject. You don't have much faith in this recommendation; it actually makes M a less attractive alternative.
○ Fully reject. You will definitely not watch M.
○ Don't know. This recommendation confuses you: it gives you reasons both to see M, and not to see it.

Fig. 3.7 Example of the questionnaire about the role of ignorance and distrust in the propagation process.

Obviously, this was a very small experiment, and we are well aware that no strong conclusions can be drawn from the answers to the questionnaire; to be able to do this, one would need to construct more well-founded questionnaires (also with other scenarios, e.g. where more risk is involved), take more care of the underlying sociological and psychological interpretations (e.g. the effect of positive versus negative recommendations), and involve more participants. However, this goes beyond the scope of this book. The goal of the experiment was to shed some more light on the possible role of distrust, and to give us an indication on how trust, distrust and ignorance can be propagated. There is no ready-made answer to this question, as the experiment clearly illustrates, but it did give us inspiration for the creation of new trust score propagation operators that can handle trust, distrust and ignorance (which we will discuss in detail in Sec. 3.3.2).

3.3   Trust Score Propagation Operators

In the previous section, we discussed several desirable propagation properties and practical propagation patterns. In this section, we bring these two sides together and create a set of propagation operators that satisfy them as much as possible. Along the way, it will turn out that some theoretical properties have to be sacrificed to ensure that an operator's behavior is in accordance with the underlying propagation profile.

3.3.1   *Preliminaries*

As explained in Sec. 3.1, when dealing with trust only, the multiplication operator is omnipresent, for probabilistic as well as gradual settings. However, in gradual (fuzzy) settings, where trust is a number in $[0, 1]$, there is a wider range of possibilities, as the following example illustrates.

Example 3.5. Suppose that, on a scale from 0 to 1, user a trusts user b to the degree 0.5, and that b trusts user x to the degree 0.7. Then, in a probabilistic setting (using standard multiplication), trust propagation yields 0.35. In a fuzzy logic approach however, the final trust estimate depends on the choice of the operator: for instance, the rationale that a propagation chain is only as strong as its weakest link leads to the use of the minimum as propagation operator, hence yielding 0.5 as the propagated trust estimate. The use of the Łukasiewicz conjunction operator on the other hand, i.e. $\max(t_1 + t_2 - 1, 0)$, will yield 0.2. Like with multiplication, this propagated trust value reflects the individual influences of both composing links, as opposed to only the weakest link.

The operators in this example can be generalized by the concept of triangular norms, or t-norms for short [68, 126], representing large families of conjunctive operators.

Definition 3.6 (Triangular norm). A t-norm $\mathcal{T}$ is an increasing, commutative and associative $[0, 1]^2 \rightarrow [0, 1]$ mapping satisfying $\mathcal{T}(1, x) = x$ for all x in $[0, 1]$.

Table 3.1   Examples of dual t-norms and t-conorms w.r.t. the standard negator, with x and y in $[0,1]$.

t-norms	t-conorms
$T_M(x,y) = \min(x,y)$	$S_M(x,y) = \max(x,y)$
$T_P(x,y) = x \cdot y$	$S_P(x,y) = x + y - x \cdot y$
$T_L(x,y) = \max(x+y-1,0)$	$S_L(x,y) = \min(x+y,1)$
$T_D(x,y) = \begin{cases} \min(x,y) & \text{if } \max(x,y) = 1 \\ 0 & \text{otherwise} \end{cases}$	$S_D(x,y) = \begin{cases} \max(x,y) & \text{if } \min(x,y) = 0 \\ 1 & \text{otherwise} \end{cases}$

Table 3.1 contains some well-known and often used t-norms. Note that the largest t-norm is T_M, and the smallest the drastic t-norm T_D.

For distrust degrees too, this generalized approach might be followed. However, according to our discussion in the last pages, the picture gets more complicated when we also allow distrust as the first link in a propagation chain. Agent a might e.g. follow the principle of 'the enemy of your enemy is your friend', but another interpretation is to say that a should distrust x because a thinks that someone that is distrusted by a user that he distrusts certainly must be distrusted. Guha *et al.* call the latter strategy additive distrust propagation, and the former multiplicative distrust propagation [50]. They discuss the negative side effects (for example, cycles can lead to an agent distrusting himself) of multiplicative propagation (also see [158]), but conclude that it cannot be ignored because it has some philosophical defensibility; the enemy of your enemy may well be your friend. Besides Guha *et al.*, other researchers also proposed operators that adhere to the first strategy, such as Jøsang *et al.*'s opposite belief favoring discount operator [64], and also some of the operators we will introduce in Sec. 3.3.2.

Propagation operators that take into account two values (trust and distrust) are scarce. The standard gradual example is the approach of Guha *et al.* [50], while Jøsang's subjective logic operators [62, 64] are classic probabilistic examples; we discuss both of them in the following two examples.

Example 3.6. A trust score $(0.5, 0.2)$ denotes partial trust 0.5, partial distrust 0.2 and partial lack of knowledge $1 - 0.5 - 0.2 = 0.3$. Assume that the trust score of user a in user b is (t_1, d_1) and, likewise, that the trust score of user b in user x is (t_2, d_2). The trust score (t_3, d_3) of user a in user x can then be computed as the minimum of the trust degrees (as in Example 3.5), and the maximum of the distrust degrees, reflecting that any evidence of distrust should be retained (the additive approach). Another possibility is to calculate (t_3, d_3)

as follows:

$$(t_3, d_3) = (t_1 \cdot t_2, t_1 \cdot d_2)$$

This propagation strategy reflects the attitude of listening to whom you trust and not deriving any knowledge through a distrusted or unknown third party. In [62], Jøsang uses the same propagation technique to combine pairs of beliefs and disbeliefs. Furthermore, subtracting the distrust degree from the trust degree, the propagated trust score collapses to $t_1 \cdot (t_2 - d_2)$, a propagation scheme proposed by Guha *et al.* [50].

Example 3.7. Alternatively, the trust score (t_3, d_3) of a in x can be calculated as:

$$(t_3, d_3) = (t_1 \cdot t_2 + d_1 \cdot d_2 - t_1 \cdot t_2 \cdot d_1 \cdot d_2, t_1 \cdot d_2 + d_1 \cdot t_2 - t_1 \cdot d_2 \cdot d_1 \cdot t_2)$$

In this propagation strategy, t_3 is computed as the probabilistic sum of $t_1 \cdot t_2$ and $d_1 \cdot d_2$, while d_3 is the probabilistic sum of $t_1 \cdot d_2$ and $d_1 \cdot t_2$.

The underlying assumption is that a distrusted user is giving the wrong information on purpose. Hence user a trusts user x if a trusted third party tells him to trust x, *or*, if a distrusted third party tells him to distrust x (i.e. the enemy of your enemy is your friend). Subtracting the distrust degree from the trust degree yields $(t_1 - d_1) \cdot (t_2 - d_2)$, a distrust propagation scheme put forward by Guha *et al.* in [50].

Analogous to triangular norms, the maximum, probabilistic sum, etc. can be generalized by triangular conorms, or t-conorms for short [68], representing large families of disjunctive operators:

Definition 3.7 (Triangular conorm). A t-conorm $\mathscr{S}$ is an increasing, commutative and associative $[0,1]^2 \rightarrow [0,1]$ mapping satisfying $\mathscr{S}(x,0) = x$ for all x in $[0,1]$.

In the right part of Table 3.1, we summarized some well-known and often used t-conorms. The largest t-conorm is S_D, and the smallest S_M. Note that t-norms and t-conorms often appear in pairs:

Definition 3.8 (Negator). An involutive negator $\mathscr{N}$ is a decreasing $[0,1] \rightarrow [0,1]$ mapping satisfying $\mathscr{N}(0) = 1$, $\mathscr{N}(1) = 0$ and $\mathscr{N}(\mathscr{N}(x)) = x$ for all x in $[0,1]$.

Definition 3.9 (Dual t-norm and t-conorm). The t-norm $\mathscr{T}$ is called the dual of the t-conorm $\mathscr{S}$ w.r.t. the involutive negator $\mathscr{N}$ iff $\mathscr{T}(x,y) = \mathscr{N}(\mathscr{S}(\mathscr{N}(x), \mathscr{N}(y)))$ for all x and y in $[0,1]$.

The most commonly used involutive negator is $\mathcal{N}_s(x) = 1 - x$, called the standard negator; the t-norms and t-conorms in Table 3.1 are duals w.r.t. the standard negator. Note that the concept of dual t-norms and t-conorms is a generalization of the De Morgan's Laws for bivalent inputs.

3.3.2 *New Trust and Distrust Propagation Families*

Our questionnaire experiment revealed one basic trust propagation profile and several distrust propagation patterns. To study these propagation schemes, let us first consider the bivalent case, i.e. when trust and distrust degrees assume only the values 0 or 1. For agents a and b, we use $R^+(a,b)$, $R^-(a,b)$, and $\sim R^-(a,b)$ as shorthands for respectively $R^+(a,b) = 1$, $R^-(a,b) = 1$ and $R^-(a,b) = 0$. We consider the following four, different propagation schemes:

(1) $R^+(a,x) \equiv R^+(a,b) \wedge R^+(b,x)$
 $R^-(a,x) \equiv R^+(a,b) \wedge R^-(b,x)$
(2) $R^+(a,x) \equiv R^+(a,b) \wedge R^+(b,x)$
 $R^-(a,x) \equiv \sim R^-(a,b) \wedge R^-(b,x)$
(3) $R^+(a,x) \equiv (R^+(a,b) \wedge R^+(b,x)) \vee (R^-(a,b) \wedge R^-(b,x))$
 $R^-(a,x) \equiv (R^+(a,b) \wedge R^-(b,x)) \vee (R^-(a,b) \wedge R^+(b,x))$
(4) $R^+(a,x) \equiv R^+(a,b) \wedge R^+(b,x)$
 $R^-(a,x) \equiv (R^+(a,b) \wedge R^-(b,x)) \vee (R^-(a,b) \wedge R^+(b,x))$

In scheme (1) agent a only listens to whom he trusts, and ignores everyone else; this behavior corresponds to a combination of the basic trust profile and the basic ignorance profile from Sec. 3.2.2. Scheme (2) is similar, but in addition agent a takes over distrust information from a not distrusted (hence possibly unknown) third party (in other words, we preserve the basic trust profile but change the attitude towards ignorance). Scheme (3) corresponds to an interpretation in which the enemy of an enemy is considered to be a friend, and the friend of an enemy to be an enemy too (a combination of the basic trust profile and one of the distrust patterns found in the experiment). Finally, scheme (4) is an alteration of (3) which models the second distrust pattern in combination with the trust propagation profile; a mitigation of scheme (3).

In the trust score space, besides 0 and 1, we also allow partial trust and distrust. Hence we need suitable extensions of the logical operators that are used in schemes (1)–(4). For conjunction, disjunction and negation, we use respectively a t-norm $\mathcal{T}$, a t-conorm $\mathcal{S}$ and a negator $\mathcal{N}$. They represent large classes of logic connectives, from which specific operators, each with their own behavior, can be chosen, according to the application or context. In the remainder of this section, we use t_1 as an abbreviation for the trust degree $R^+(a,b)$ of agent a in agent b, and d_1 for the corresponding distrust degree $R^-(a,b)$. Similarly, we use (t_2,d_2) to denote the trust score from agent b in agent x. In other words $R(a,b) = (t_1,d_1)$ and $R(b,x) = (t_2,d_2)$.

Definition 3.10 (Propagation operators in $\mathscr{BL}^\square$). Let $\mathscr{T}$ be a t-norm, $\mathscr{S}$ a t-conorm and $\mathcal{N}$ a negator. The propagation operators P_1, P_2, P_3 and P_4 are defined by (for (t_1,d_1) and (t_2,d_2) in $[0,1]^2$):

$$P_1((t_1,d_1),(t_2,d_2)) = (\mathscr{T}(t_1,t_2), \mathscr{T}(t_1,d_2))$$

$$P_2((t_1,d_1),(t_2,d_2)) = (\mathscr{T}(t_1,t_2), \mathscr{T}(\mathcal{N}(d_1),d_2))$$

$$P_3((t_1,d_1),(t_2,d_2)) = (\mathscr{S}(\mathscr{T}(t_1,t_2), \mathscr{T}(d_1,d_2)), \mathscr{S}(\mathscr{T}(t_1,d_2), \mathscr{T}(d_1,t_2)))$$

$$P_4((t_1,d_1),(t_2,d_2)) = (\mathscr{T}(t_1,t_2), \mathscr{S}(\mathscr{T}(t_1,d_2), \mathscr{T}(d_1,t_2)))$$

People are likely to listen to whom they trust; this attitude is reflected by the first propagation operator. An agent with this profile (P_1) exhibits a skeptical behavior in deriving no knowledge through a distrusted or unknown third party. In the left hand side of Table 3.2, the behavior of P_1 for bivalent inputs is shown. Note that the results for inconsistency in the last link are also in accordance with this behavior. We do not consider results for inconsistency in the first link, because we assume that all agents behave in a consistent way; in fact, it is only useful to propagate inconsistency when it occurs in the last link of the propagation chain (where information is possibly aggregated).

It follows from the monotonicity of $\mathscr{T}$ that P_1 is knowledge and trust monotonic, while associativity of the t-norm leads to P_1 being associative. a quasi-ordering, and hence nothing can be said about the trust degrees involved. If there occurs a "missing link" $(0,0)$ anywhere in the propagation chain, the result will contain no useful information. In other words, P_1 is knowledge absorbing. Note that the same conclusion (i.e. ignorance) can be drawn if at any position in the chain, except the last one, there occurs complete distrust $(0,1)$.

P_1 neglects all information coming from an unknown agent. However, some agents might be willing to take over some information coming from whatever party, as long as it is not distrusted.

Table 3.2   Propagation operators P_1 and P_2, using TTP b with $R(a,b) = (t_1,d_1)$ (rows) and $R(b,x) = (t_2,d_2)$ (columns).

P_1	(0,0)	(0,1)	(1,0)	(1,1)	P_2	(0,0)	(0,1)	(1,0)	(1,1)
(0,0)	(0,0)	(0,0)	(0,0)	(0,0)	(0,0)	(0,0)	(0,1)	(0,0)	(0,1)
(0,1)	(0,0)	(0,0)	(0,0)	(0,0)	(0,1)	(0,0)	(0,0)	(0,0)	(0,0)
(1,0)	(0,0)	(0,1)	(1,0)	(1,1)	(1,0)	(0,0)	(0,1)	(1,0)	(1,1)

Table 3.3   Propagation operators P_3 and P_4, using TTP b with $R(a,b) = (t_1,d_1)$ (rows) and $R(b,x) = (t_2,d_2)$ (columns).

P_3	(0,0)	(0,1)	(1,0)	(1,1)	P_4	(0,0)	(0,1)	(1,0)	(1,1)
(0,0)	(0,0)	(0,0)	(0,0)	(0,0)	(0,0)	(0,0)	(0,0)	(0,0)	(0,0)
(0,1)	(0,0)	(1,0)	(0,1)	(1,1)	(0,1)	(0,0)	(0,0)	(0,1)	(0,1)
(1,0)	(0,0)	(0,1)	(1,0)	(1,1)	(1,0)	(0,0)	(0,1)	(1,0)	(1,1)

For instance, when agent b warns a about an agent x that is to be distrusted, agent a might listen to the advice even when he does not know b. In this way we arrive at a propagation operator reflecting that a trusts x when a trusts b and b trusts x (in other words, the classical behavior), and a distrusts x because b distrusts x and a does *not* distrust b. This attitude is represented by propagation operator P_2.

Note how P_2 only differs from P_1 in the computation of the propagated distrust degree. Agents with this second profile display a paranoid behavior in taking some distrust information even from an unknown third party: suppose you meet someone that tells you a movie was dreadful. Even though you do not know this person and whether to trust him, it may happen that you retain some of this negative information. This paranoid behavior also occurs when the unknown third party receives inconsistent information. The following example illustrates that P_2 is not knowledge monotonic.

Example 3.8. In this example we use the standard negator $\mathcal{N}_s$ and an arbitrary t-norm. To see that P_2 is not knowledge monotonic, consider

$$P_2((0.2,0.7),(0,1)) = (0,0.3)$$
$$P_2((0.2,0.8),(0,1)) = (0,0.2)$$

Going from the first to the second situation, all trust degrees remain the same but the distrust degree of agent a in agent b has increased slightly. In other words, a has formed a slightly more informed opinion about b:

$$(0.2,0.7) \leqslant_k (0.2,0.8)$$

and trivially also $(0,1) \leqslant_k (0,1)$. However, the propagated trust score in the second situation now contains less knowledge:

$$(0,0.3) \nleq_k (0,0.2),$$

since the propagated distrust degree of a in x in the second situation has dropped slightly, while the propagated trust degree of a in x did not change.

The intuitive explanation behind the non knowledge monotonic behavior of P_2 is that, using this propagation operator, agent a takes over distrust from a stranger b, hence giving b the benefit of the doubt, but when a starts to distrust b (thus knowing b better), a will adopt b's opinion to a lesser extent, or in other words, derive less knowledge.

P_2 is trust monotonic, but not knowledge absorbing (due to the role of ignorance in the first link), nor associative as the following example shows.

Example 3.9. Using the standard negator $\mathcal{N}_s$ and the product t-norm $\mathcal{T}_P$ we obtain:

$$P_2((0.3,0.6), P_2((0.1,0.2),(0.8,0.1))) = (0.024,0.032)$$
$$P_2(P_2((0.3,0.6),(0.1,0.2)),(0.8,0.1)) = (0.024,0.092)$$

The following example illustrates the effects of gradual trust and gradual distrust degrees.

Example 3.10. In this example we use the product t-norm $\mathcal{T}_P$ and the standard negator $\mathcal{N}_s$. Assume that, although agent a highly trusts b, there is also evidence to slightly distrust b, e.g.

$$(t_1,d_1) = (0.8,0.2)$$

Furthermore assume that b highly distrusts x, i.e.

$$(t_2,d_2) = (0.1,0.9)$$

Then, if agent a matches the second profile, we obtain

$$P_2((t_1,d_1),(t_2,d_2)) = (0.08,0.72)$$

In other words, agent a takes over most of the information that b provides; however, the final trust score is mitigated because a also slightly distrusts b.

Unlike the first profiles, it is in fact possible that some agents will use information coming from a distrusted agent. Propagation operator P_3 is an extension of P_1 and the implementation of the third scheme on page 38.

Agents that fit this profile consider an enemy of an enemy to be a friend and a friend of an enemy to be an enemy, i.e., $P_3((0,1),(0,1)) = (1,0)$ and $P_3((0,1),(1,0)) = (0,1)$.

Due to the monotonicity of $\mathcal{T}$ and $\mathcal{S}$, P_3 is knowledge monotonic. Examples can be constructed to prove that P_3 is not trust monotonic or associative. Knowledge absorption holds for P_3, despite the fact that it is not associative.

The last profile (P_4) is a moderation of P_3. While a friend of an enemy is still considered to be an enemy, no information is derived about an enemy of an enemy: $P_4((0,1),(1,0)) = (0,1)$ and $P_4((0,1),(0,1)) = (0,0)$. In a situation in which the first agent of the chain is distrusted, the trust degree of the second link is transferred to the distrust component of the propagated result, while the distrust degree is ignored (i.e., $P_4((0,1),(t,d)) = (0,t)$). Note that this is also the case when inconsistency is involved. The properties of the third profile apply to P_4 as well. In addition, P_4 is also trust monotonic.

In summary, as Prop. 3.1 shows, all the proposed propagation operators copy information from a fully trusted TTP. All of them ignore information coming from an unknown party, except P_2 which takes over the distrust information from a stranger.

Proposition 3.1. *For all (t,d) in $[0,1]^2$ it holds that*

$$P_1((1,0),(t,d)) = (t,d) \quad P_1((0,0),(t,d)) = (0,0) \quad P_1((0,1),(t,d)) = (0,0)$$
$$P_2((1,0),(t,d)) = (t,d) \quad P_2((0,0),(t,d)) = (0,d) \quad P_2((0,1),(t,d)) = (0,0)$$
$$P_3((1,0),(t,d)) = (t,d) \quad P_3((0,0),(t,d)) = (0,0) \quad P_3((0,1),(t,d)) = (d,t)$$
$$P_4((1,0),(t,d)) = (t,d) \quad P_4((0,0),(t,d)) = (0,0) \quad P_4((0,1),(t,d)) = (0,t)$$

In these basic cases, it is clear that all propagation operators preserve the consistency. In general, only P_1 and P_2 are consistency preserving for arbitrary choices of the fuzzy logical operators involved; however, when using the minimum/maximum, product/probabilistic sum, or the Łukasiewicz duals, the property also holds for P_3 and P_4.

Proposition 3.2. P_1 *and* P_2 *preserve the consistency.*

Proof. Assume that (t_1,d_1) and (t_2,d_2) are consistent. Due to the monotonicity of $\mathcal{T}$ it holds that $\mathcal{T}(t_1,t_2) \leqslant \mathcal{T}(1,t_2) = t_2$, and analogously $\mathcal{T}(t_1,d_2) \leqslant d_2$, hence $\mathcal{T}(t_1,t_2) + \mathcal{T}(t_1,d_2) \leqslant t_2 + d_2 \leqslant 1$, since (t_2,d_2) is consistent. This shows that P_1 is consistent. Analogously for P_2. $\qquad\qquad\square$

Propagation operators P_3 and P_4 are not consistency preserving in general. As a counterexample for P_3 and P_4, take $\mathcal{T} = T_M$ and $\mathcal{S} = S_D$ with $(t_1,d_1) = (0.3,0.6)$ and $(t_2,d_2) = (0.8,0.1)$.

Table 3.4 Properties of the propagation operators in Def. 3.10.

Property	P_1	P_2	P_3	P_4
Knowledge monotonicity	x		x	x
Trust monotonicity	x	x		x
Associativity	x			
Knowledge absorption	x		x	x
Consistency perserving	x	x		

Proposition 3.3. *P_3 and P_4 preserve the consistency if $\mathscr{T} = T_M$ and $\mathscr{S} = S_M$, or $\mathscr{T} = T_P$ and $\mathscr{S} = S_P$, or $\mathscr{T} = T_L$ and $\mathscr{S} = S_L$.*

Proof. We show that P_4 preserves the consistency; proofs for P_3 can be constructed analogously.

For T_M & S_M, we need to demonstrate that $\min(t_1,t_2) + \max(\min(t_1,d_2), \min(d_1,t_2))$ $[*] \leqslant 1$. From the monotonicity of the minimum and maximum and the consistent nature of the trust scores, it follows that $[*] \leqslant \min(t_1,t_2) + \max(\min(t_1, 1 - t_2), \min(1 - t_1, t_2))$ $[**]$. Suppose (i) $t_1 \geqslant 1 - t_2$, then $[**] = \min(t_1,t_2) + \max(1 - t_1, 1 - t_2)$ $[***]$. If $1 - t_1 \leqslant 1 - t_2$ (and hence $t_1 \geqslant t_2$), then $[***] = t_2 + 1 - t_2 = 1$ (and analogously for the other case). Suppose that (ii) $t_1 < 1 - t_2$ (or $t_1 + t_2 < 1$), then $[**] = \min(t_1,t_2) + \max(t_1,t_2) = t_1 + t_2 < 1$.

For T_P & S_P, we prove that $t_1 t_2 + t_1 d_2 + d_1 t_2 \leqslant 1$, and hence that $t_1 t_2 + t_1 d_2 + d_1 t_2 - t_1 d_2 d_1 t_2 \leqslant 1$. Since we assume consistent trust scores, $t_1 t_2 + t_1 d_2 + d_1 t_2 \leqslant t_1 t_2 + t_1(1 - t_2) + (1 - t_1)t_2 = t_1 + t_2(1 - t_1)$ $[*]$. Since t_1 and t_2 in $[0,1]$, $[*] = t_1 + t_2 - t_1 t_2 = \mathscr{S}_P(t_1,t_2) \leqslant 1$.

Finally, for T_L & S_L, $\max(t_1 + t_2 - 1, 0) + \min(\max(t_1 + d_2 - 1, 0) + \max(d_1 + t_2 - 1, 0), 1) \leqslant \max(t_1 + t_2 - 1, 0) + \min(\max(t_1 - t_2, 0) + \max(t_2 - t_1, 0), 1)$ $[*]$, due to the monotonicity of min and max and the consistent trust scores. Either $t_1 - t_2$ or $t_2 - t_1$ will be less than or equal to zero. Without loss of generality, let us pick $t_2 - t_1$. Then we can say that $[*] = \max(t_1 + t_2 - 1, 0) + \max(t_1 - t_2, 0) \leqslant 2t_1 - 1 \leqslant 1$. $\square$

Table 3.4 gives an overview of the properties in Sec. 3.2.1 that are fulfilled by the propagation operators. Note that P_1 satisfies all properties and is the only operator that is associative. P_2 is the only one that is not knowledge monotonic or knowledge absorbing (due to the role of ignorance), whereas P_3 is the only operator that does not satisfy trust monotonicity (due to the role of distrust in the first link of the propagation chain).

Table 3.5   Distribution of trust statements in the Epinion-s-reviews data set.

Type of statement	Trust score	#	%
all		840 799	100
full distrust	(0,1)	123 670	14.71
complete trust	(1,0)	717 129	85.29

3.4 Experimental Results

The choice of which propagation operator and t-(co)norms are appropriate mainly depends on the kind of application and the type of data that is available. In this section, we discuss data sets from CouchSurfing and Epinions , two web applications with a strong social networking component. We will continue to use these data sets throughout the book. In this section, we conduct experiments on them, illustrate that there does not exist one universal propagation operator which performs best for every application, and demonstrate that distrust-enhanced propagation strategies can be useful to obtain accurate trust estimations in agent networks.

3.4.1 *The Epinions.com and CouchSurfing.org Data Sets*

Epinions[8] is a popular e-commerce site where users can evaluate products and users, see Sec. 1.1. users to evaluate other users based on the quality of their reviews, and to provide trust and distrust evaluations in addition to their ratings: Users can include other users in their personal 'web of trust' (i.e., a list of reviewers whose reviews and ratings were consistently found to be valuable[8]), or put them on their 'block list' (a list of authors whose reviews were consistently found to be offensive, inaccurate or low quality[8], thus indicating distrust). The data set we use in our experiments was collected by Guha *et al.* [50] and consists of 131 829 users and 840 799 non self-referring trust relations. Remark that the Epinions data set only contains bivalent values (i.e., contains only full trust and full distrust, and no gradual statements), and that the users do not have the possibility to explicitly indicate ignorance. Also note that the complete distrust statements constitute only a small portion of the data set, namely about 15%; see Table 3.5.

CouchSurfing[9] is a large online hospitality network. Its members use the social network

---

[8]See www.epinions.com and www.epinions.com/help/faq
[9]See www.couchsurfing.org

to form friendships, exchange ideas and impressions, and in the first place, to find or offer free accommodation (also see Sec. 1.1). One of the questions assesses the trust relationship between the parties involved: Users can indicate whether they 'don't trust', 'somewhat', 'generally' or 'highly' trust another CouchSurfer, trust him/her 'with his life', or have no idea ('don't know this person well enough to decide'). The trust field is kept private to other members of CouchSurfing and is not mandatory. Nonetheless, these relationships constitute a large trust network of 397 471 users and 2 697 705 trust statements. The distribution of the trust statements in the network is given in Table 3.6. Furthermore, the users can also indicate how well they know each other, using one of the following options: 'not at all', 'a little bit', 'somewhat', 'fairly well', 'very well', 'extremely well' or 'could not know any better'.

This data set is very suitable for our purposes, since it contains gradual trust, distrust, and gradual knowledge levels. Unfortunately, the CouchSurfing data does not perfectly align with our trust score space setting (for instance, the latter requires cardinal values, whereas the data set only provides ordinal ones); hence, we need a heuristic method to map the available information into trust scores. Such heuristics are often used in link (strength) prediction problems where the relations (and weights) are not numerical values; see e.g. [52] or [88] in which the trust statements from Advogato are translated to numerical values, and the bivalent statements from Epinions to distances w.r.t. a certain horizon (also see chapter 6).

Our translation of the trust and knowledge statements into $[0,1]$ can be found in Table 3.6. We chose to translate the three highest knowledge levels to the maximum knowledge value 1 due to pragmatic reasons, to ensure a more balanced distribution of the trust scores over the trust score space. We propose to map the available trust and knowledge information to trust scores according to the following formula: $(t,d) = \left(k \cdot t', k \cdot (1 - t') \right)$, with t' (k) the translation of the trust (knowledge) statement[10]. In this way, we obtain a data set with a high variety of knowledge defects and gradual trust and distrust degrees, containing consistent trust scores with the desirable properties $t + d = k$ and $1 - k = kd(t,d)$; recall that for consistent trust scores, 1 and k represent the perfect and actual knowledge contained in a trust score, and kd the missing information, i.e., the knowledge defect.

---

[10]Records that contain a 'not at all' knowledge statement or a 'dont know well enough to decide' trust statement are translated to $(0, 0)$.

Table 3.6   Distribution of trust and knowledge statements in the CouchSurfing data set.

trust statements				knowledge statements			
type	t'	#	%	type	k	#	%
all		2 697 705	100	all		2 697 705	100
don't know	0	152 443	5.65	not at all	0	88 808	3.29
don't trust	0	6 429	0.24	a little bit	0.25	573 517	21.26
somewhat trust	0.25	331 061	12.27	somewhat	0.5	761 085	28.21
generally trust	0.5	994 476	36.86	fairly well	0.75	658 996	24.43
highly trust	0.75	893 428	33.12	very well	1	341 529	12.66
trust with my life	1	319 868	11.86	extremely well	1	177 001	6.56
				couldn't know any better	1	96 770	3.59

3.4.2   Propagation Operators for Epinions and CouchSurfing

The goal of our experiments is to find out which of the propagation behaviors exhibited by the operators of Def. 3.10 occur in real-world data sets, and how well the operators perform in a trust estimation problem. In this section, we focus on propagation chains of length 2 (i.e., with one intermediate agent), by analogy with the atomic propagation examples in the previous sections on which we have based our propagation operators[11]. The propagation chains that we consider consist of $R(a,b)$ and $R(b,x)$, for which the trust score $R(a,x)$ is also available in the data set. Like this, we are able to compare the propagated value with the actual value.

To measure the performance of the propagation operators, we use the leave-one-out method, which consists of hiding a trust relation and trying to predict its hidden value (i.e., the trust score). Figure 3.8 depicts an example of a data instance which contains three users with three trust relations (denoted by the solid lines): we hide the trust relation from agent a to agent x and try to estimate its trust score by propagating the opinion of a's acquaintance b. Therefore, we need to propagate a's trust score in b and b's trust score in x; this process is represented by the dotted line. The Epinions and CouchSurfing data set contain respectively 10 961 993 and 6 271 259 of these configurations for which we can apply the leave-one-out method.

To measure the accuracy of the propagation operators, we work with a variation on the classical mean absolute error (MAE). The computation of the MAE is done by determining the deviation between the hidden trust score and the predicted trust score for each leave-one-out experiment. Since the MAE is defined for scalar values, but we work with

---

[11] In chapter 6, we experiment with longer propagation paths as well.

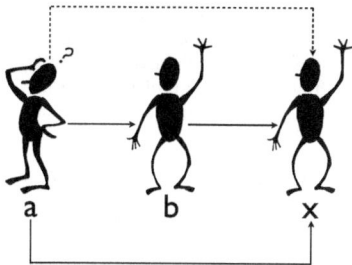

Fig. 3.8   Example of a leave-one-out scenario for propagation. Solid lines denote existing trust relations in the data set, the dotted line represents the predicted $R(a,x)$.

trust scores which have two components, we define the trust score MAE as the average of the Manhattan distances. Since the trust and distrust degrees range between 0 and 1, the extreme values that T-MAE can reach are 0 and 2.

Definition 3.11 (T-MAE). We define the trust score MAE in a leave-one-out experiment with n trust score predictions as

$$\text{T-MAE} = \frac{\sum_{i=1}^{n} |t_{r_i} - t_{p_i}| + |d_{r_i} - d_{p_i}|}{n}$$

with (t_{r_i}, d_{r_i}) the real trust score and (t_{p_i}, d_{p_i}) the predicted trust score.

We work with T-MAE instead of two MAEs (one for the trust degree and one for the distrust degree), since a trust score consists of two separate albeit dependent components which must be considered together: a trust degree of 0.8 e.g. has a completely different meaning when combined with a distrust degree of 0 or 0.8; in the former case this represents almost complete trust, while in the latter it denotes highly conflicting information.

Table 3.7 and 3.8 contain the results of the propagation leave-one-out experiments for P_1, P_2, P_3 and P_4 on the Epinions and CouchSurfing data set resp. Let us first focus on the results for the Epinions application. Since this data set contains bivalent trust and distrust degrees, we cannot distinguish between different $\mathscr{T}$ and $\mathscr{S}$, as their behavior on bivalent inputs is the same. Furthermore, P_1 and P_2 yield the same results because $\mathscr{T}(t_1, d_2) = \mathscr{T}(\mathscr{N}(d_1), d_2)$ due to the fact that the data set does not take into account explicit ignorance.

Note that it is no surprise that the trust-oriented propagation operators P_1 and P_2 perform more or less the same as the distrust-enhanced operators P_3 and P_4 due to the trust-distrust ratio in the data set (only 15% of all relations denote distrust), and the fact that the behavior of following the opinion of a trusted third party (which is embodied by P_1 and is at the

Table 3.7 T-MAE performance of the propagation operators in the Epinions data set, values are on a scale from 0 to 2; due to the bivalent nature of the data, the choice of $\mathcal{T}$ and $\mathcal{S}$ is irrelevant.

Operator	$\mathcal{T} = T_M = T_P = T_L$
P_1	0.142
P_2	0.142
P_3	0.136
P_4	0.134

basis of all other operators as well) is omnipresent: from all leave-one-out experiments with $R(a,b) = (1,0)$ and $R(b,x) = (1,0)$, 98.67% results in $R(a,x) = (1,0)$.

The T-MAE differences in Table 3.7 are small indeed, but note that we can nevertheless clearly make a distinction between the two approaches. P_3 and P_4 achieve the best T-MAEs, which indicates that distrust can be used to improve the trust score prediction process ('enemy of a friend is an enemy').

Unlike Epinions, the CouchSurfing data set contains gradual trust and distrust degrees. This enables us to investigate the usefulness of the t-norm and t-conorm pairs. Table 3.8 contains the results of the propagation leave-one-out experiment for P_1, P_2, P_3 and P_4, with $\mathcal{T} = T_M$, T_P and T_L. If a propagation operator requires a t-conorm $\mathcal{S}$, we chose the dual of $\mathcal{T}$ w.r.t. $\mathcal{N}_s$. First note that the minimum achieves the best results for all operators, and the Łukasiewicz the worst (recall that most classical approaches use T_P). This indicates that the trust score prediction task for CouchSurfing requires a propagation operator that penalizes weak links (i.e., low trust and distrust degrees), rather than an operator with a more compensating behavior.

We can easily observe that the best overall propagation attitude is exhibited by P_3, which considers 'the enemy of an enemy as a friend', and 'a friend of an enemy as an enemy'. This is also illustrated by the results of P_4: the only difference between P_3 and P_4 lies in the trust propagation process (where P_4 does not consider the enemy of an enemy to be a friend), and P_4 results in higher T-MAE's than P_3. Note that the most extreme option (P_3) performs best for the CouchSurfing application.

The experiments on the two data sets with different characteristics (bivalent versus gradual data, availability of explicit ignorance or not) demonstrate that the Epinions and CouchSurfing applications gain most by an operator that actively incorporates distrust. Studies on other social data sets have also revealed that several types of trust-enhanced

Table 3.8   T-MAE performance of the propagation operators in the CouchSurfing data set, values
are on a scale from 0 to 2; for $\mathscr{S}$ we choose the
dual of $\mathscr{T}$ w.r.t $\mathscr{N}_s$.

Operator	$\mathscr{T} = T_M$	$\mathscr{T} = T_P$	$\mathscr{T} = T_L$
P_1	0.357	0.425	0.508
P_2	0.364	0.405	0.496
P_3	0.336	0.381	0.498
P_4	0.341	0.404	0.498

applications may benefit from such operators. E.g., recent publications have shown that
'the enemy of an enemy is a friend' propagation pattern (in line with our P_3) is applicable
in the technology news website Slashdot [70] and the political forum Essembly [56]; this
is the pattern with the best performance for the CouchSurfing experiment. The Epinions
application, too, asks for a distrust-based propagation strategy such as P_3 or P_4.

However, one cannot jump to conclusions, because propagation and aggregation must
be considered together: in large data sets, it is very likely that there exists not one, but several paths between agents a and x (see for example Fig. 4.1). In other words, the results in
this section may give us an indication of the best propagation method for the CouchSurfing
and Epinions data set, but to determine the most optimal prediction strategies we need to
involve trust score aggregation operators as well.

3.5   Conclusions

The need for propagation operators is becoming increasingly important, especially now that
many online trust networks are very large and rarely fully connected. The design of suitable
trust propagation operators is not an easy task when distrust is involved. Unlike with trust,
there are several intuitive possibilities to model an agent's behavior towards distrust.

The study of distrust propagation is scarcely out of the egg, and the question whether
distrust can be propagated, and if so, how it should be, is still unanswered. Our goal in
this chapter was to contribute to a better understanding of the problem. Firstly, we introduced four new families of propagation operators that can be used to model different
kinds of distrust behavior: P_1 which is at the basis of all propagation strategies, and which
represents the most skeptical agents who only derive information coming from a trusted
acquaintance, while P_2 extends this behavior by also taking over distrust information coming from unknown parties. The other two families actively incorporate distrust by allowing

distrust to propagate throughout the propagation chain; they infer information coming from all kinds of agents, whether they are (partially) trusted, unknown, or distrusted. Operator P_4 considers a friend (trusted agent) of an enemy (distrusted agent) to be an enemy, and P_3 exhibits a somewhat more extreme attitude by also considering an enemy of an enemy to be a friend.

Secondly, we studied their behavior on a theoretical level by focusing on useful propagation properties such as knowledge and trust monotonicity, associativity, knowledge absorption and consistency preservation. Associativity turns out to be a hard condition to obtain; it is only satisfied by P_1. This is also the only operator that always satisfies all properties, while P_2 fulfills the fewest conditions. Finally, we also investigated their usefulness in practice by a large leave-one-out experiment for propagation paths of length 2 on real-world data sets from Epinions.com and CouchSurfing.org; we showed that the distrust-oriented operators P_3 and P_4 perform best for such social web applications, better than the standard trust-only approaches.

In chapter 6, we will focus on longer propagation paths (with a focus on trust-enhanced recommendations), while the combination of propagation and aggregation will be discussed in detail in chapter 4 (Sections 4.1 and 4.4).

Chapter 4

Trust Aggregation

In the previous chapter, we thoroughly discussed the trust propagation problem. However, besides propagation, a trust metric must also include an aggregation strategy. After all, in large networks it will often be the case that not one, but several paths lead to the user for whom we want to obtain a trust estimate. When this is the case, the trust estimates that are generated through the different propagation paths must be combined into one aggregated estimation; see for instance the situation depicted in Fig. 4.1.

As was the case with propagation too, the research on aggregation of both trust and distrust as separate concepts is almost non existent. After a review of related aggregation work and a discussion of issues related to the combination of propagation and aggregation (Sec. 4.1), we embark on the trust score aggregation problem. Our goal in this chapter is not only to study the problem on a theoretical basis, but also from a practical point of view. Like this, we hope to bridge the gap between theoretical research on aggregation operators and trust-enhanced aggregation applications. In Sec. 4.2, we first postulate desirable trust score aggregation properties, and then set out to define a number of aggregation operators fulfilling these properties in Sec. 4.3. Subsequently, in Sec. 4.4, we show that the best operators from a theoretical perspective are not always the most suitable ones in practice, and that the can outperform the sacrifice of certain theoretical properties may lead to better performing approaches. We conclude the chapter with a discussion of future research directions in Sec. 4.5.

4.1 Aggregation Preliminaries and Context

A whole range of aggregation operators are available when we need to model an aggregation process with scalar values in $[0, 1]$. For example, we can work with a simple minimum,

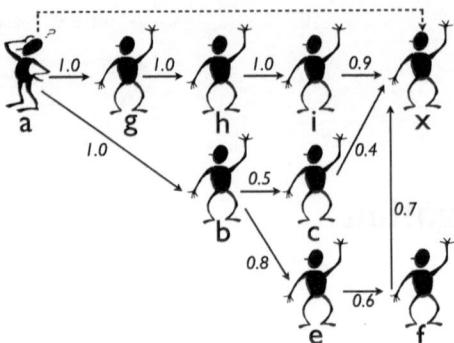

Fig. 4.1   Aggregation example: prediction of agent a's trust in agent x (dotted line) via three propagation paths; for simplicity only the trust degrees are displayed.

maximum or average, or use the more complicated fuzzy integrals [18, 131]. For a good overview of several aggregation operator families, we refer to [24] or [44].

One particularly interesting set of operators are the *weighted aggregation operators*, because they allow us to model the aggregation process more flexibly: they give us the opportunity to consider some inputs (agents or propagation paths) as more important than others. For example, in a weighted average, weights are associated with an information source. Like this, we can e.g. favor values that result from shorter propagation chains (remember our discussion on page 28).

A well-known type of weighted operators that is very often used in all kinds of applications [147, 149] is the *Ordered Weighted Averaging (OWA) family*. The OWA family can model a whole range of aggregation operators, among which also the minimum, maximum and arithmetic mean. The OWA weights are not associated to a source, but to an ordered position. This kind of aggregation is e.g. used for the judging of several olympic sports such as gymnastics: the most extreme scores (the lowest and highest) do not count for the final score, i.e., they receive weight 0 in the aggregation process.

The standard OWA operator models an aggregation process in which a sequence V of n scalar values are ordered decreasingly and then weighted according to their ordered position by means of a weight vector W [145]:

Definition 4.1 (Ordered weighted averaging aggregation family). Suppose $W = \langle w_1, \ldots, w_n \rangle$ is a weight vector for which it holds that $w_i \in [0,1]$ and $\sum_{i=1}^{n} w_i = 1$. The OWA operator associated with weight vector W is then defined as

$$OWA_W(V) = \sum_{i=1}^{n} w_i c_i,$$

in which c_i represents the ith largest value in V.

The OWA's main strength is its flexibility, since it enables us to model a spectrum of aggregation strategies: for example, if $W_1 = \langle 0, \ldots, 0, 1 \rangle$, then OWA_{W_1} equals the minimum; the average is modeled by $W_2 = \langle 1/n, \ldots, 1/n \rangle$, etc. OWA operators can be analyzed by several measures, among which the orness-degree that computes how similar its behavior is to that of the maximum:

Definition 4.2 (OWA Orness degree). The orness degree of OWA_W is defined as

$$orness(W) = \frac{1}{n-1} \sum_{i=1}^{n} ((n-i) \cdot w_i)$$

E.g., $orness(W_1) = 0$, while the weight vector $\langle 0.8, 0.1, 0.1, 0, 0 \rangle$ yields an orness-degree of 0.925, meaning that its behavior is very maximum-like. Yager proved that the higher the orness, the more the operator approaches the maximum [146]. OWA operators with an orness degree less than 0.5 approach the minimum operator.

Compared to classical aggregation approaches, the reordering of the arguments in the OWA process introduces an element of non-linearity into an otherwise linear process. However, in some cases it might not be possible to reorder the arguments because no useful/obvious order exists. One solution to this problem is the induced OWA operator (IOWA, [148]), in which the ordering of the arguments is not based on their value, but on that of an induced ordering variable which is associated to them:

Definition 4.3 (Induced OWA). Let V and W be defined as in Definition 4.1, and let U be a sequence of (not necessarily scalar) values, drawn from a linearly ordered space $(\mathscr{L}, \leqslant_{\mathscr{L}})$. If c_i represents the value in V associated with the ith largest value in U, then the induced ordered weighted averaging aggregation operator is defined by

$$IOWA_W(V, U, \leqslant_{\mathscr{L}}) = \sum_{i=1}^{n} w_i c_i$$

Since the values of the induced ordering variable need not be scalars, IOWA operators offer even more flexibility than their standard counterparts.

Trust metrics that only take into account trust mostly use classical aggregation operators such as the minimum, maximum, average, or weighted average [1, 4, 42, 66, 99, 102, 123]. Aggregation of both trust and distrust has not received much attention so far. Guha *et al.*'s approach [50] uses matrix multiplications to model the propagation and aggregation process, and needs mechanisms to round to one binary value. In other words, as with propagation, the two values are merged into one. In our trust score space setting, however, the goal is to treat trust and distrust as two separate concepts throughout the whole aggregation process. This strategy is also followed by Jøsang *et al.* for the subjective logic framework. They proposed three probabilistic aggregation operators, called consensus operators, for the fusion of dependent, independent or partially dependent opinions [64]. However, these operators assume equally important users (equal weights), and hence lack flexibility.

Note that propagation and aggregation very often need to be combined, and that the final trust estimation might depend on the way their interaction is implemented. Let us again take a look at Fig. 4.1; for simplicity we only include the trust values, a similar strategy can be followed to obtain a distrust estimate. There are three propagation paths leading to agent x; the two lowest paths have one chain in common. For these two paths, there are two scenarios to combine the values on the paths to obtain a trust estimate about agent x from agent b. The first possibility is to propagate trust to agent x, i.e., to apply a propagation operator on the trust from b to c and from c to x, and to apply one from b to e, from e to f, and from f to x, and then to aggregate the two propagated trust results. In this scenario, trust is first propagated, and afterwards aggregated (i.e., first propagate then aggregate, or FPTA). A second possibility is to follow the opposite process, i.e., first aggregate and then propagate (FATP). In this scenario, b must aggregate the estimates that he receives via c and e, and pass on the new estimate to a. Consequently, the FATP strategy must be implemented as a recursive process.

Example 4.1 (FATP vs. FPTA). In Fig. 4.1 there are three different paths from a to x. For the upper path, the problem of FATP versus FPTA does not pose itself since the path only consists of successive links. Assume that all trust degrees on the upper chain (a-g-h-i-x) are 1, except for the last link which has a trust weight of 0.9. Hence, using multiplication as propagation operator, the propagated trust value resulting from that chain is 0.9. Now, suppose that a trusts b to degree 1, and that b trusts c to the degree 0.5 and e to the degree 0.8. That means that the propagated trust value over the two chains from a to x through b are $1 \times 0.5 \times 0.4 = 0.2$ and $1 \times 0.8 \times 0.6 \times 0.7 \approx 0.34$ respectively. Using the classical average as aggregation operator, FPTA yields a final trust estimate of $(0.9 + 0.2 + 0.34)/3 = 0.48$. On the other hand, if we would allow b to first aggregate the information coming from his trust network, then b would pass the value $(0.2 + 0.34)/2 = 0.27$ on to a. In a FATP strategy, this would then be combined with the information derived through the upper chain in Fig. 4.1, leading to an overall final trust estimate of $(0.9 + 0.27)/2 \approx 0.59$.

It is easy to see that in the latter case (FATP) the agents in the network receive much more responsibility than in the former scenario (FPTA), and that the trust computation can be done in a distributed manner, without agents having to expose their personal trust and/or distrust information. In other words, FATP is more suitable for privacy-preserving environments. Also note that the privacy-preserving FATP strategy implies a right-to-left direction for the propagation; remember our discussion in Sec. 3.2.1. On the other hand, the FPTA approach can easily be used in applications with a central authority, and one can choose which order to use for the propagation. A last remark can be made w.r.t. the influence of an agent's opinion on the final trust estimate, which is smaller in the FATP than in the FPTA approach: in FPTA, all paths count just as much, while in FATP the paths are merged so that there is only one trust estimation for every neighbor of the inquiring agent.

In the remainder of this book, we assume the FPTA approach in experiments where we have to combine aggregation with propagation paths of more than one intermediate agent. In this chapter, we limit ourselves to propagation paths of length 2 (one intermediate agent)[1]. Like this, we can reduce the effect of different propagation lengths and the FPTA vs. FATP issue, and hence fully concentrate on the performance of the aggregation techniques themselves. In the following section, we start our search for operators that can handle both trust and distrust by investigating several useful properties for an aggregation operator in the trust score space.

4.2 Trust Score Aggregation Properties

For a discussion of common properties for aggregation operators for scalar values, we refer to [43]. Some of the most often imposed conditions for such operators are the boundary condition, the monotonicity property, and commutativity. The boundary condition ensures that the aggregated value cannot be higher (lower) than the maximum (minimum) among the aggregates, while respecting the monotonicity means that the aggregated result cannot decrease when one of the aggregates increases. In this section, we begin by investigating whether these conditions can be meaningfully extended for use in our trust score framework, and whether they can be justified intuitively.

Let $\mathscr{BL}^{\square} = ([l, \infty]^{\in}, \leqslant_{\sqcup\Gamma}, \leqslant_k, \neg)$ be the trust score space introduced in Sec. 2.3. In this

---

[1] The effect of longer propagation paths will be studied in the context of trust-enhanced recommenders in Chap. 6.

space, we look for a trust score aggregation operator $A : ([0,1]^2)^n \rightarrow [0,1]^2$ $(n \geqslant 1)$ satisfying as many of the following characteristics pinned down in Definitions 4.4–4.15 as possible.

Since an aggregated trust score should reflect a consensus about the trust estimation, it is only natural that it should not contain more trust than the maximum trust value among the aggregates. In the same respect, the aggregated distrust value should not be higher than the maximum of the aggregates' distrust values. Analogously, the aggregated trust score should contain at least as much distrust and trust as the minimum among the aggregates.

Definition 4.4 (Trust boundary preservation). We say that aggregation operator A satisfies the trust boundaries iff $A((t_1,d_1),\ldots,(t_n,d_n)) = (p,q)$, with $\min(t_1,\ldots,t_n) \leqslant p \leqslant \max(t_1,\ldots,t_n)$, $\forall (t_1,d_1),\ldots,(t_n,d_n) \in [0,1]^2$.

Definition 4.5 (Distrust boundary preservation). We say that aggregation operator A satisfies the distrust boundaries iff $A((t_1,d_1),\ldots,(t_n,d_n)) = (p,q)$, with $\min(d_1,\ldots,d_n) \leqslant q \leqslant \max(d_1,\ldots,d_n)$, $\forall(t_1,d_1),\ldots,(t_n,d_n) \in [0,1]^2$.

Note that these conditions imply aggregation operators that cannot be used in an additive context. For instance, in situations where risk is involved, if a lot of the agents highly distrust x, the aggregated distrust degree about x could be experienced on a higher level than the maximum among the distrust degrees, to emphasize the fact that many agents really distrust x (which cannot be modeled due to the upper distrust boundary).

If agent a receives the same trust score $(t,d) \in [0,1]^2$ from all paths linking it to agent x, i.e., $(t_1,d_1) = (t,d),\ldots,(t_n,d_n) = (t,d)$, then the opinion of a about x should be that same trust score:

Definition 4.6 (Idempotency). An aggregation operator A is idempotent iff, $\forall (t,d) \in [0,1]^2$, $A((t,d),\ldots,(t,d)) = (t,d)$.

Proposition 4.1. *If an aggregation operator A satisfies the trust and distrust boundaries, A also fulfills the idempotency condition.*

When aggregating additional trust scores, the knowledge contained in the aggregated trust score should not decrease. In other words, the aggregated trust score should contain at least as much knowledge as the most knowledgeable aggregate:

Definition 4.7 (Knowledge boundary preservation). We say that an aggregation operator A satisfies the knowledge boundary iff $A((t_1, d_1), \ldots, (t_n, d_n)) = (p, q)$, with $p + q \geq \max(t_1 + d_1, \ldots, t_n + d_n)$, $\forall (t_1, d_1), \ldots, (t_n, d_n) \in [0,1]^2$.

Recall that we assume that all agents are consistent. If we use propagation operators that preserve consistency, this means that all aggregates will also be consistent, and can be represented as intervals. Hence, in the latter spirit, the knowledge boundary condition implies more narrow aggregated intervals, i.e., the uncertainty should not increase. E.g., consider (t_1, d_1) and (t_2, d_2) with $t_1 = t_2$ and $d_1 > d_2$, which means that $[t_1, 1 - d_1]$ is included in $[t_2, 1 - d_2]$. In other words, the latter contains more uncertainty than the former. Due to the trust boundary condition and $t_1 = t_2$, the aggregated trust degree p must be t_1. W.r.t. the aggregated distrust degree q, from the knowledge boundary condition $(p + q \geq \max(t_1 + d_1, t_2 + d_2))$ it follows that $q \geq d_1$. Hence, $[p, 1 - q]$ must be at least as narrow as $[t_1, 1 - d_1]$, and certainly less wide than $[t_2, 1 - d_2]$.

Since we are using a trust score space with two orderings, two monotonicity conditions arise; one for the trust-distrust and one for the knowledge ordering. Intuitively, each of these conditions makes sense, as for instance, the more information/less doubt (resp., the more trust and the less distrust) the individual sources provide, the more information (resp., the more trust/less distrust) the aggregated outcome should contain. Therefore, a trust score aggregation operator A should be be monotonously increasing with respect to both $\leq_{td}$ and $\leq_k$.

Definition 4.8 (Trust-Distrust monotonicity). We say that an aggregation operator A respects trust-distrust monotonicity iff $\forall (t_j, d_j), (t'_j, d'_j) \in [0,1]^2$, with $j \in \{1, \ldots, n\}$, it holds that, if $(t_j, d_j) \leq_{td} (t'_j, d'_j)$, then

$$A((t_1, d_1), \ldots, (t_j, d_j), \ldots, (t_n, d_n)) \leq_{td} A((t_1, d_1), \ldots, (t'_j, d'_j), \ldots, (t_n, d_n))$$

Definition 4.9 (Knowledge monotonicity). We say that an aggregation operator A respects knowledge monotonicity iff $\forall (t_j, d_j), (t'_j, d'_j) \in [0,1]^2$, with $j \in \{1, \ldots, n\}$: if $(t_j, d_j) \leq_k (t'_j, d'_j)$, then

$$A((t_1, d_1), \ldots, (t_j, d_j), \ldots, (t_n, d_n)) \leq_k A((t_1, d_1), \ldots, (t'_j, d'_j), \ldots, (t_n, d_n))$$

Proposition 4.2. *If A is an idempotent trust score aggregation operator that satisfies the trust-distrust monotonicity, then A respects the trust and distrust boundaries.*

Proof. Since we assume that the trust-distrust monotonicity is valid, it holds that $A((t_1,d_1),\ldots,(t_j,d_j),\ldots,(t_n,d_n)) \leqslant_{td} A((t_l,d_m),\ldots,(t_l,d_m))$ [*], with $t_l = \max(t_1,\ldots,t_n)$ and $d_m = \min(d_1,\ldots,d_n)$. Since A is idempotent, $[*] = (t_l,d_m)$. From the definition of $\leqslant_{td}$ it follows that if $A((t_1,d_1),\ldots,(t_j,d_j),\ldots,(t_n,d_n)) = (p,q)$ then $p \leqslant t_l \wedge q \geqslant d_m$, or in other words, $p \leqslant \max(t_1,\ldots,t_n)$ and $q \geqslant \min(d_1,\ldots,d_n)$. Analogously for $p \geqslant \min(t_1,\ldots,t_n)$ and $q \leqslant \max(d_1,\ldots,d_n)$. □

Definition 4.10 (Trust monotonicity). We say that an aggregation operator A respects trust monotonicity iff, $\forall \ (t_j,d_j),(t'_j,d'_j) \in [0,1]^2$ with $j \in \{1,\ldots,n\}$, it holds that, if $(t_j,d_j) \leqslant_t (t'_j,d'_j)$, then

$$A((t_1,d_1),\ldots,(t_j,d_j),\ldots,(t_n,d_n)) \leqslant_t A((t_1,d_1),\ldots,(t'_j,d'_j),\ldots,(t_n,d_n)).$$

Definition 4.11 (Distrust monotonicity). We say that an aggregation operator A respects distrust monotonicity iff, $\forall \ (t_j,d_j),(t'_j,d'_j) \in [0,1]^2$ with $j \in \{1,\ldots,n\}$, it holds that, if $(t_j,d_j) \leqslant_d (t'_j,d'_j)$, then

$$A((t_1,d_1),\ldots,(t_j,d_j),\ldots,(t_n,d_n)) \leqslant_d A((t_1,d_1),\ldots,(t'_j,d'_j),\ldots,(t_n,d_n)).$$

Proposition 4.3. *Trust-distrust and knowledge monotonicity are fulfilled iff trust and distrust monotonicity hold.*

Proof. If trust and distrust monotonicity hold, it can easily be shown that trust-distrust and knowledge monotonicity also hold by taking into account Prop. 2.1.

For the opposite direction, we show the connection for trust monotonicity; the proof for distrust monotonicity can be obtained analogously. Let $(t_j,d_j) \leqslant_t (t'_j,d'_j)$. Suppose now that $d_j \leqslant d'_j$, and hence $(t_j,d_j) \leqslant_k (t'_j,d'_j)$. Since we assume that knowledge monotonicity is valid, it holds that

$$A((t_1,d_1),\ldots,(t_j,d_j),\ldots,(t_n,d_n)) \leqslant_k A((t_1,d_1),\ldots,(t'_j,d'_j),\ldots,(t_n,d_n)). \qquad (*)$$

From (*) and by the definition of knowledge monotonicity it follows that, if $A((t_1,d_1),\ldots,(t_j,d_j),\ldots,(t_n,d_n)) = (p,q)$ and $A((t_1,d_1),\ldots,(t'_j,d'_j),\ldots,(t_n,d_n)) = (r,s)$,

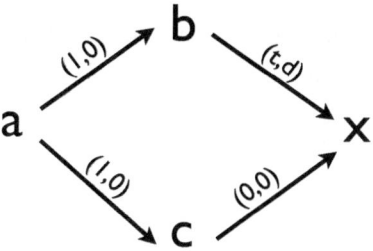

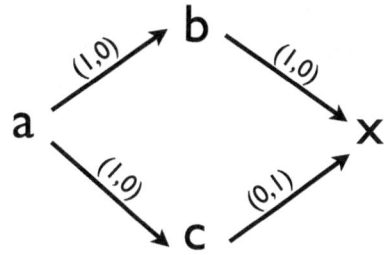

Fig. 4.3   Aggregation scenario with total inconsistency

Fig. 4.2   Aggregation scenario with ignorance

$p \leqslant r$ and $q \leqslant s$. Consequently, according to the definition of trust monotonicity, $(p,q) \leqslant_t (r,s)$, which shows that A respects trust monotonicity if $d_j \leqslant d_j'$ (or $(t_j,d_j) \leqslant_k (t_j',d_j')$). In a similar way, we can prove that A also respects the trust monotonicity if $d_j > d_j'$ (or $(t_j,d_j) \leqslant_{td} (t_j',d_j')$) by assuming that trust-distrust monotonicity is valid.   □

To compute the opinion of agent a about agent x, the order of the trust scores should not matter.

Definition 4.12 (Commutativity). An aggregation operator A is commutative iff $A((t_1,d_1),\dots,(t_n,d_n)) = A((t_{\pi(1)},d_{\pi(1)}),\dots,(t_{\pi(n)},d_{\pi(n)}))$, $\forall$ $(t_j,d_j) \in [0,1]^2$, $j \in \{1,\dots,n\}$, and π a permutation of $\{1,\dots,n\}$.

The associativity ensures that the operator can be extended unambiguously for more operands.

Definition 4.13 (Associativity). An aggregation operator A is associative iff

$$A((t_1,d_1),\dots,(t_n,d_n)) = A((t_1,d_1),A((t_2,d_2),\dots,(t_n,d_n))) =$$
$$\dots = A(A((t_1,d_1),\dots,(t_{n-1},d_{n-1})),(t_n,d_n)), \ \forall \ (t_j,d_j) \in [0,1]^2.$$

Besides these mathematical properties that have well-known intuitive rationales, we also propose a number of additional requirements to further guarantee the correct/intuitive behavior of the trust score aggregation process. to guarantee the intuitive behavior of the trust score aggregation process. We motivate these requirements by examples.

Example 4.2 (Ignorance). In the scenario in Fig. 4.2, b and c are both fully trusted acquaintances of a that are connected to x. Propagation with any of the four operators from

Chap. 3 results in the two trust scores (t,d) and $(0,0)$. However, it can be argued that c's opinion of x (ignorance) should not contribute to the final outcome; indeed, a $(0,0)$ edge can be considered as no edge at all, as it carries no information.

In other words, $(0,0)$ should act as a neutral element of the aggregation:

Definition 4.14 (Neutrality). We say that an aggregation operator A satisfies the neutrality condition iff $\forall\ (t_j,d_j) \in [0,1]^2$ and $j \in \{1,\dots,n\}$,

$$A((t_1,d_1),\dots,(t_{i-1},d_{i-1}),(0,0),(t_{i+1},d_{i+1}),\dots,(t_n,d_n)) =$$
$$A((t_1,d_1),\dots,(t_{i-1},d_{i-1}),(t_{i+1},d_{i+1}),\dots,(t_n,d_n)).$$

Example 4.2 also shows why a naive average of trust and distrust degrees, leading to $\left(\frac{t}{2},\frac{d}{2}\right)$, would be a poor aggregation strategy in this case.

Proposition 4.4. *If A is an idempotent trust score aggregation operator that satisfies the knowledge monotonicity and the neutral element condition, then A respects the knowledge boundary.*

Proof.   Due to knowledge monotonicity, it holds that

$$A((t_1,d_1),\dots,(t_i,d_i),\dots,(t_n,d_n)) \geqslant_k A((0,0),\dots,(t_i,d_i),\dots,(0,0)) = [*].$$

Since A is idempotent and satisfies the neutrality condition, it holds that $[*]= A((t_i,d_i)) = (t_i,d_i)$.   Hence, from the definition of $\leqslant_k$ it follows that if $A((t_1,d_1),\dots,(t_i,d_i),\dots,(t_n,d_n)) = (p,q)$ then $p \geqslant t_i$ and $q \geqslant d_i$, hence $p+q \geqslant t_i + d_i$, and this for all $i = 1,\dots,n$. In other words, $p+q \geqslant \max(t_1 + d_1,\dots,t_i + d_i,\dots,t_n + d_n)$ which shows that A respects the knowledge boundary. $\square$

Example 4.3 (Total inconsistency). In Figure 4.3, two fully trusted acquaintances of agent a express completely opposite trust opinions of agent x. Again, a simple average of trust and distrust degrees, yielding $(0.5,0.5)$, is unsuitable, since it does away with the conflicting information a receives, and cannot be distinguished from a scenario in which a receives information that x is half to be trusted and half to be distrusted. In other words, we lose too much provenance information. A more intuitive result seems to be $(1,1)$, reflecting the inconsistency agent a faces in his assessment of agent x.

This brings us to a final requirement for trust score aggregation operators: an equal number of $(1,0)$ and $(0,1)$ arguments should yield contradiction.

Definition 4.15 (Opposite arguments). We say that an aggregation operator A fulfills the opposite arguments condition iff

$$A(\underbrace{(1,0),\ldots,(1,0)}_{n/2 \; times},\underbrace{(0,1),\ldots,(0,1)}_{n/2 \; times}) = (1,1).$$

Note that we have formulated the aggregation conditions for n arguments, as opposed to the propagation properties in Sec. 3.2.1 where we worked with two arguments. This is because propagation operators with two arguments can easily be extended for more arguments by agreeing on left associativity (central authority) or right associativity (e.g. needed in a privacy-preserving environment, or can also be applied within a central authority context). On the other hand, this has little use in an aggregation context since many aggregation operators are not associative, as will also be the case with the operators in Sec. 4.3.2.

4.3   Trust Score Aggregation Operators

In this section, we investigate several operators satisfying one or more of the conditions proposed in the previous section. In particular, we start by defining trust score aggregation operators that preserve the trust, distrust and knowledge boundaries (Sec. 4.3.1), and then proceed by introducing more advanced techniques that are based on the OWA operator and the incorporation of knowledge defects (Sec. 4.3.2).

4.3.1   *Bilattice-Based Aggregation Operators*

Figure 4.4 depicts two possible scenarios, both for aggregating two trust scores (denoted by dots): (t_1,d_1) and (t_2,d_2) (Example 4.4), and (t_3,d_3) and (t_4,d_2) (Example 4.5). Note that all trust scores are consistent since they reside under or on the $kd(t,d) = 0$ line (lower triangle); hence, we can also represent them as intervals.

Example 4.4 (Aggregation with overlap). Agent a asks two of his acquaintances (whom he trusts completely) for an opinion about agent x. The first agent returns the trust score (t_1,d_1) and the second one (t_2,d_2) (dots). Since agent a has complete faith in the two trusted third parties, the propagated trust scores to be aggregated remain (t_1,d_1) and (t_2,d_2) . Note that, in Fig. 4.4, $t_1 < t_2$, $d_1 > d_2$ and $t_2 < 1 - d_1$; in other words, $t_1 < t_2 < 1 - d_1 < 1 - d_2$.

Since it is desirable that a standard trust score aggregation operator should fulfill at least Definitions 4.4 and 4.5 (trust and distrust boundaries), the aggregated result must be in the

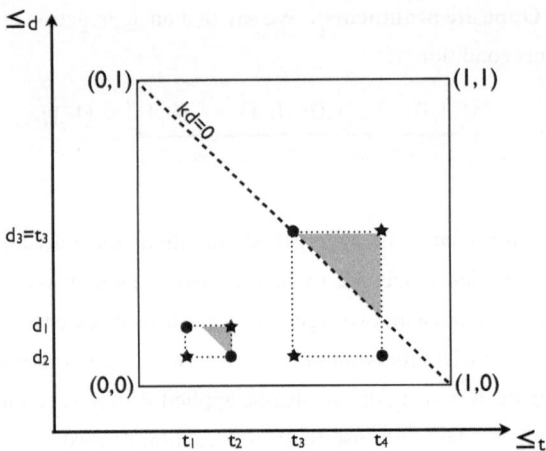

Fig. 4.4 Possible aggregation results of (t_1, d_1) and (t_2, d_2), and (t_3, d_3) and (t_4, d_2), for operators satisfying the trust and distrust boundaries (within the dotted lines) and the knowledge boundary (gray area).

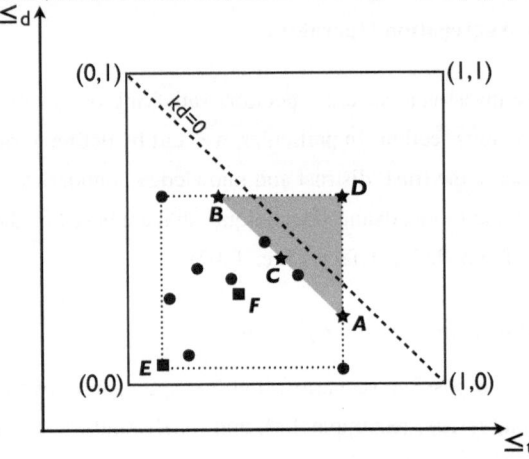

Fig. 4.5 Possible aggregation results of several trust scores, for operators fulfilling the trust, distrust and knowledge boundary conditions.

area marked out by the dotted lines. Hence, the extremes w.r.t. $\leq_t$ and $\leq_d$ for the aggregated trust score are (t_2, d_1) and (t_1, d_2) (stars). By also imposing Definition 4.7, however, only part of the possible results remain: as can be seen in the figure, $t_2 + d_2 > t_1 + d_1$, and hence all possible results should reside above or on the $kd(t, d) = kd(t_2, d_2)$ line (formed by all trust scores that have the same knowledge defect as (t_2, d_2)), in other words, in the gray area. In this way, only one extreme remains, namely (t_2, d_1).

The same conclusion can be obtained when reasoning in the interval representation, even without focusing on the boundary conditions. The interval representations of (t_1, d_1) and (t_2, d_2) are $[t_1, 1 - d_1]$ and $[t_2, 1 - d_2]$ respectively. Note that in Example 4.4 the two intervals overlap $(t_1 < t_2 < 1 - d_1 < 1 - d_2)$. As the aggregated trust interval must reflect the consensus among the two intervals, it should represent the trust estimation on which both agents agree, which is usually modeled as the intersection of the two intervals. This strategy results in a narrower interval, or analogously, a trust score that contains less uncertainty (recall our discussion about knowledge monotonicity). Hence, $[t_2, 1 - d_1]$ is indeed the most logical choice for the aggregation extreme w.r.t. $\leqslant_t$ and $\leqslant_d$.

Example 4.5 (Aggregation with no overlap). In the second scenario of Fig. 4.4, a makes inquiries about agent z, resulting in (t_3, d_3) (or $[t_3, 1 - d_3]$) and (t_4, d_2) (or $[t_4, 1 - d_2]$). Note that $t_3 = 1 - d_3 < t_4 < 1 - d_2$. This time, a's acquaintances do not agree at all: there is no overlap between the two trust intervals.

The example illustrates how inconsistent trust scores can arise, even when the agents are consistent. In this case, the extreme aggregated trust score is (t_4, d_3), reflecting the disagreement that exists between the aggregates.

These two-points-examples can be generalized to scenarios with more inputs; see Fig. 4.5 for an example with eight aggregates, represented by dots. Imposing trust, distrust and knowledge boundary conditions yields a limited number of possible aggregation results, depicted in the figure by the gray area. Each of the trust scores marked by stars makes sense as aggregated score: A is the most optimistic choice (maximum trust degree for the lowest possible knowledge level), B the most pessimistic one (maximum distrust), C the moderating approach (average of the most knowledgeable trust scores; only trust scores that have the highest amount of knowledge, or the smallest knowledge defect, take part) and D the most extreme, knowledge maximizing, option: maximum trust and distrust degree, often resulting in an inconsistent trust estimation.

We call A the trust maximizing and B the distrust maximizing operator, C the knowledge preference averaging operator and D the knowledge maximizing trust score aggregation operator.

Definition 4.16 (TMAX). We define the trust maximizing trust score aggregation operator *TMAX* as

$$TMAX\left((t_1, d_1), \ldots, (t_n, d_n)\right) = (\max(t_1, \ldots, t_n), \max(t_1 + d_1, \ldots, t_n + d_n) - \max(t_1, \ldots, t_n)).$$

Definition 4.17 (DMAX). We define the distrust maximizing trust score aggregation operator *DMAX* as

$$DMAX\left((t_1,d_1),\ldots,(t_n,d_n)\right) =$$
$$\left(\max(t_1+d_1,\ldots,t_n+d_n) - \max\left(d_1,\ldots,d_n\right), \max(d_1,\ldots,d_n)\right).$$

Definition 4.18 (KAV). We define the knowledge preference averaging trust score aggregation operator *KAV* as

$$KAV\left((t_1,d_1),\ldots,(t_n,d_n)\right) = (p,q)$$

with (p,q) such that

$$p = \frac{\sum\limits_{i=1}^{n} w_i \cdot t_i}{\sum\limits_{i=1}^{n} w_i}, \quad q = \frac{\sum\limits_{i=1}^{n} w_i \cdot d_i}{\sum\limits_{i=1}^{n} w_i}$$

$$w_i = \begin{cases} 1 & \text{if } t_i+d_i = \max(t_1+d_1,\ldots,t_n+d_n) \\ 0 & \text{otherwise} \end{cases}$$

Definition 4.19 (KMAX). We define the knowledge maximizing trust score aggregation operator *KMAX* as

$$KMAX\left((t_1,d_1),\ldots,(t_n,d_n)\right) = \left(\max(t_1,\ldots,t_n), \max(d_1,\ldots,d_n)\right).$$

Note that this operator corresponds to $\oplus$, the join of the information lattice $([0,1]^2, \leqslant_k)$ in the trust score space.

The following proposition shows how the four operators perform w.r.t. the criteria set out in the previous section:

Proposition 4.5. *TMAX, DMAX, KAV and KMAX fulfill Definitions 4.4-4.7 and 4.12-4.14. Furthermore, KMAX also satisfies Definitions 4.8-4.11 and 4.15, while TMAX and DMAX fulfill Definitions 4.10, 4.11 respectively.*

4.3.2 Advanced Trust Score Aggregation Operators

Although the four operators from the previous section are perfectly justifiable, it will often be the case that they are too extreme. For example, in some situations, agents might prefer also to take into account the opinions from agents who have more doubt about their opinions, while in other scenarios they might prefer to listen to less marked opinions instead of only retaining the 'best' and the 'worst' among the opinions.

In this section, we will present several families of aggregation operators which mitigate the behavior of KMAX and KAV. This can be achieved by introducing maximum-like weights, or through the incorporation of knowledge defects. Along the way, it will turn out that some of the postulated properties need to be sacrificed, or at least adjusted.

4.3.2.1 *Fixed Weight OWA Trust Score Aggregation*

A straightforward solution for mitigating KMAX's behavior is to introduce weights in the aggregation process. The weights can then be chosen in such a way that KMAX's behavior is alleviated, but without harming the underlying maximum thought. The ordered weighted averaging aggregation family (Definition 4.1) is one of the best-known weighted aggregation strategies. However, the application of an OWA operator requires scalar values as arguments. As such, OWA operators are not directly applicable to aggregate trust scores. Therefore, we propose to perform trust aggregation by means of two separate OWA operators, one for the trust and one for the distrust degrees.

Below, we describe a generic procedure for applying (standard) OWA operators to the trust score aggregation problem:

(1) Determine n, the number of trust score arguments distinct from $(0,0)$. Trust scores that represent complete ignorance do not take part in the aggregation process[2] to preserve their role as neutral element.

(2) Construct sequences T and D, containing the n trust values (resp., the n distrust values) of the trust score arguments.

(3) Construct n-dimensional weight vectors W_T and W_D.

(4) Compute the aggregated trust score as $(OWA_{W_T}(T), OWA_{W_D}(D))$.

If we add an extra restriction to the construction of W_T and W_D which ensures that the orness degree of both weight vectors is at least 0.5 (so that they exhibit a maximum-like behavior), the above procedure can be generalized into a class of trust score aggregation operators that can be seen as alternate, mitigated, versions of KMAX.

---

[2]If all trust scores equal $(0,0)$, the final result is also set to $(0,0)$ and the aggregation process terminates at this step.

Definition 4.20 (K-OWA). We define the trust score OWA operator $K\text{-}OWA_{W_T,W_D}$ associated with the trust weight vector W_T and distrust weight vector W_D as

$$K\text{-}OWA_{W_T,W_D}\left((t_1,d_1),\ldots,(t_n,d_n)\right) =$$

$$\left(OWA_{W_T}(t_1,\ldots,t_n), OWA_{W_D}(d_1,\ldots,d_n)\right),$$

with $W_T = \langle w_{T_1},\ldots,w_{T_n}\rangle$ and $W_D = \langle w_{D_1},\ldots,w_{D_n}\rangle$ such that

$$orness(W_T) \geqslant 0.5 \text{ and } orness(W_D) \geqslant 0.5$$

$$\sum_{i=1}^{n} w_{T_i} = 1 \text{ and } \sum_{i=1}^{n} w_{D_i} = 1$$

with $(t_j,d_j) \neq (0,0)$ for all $j \in \{1,\ldots,n\}$; trust scores $(t_j,d_j) = (0,0)$ do not take part in the aggregation process.

Proposition 4.6. *K-OWA always fulfills Definitions 4.4, 4.5, 4.6, 4.12 and 4.14 (regardless of the weight choice). In order for Definition 4.15 to hold, it suffices that* $w_{T_i} = 0$ *and* $w_{D_i} = 0$ *as soon as* $i > \frac{n}{2}$. *If we add the restriction to Definitions 4.8 and 4.9 that* $(t_j,d_j) \neq (0,0)$ *and* $(t'_j,d'_j) \neq (0,0)$, *the property holds, regardless of the weight vectors* W_T *and* W_D. *Analogously for Definitions 4.10 and 4.11.*

This can be verified by construction and by the properties of an OWA operator. The reason for the failure of the monotonicity properties for K-OWA is due to the presence (and subsequent alteration) of $(0,0)$ trust score arguments, which causes the application of the OWA operators to a different number of arguments. This is demonstrated by the following example.

Example 4.6. If the trust scores to aggregate are $(1,0)$, $(0,0)$, $(0,0)$ and $(0,0)$, then the outcome by the K-OWA procedure is $(1,0)$ (regardless of the choice of weights vectors, because $n = 1$). If we change these trust scores to $(1,0)$, $(0.1,0)$, $(0.1,0)$ and $(0.1,0)$, the number of arguments that take part in the OWA aggregation equals 4. If we compute the weights for instance as $W_T = \langle \frac{2}{3},\frac{1}{3},0,0\rangle$ and $W_D = \langle 1,0,0,0\rangle$, the final result of the aggregation equals $(0.7,0)$. So, although $(0,0) \leqslant_t (0.1,0)$ and $(0,0) \leqslant_k (0.1,0)$, $(1,0) \not\leqslant_t (0.7,0)$ and $(1,0) \not\leqslant_k (0.7,0)$.

Note that the associativity condition 4.13 will not always be fulfilled, since this depends on the weighting scheme (see Example 4.7). Because of the averaging nature of K-OWA, the knowledge boundary condition 4.7 does not always hold either: take e.g. $(1,0)$, $(0.5,0)$ and $(0.6,0)$ and $W_T = \langle 1/3,1/3,1/3\rangle$, which yields $(0.7,0)$ as aggregated result, and $0.7+0 < 1+0$. In other words, the result of the aggregation will not always reside in the gray triangle of Fig. 4.5. However, it will remain in the area that is marked out by the minimum and maximum among the trust and distrust degrees (since the trust and distrust boundaries are always satisfied).

As is clear from the above, the actual way of aggregating the trust scores is determined by the choice of the weight vectors. One strategy is to construct W_T and W_D beforehand. For instance, the final trust (resp., distrust) value can be evaluated as the extent to which a predefined fraction (at least one, all of them, a majority, ...) of the trust score arguments exhibits trust (resp., distrust).

Example 4.7 (Fixed weights). Given n trust score arguments to aggregate (all distinct from $(0,0)$), the trust and distrust weights can be computed by

$$w_{T_i} = \frac{2 \cdot \max(0, \lceil \frac{n}{2} \rceil - i + 1)}{\lceil \frac{n}{2} \rceil (\lceil \frac{n}{2} \rceil + 1)} \quad , \quad w_{D_i} = \frac{2 \cdot \max(0, \lceil \frac{n}{4} \rceil - i + 1)}{\lceil \frac{n}{4} \rceil (\lceil \frac{n}{4} \rceil + 1)}$$

The disparity between trust and distrust weights can be motivated by the observation that a few distrust statements about x (in particular, a quarter of them) may suffice to reach a final conclusion of distrust, while the evaluation of trust depends on the majority of the arguments; distrust is easier established than trust. Note that weights are decreasing, in the sense that the higher trust/distrust values have a stronger impact than the lower ones.

This example also illustrates why K-OWA does not always satisfy the associativity condition: let $n = 3$, if we aggregate all three trust scores at once, two of them will take part in the trust degree computation; however, when we perform the aggregation in two phases, only one trust score will take part in each trust degree computation. For example, $K\text{-}OWA((1,0),(0.5,0),(0.3,0)) = 5/6$, while $K\text{-}OWA(K\text{-}OWA((1,0),(0.5,0)),(0.3,0)) = K\text{-}OWA((1,0),(0.3,0)) = (1,0)$.

The above example can be generalized into an implementation of the K-OWA family, where the weight vectors are determined by two parameters α and β:

Example 4.8 (Fixed weights family). Let α and β in $[1,\infty]$. The weights can then be computed as (with $i \in \{1,\dots,n\}$):

$$w_{T_i} = \frac{2 \cdot \max(0, \lceil \frac{n}{\alpha} \rceil - i + 1)}{\lceil \frac{n}{\alpha} \rceil (\lceil \frac{n}{\alpha} \rceil + 1)}$$

$$w_{D_i} = \frac{2 \cdot \max(0, \lceil \frac{n}{\beta} \rceil - i + 1)}{\lceil \frac{n}{\beta} \rceil (\lceil \frac{n}{\beta} \rceil + 1)}$$

Remark that KMAX is a special case of this particular implementation of K-OWA, with $\alpha = \beta = n$.

Proposition 4.7. *The weights from Example 4.8 sum up to 1, regardless of the choice for α and β.*

Proof. We show that $\sum_{i=1}^{n} \max(0, \lceil \frac{n}{\alpha} \rceil - i + 1) = \left(\lceil \frac{n}{\alpha} \rceil (\lceil \frac{n}{\alpha} \rceil + 1) \right) / 2$. The same rationale can be followed for w_{D_i}.

$$\sum_{i=1}^{n} \max \left(0, \left\lceil \frac{n}{\alpha} \right\rceil - i + 1 \right) = \sum_{i=1}^{\lceil \frac{n}{\alpha} \rceil} \left(\left\lceil \frac{n}{\alpha} \right\rceil - i + 1 \right)$$

$$= \left\lceil \frac{n}{\alpha} \right\rceil \cdot \left(\left\lceil \frac{n}{\alpha} \right\rceil + 1 \right) - \sum_{i=1}^{\lceil \frac{n}{\alpha} \rceil} i$$

$$= \left(\left\lceil \frac{n}{\alpha} \right\rceil \cdot \left(\left\lceil \frac{n}{\alpha} \right\rceil + 1 \right) \right) / 2.$$

Proposition 4.8. *The trust score aggregation operators from Example 4.8 always exhibit a maximum-like behavior, regardless of the choice for α and β.*

Proof. We show that the orness degree of W_D and W_T will never be lower than 2/3: the lowest possible orness for W_T and W_D will be achieved when all arguments take part in the aggregation process, i.e., when $\alpha = \beta = 1$. This yields weights $W_{T_i} = W_{D_i} = \frac{2(n-i+1)}{n(n+1)}$. Consequently,

$$orness(W_T) = orness(W_D) = \frac{1}{n-1} \sum_{i=1}^{n} \left((n-i) \left(\frac{2(n-i+1)}{n(n+1)} \right) \right)$$

$$= \frac{2 \left(\sum_{i=1}^{n} (n-i)^2 + (n-i) \right)}{n(n-1)(n+1)}$$

$$= \frac{2 \left(\sum_{i=1}^{n} (n^2+n) + \sum_{i=1}^{n} (i^2-i) - 2n \sum_{i=1}^{n} i \right)}{n(n-1)(n+1)}$$

$$= \frac{2 \left(n^3 + n^2 + \frac{n^3}{3} + \frac{n^2}{2} + \frac{n}{6} - \frac{n^2}{2} - \frac{n}{2} - n^2 - n^3 \right)}{n(n-1)(n+1)}$$

$$= \frac{2 \left(\frac{n^3}{3} - \frac{n}{3} \right)}{n^3 - n}$$

$$= 2/3$$

4.3.2.2   Knowledge-Enhanced KAV Trust Score Aggregation

In Sec. 4.3.1 we explained that the KAV trust score aggregation operator exhibits the most moderating behavior among the bilattice-based strategies. However, one can argue that, for some applications/situations, even KAV might be too extreme, since it only takes into account the opinions of the most knowledgeable agents. This is illustrated by the following example.

Example 4.9. Assume that the trust scores to aggregate are $(1,0)$, $(1,0)$, $(0.7,0.29)$ and $(0.7,0.29)$. In other words, two of the trust score arguments have perfect knowledge $(kd(1,0) = 0)$, while the others only show a very small knowledge defect $(kd(0.7,0.29) \approx 0)$. Intuitively, one would expect their contribution to be almost equally important, and hence that the final trust degree lies somewhere in the middle between 0.7 and 1, and the distrust degree between 0 and 0.29. However, the KAV aggregated trust score equals $(1,0)$.

In a way, the determination of the weights for the KAV aggregation can be seen as a binary process, because only the users with the most perfect knowledge (in other words, with the lowest knowledge defect) take part in the aggregation, even if the difference with some of the other arguments is almost negligible. A possible solution to this problem is the following new family of trust score aggregation operators; they mitigate the behavior of KAV, but without harming the underlying thought of trust score discrimination w.r.t. knowledge defect.

Definition 4.21 (KAAV). We define the knowledge awarding averaging trust score aggregation operator $KAAV_\gamma$ associated with knowledge reward $\gamma \in [0,\infty]$ as

$$KAAV_\gamma((t_1,d_1),\ldots,(t_n,d_n)) = (p,q)$$

with (p,q) such that

$$p = \sum_{i=1}^{n} w_i \cdot t_i \text{ and } q = \sum_{i=1}^{n} w_i \cdot d_i$$

$$w_i = \frac{(1 - kd(t_i,d_i))^\gamma}{\sum_{i=1}^{n}(1 - kd(t_i,d_i))^\gamma}$$

If all trust scores have $kd(t,d) = 1$ and at least one trust score equals $(1,1)$, then the aggregated result is $(1,1)$; when all trust scores equal $(0,0)$ then the aggregated result is $(0,0)$.

If the knowledge reward γ equals 0, then we obtain the arithmetic mean. When $\gamma = 1$, each trust score is weighted inversely proportional to its knowledge defect: the lower $kd(t,d)$, the higher the associated weight. Note that the aggregated trust score will approximate KAV's result for $\gamma \to \infty$.

Example 4.10 (Knowledge-dependent weights). In the case of Example 4.9, with $\gamma = 1$, $W = \langle \frac{1}{3.98}, \frac{1}{3.98}, \frac{0.99}{3.98}, \frac{0.99}{3.98} \rangle$. Then the aggregated trust score $(p,q) \approx (0.85, 0.15)$, a much more intuitive result.

Proposition 4.9. *KAAV fulfills Definitions 4.4 and 4.5, 4.6, 4.12, 4.14 and 4.15.*

The following counterexample demonstrates that the associativity condition 4.13 does not hold in general: $KAAV_1 ((1,0),(0.5,0),(0.2,0.8)) = (0.58,0.32) \neq$ $KAAV_1 (KAAV_1((1,0),(0.5,0)),(0.2,0.8)) \approx (0.49,044)$. Note that, as was the case with K-OWA too, mitigating the behavior implies we have to sacrifice the knowledge boundary condition.

Trust, distrust, trust-distrust and knowledge monotonicity do not hold in general because of the way the weights are generated. Let us illustrate this with distrust monotonicity. Even if $d_j > d'_j$ and hence $1 - kd(t_j,d_j) > 1 - kd(t_j,d'_j)$ since we assume consistent agents, this does not imply that the final aggregated trust score (p,q) will contain at least as much distrust as (p,q'), since the other weights are also affected by the change in the jth weight. E.g., $(0.5,0.3) \geq_d (0,0.3)$, but $KAAV_1 ((1,0),(1,0),(0.5,0.3)) \approx (0.870,0.039) <_d KAAV_1 ((1,0),(1,0),(0,0.3)) \approx (0.857,0.086)$.

Similar examples can be constructed to show that trust, trust-distrust and knowledge monotonicity do not always hold. In fact, any attempt to award/ penalize trust scores according to their knowledge defects is incompatible with maintaining monotonicity because a knowledge-based weight may decrease even if the corresponding aggregate increases.

4.3.2.3 *Knowledge-Enhanced OWA Trust Score Aggregation*

According to the analysis in Sec. 4.3.2.1, fixed-weight OWA approaches perform well w.r.t. the criteria set out in Sec. 4.2. However, they also exhibit certain drawbacks, as the following example illustrates.

Example 4.11. Assume the trust scores to aggregate are $(1,0)$, $(\delta,0)$, $(\delta,0)$ and $(\delta,0)$, with δ a value close to 0. In other words, three of the trust score arguments are very close to ignorance. Intuitively, one would expect their contribution to the final result to be very small. However, using the same weight vector as in Example 4.7, the aggregated value will be $\left(\frac{2}{3} + \frac{1}{3}\delta, 0\right) \approx \left(\frac{2}{3}, 0\right)$, which differs significantly from $(1,0)$, the result obtained if the $(\delta, 0)$ values are replaced by $(0,0)$.

In fact, the above kind of problem occurs with any fixed-weight approach[3]; it is due to the fact that in this approach, trust scores are not discriminated w.r.t. the amount of knowledge they contain. Recall that we followed a similar rationale for Example 4.9. Hence, analogous to the knowledge-enhanced procedure of the last section, we can alter the weights based on the knowledge defect exhibited by the individual trust score arguments: given n trust score arguments (t_i, d_i), we can associate with them a weight vector W^{kd} that represents each trust score's degree of knowledge defect relative to the remaining trust scores. We cannot use W^{kd} directly as a weight vector inside the OWA operators, since the knowledge defect weights are not associated to ordered positions, but rather to the arguments themselves. We can however use them to modify existing OWA weight vectors W^T and W^D (which can be chosen as in the fixed weight approach). This leads to a new class of trust score aggregation operators:

Definition 4.22 (KK-OWA). We define the knowledge-based trust score OWA operator $KK\text{-}OWA_{\gamma, W_T, W_D}$ associated with knowledge reward γ, the trust weight vector W_T and distrust weight vector W_D as

$$KK\text{-}OWA_{\gamma, W_T, W_D}\left((t_1, d_1), \ldots, (t_n, d_n)\right) = \left(OWA_{W_T}(t_1, \ldots, t_n), OWA_{W_D}(d_1, \ldots, d_n)\right),$$

with $W_T = \langle w_{T_1}, \ldots, w_{T_n} \rangle$ and $W_D = \langle w_{D_1}, \ldots, w_{D_n} \rangle$ such that

$$W_{T_i} = \frac{W_i^T W_{\pi(i)}^{kd}}{\sum\limits_{j=1}^{n} W_j^T W_{\pi(j)}^{kd}}, \quad W_{D_i} = \frac{W_i^D W_{\pi'(i)}^{kd}}{\sum\limits_{j=1}^{n} W_j^D W_{\pi'(j)}^{kd}}$$

in which $i \in \{1, \ldots, n\}$, W_i^T and W_i^D denote the weights obtained according to the $K\text{-}OWA_{W_T, W_D}$ strategy, π and π' represent the permutations that map an ordered position i to the index of the trust score that appears at that position, and

$$W_i^{kd} = \frac{(1 - kd(t_i, d_i))^{\gamma}}{\sum\limits_{j=1}^{n} (1 - kd(t_j, d_j))^{\gamma}}.$$

If all trust scores have $kd(t, d) = 1$ and at least one trust score equals $(1, 1)$, then the aggregated result is $(1, 1)$; when all trust scores equal $(0, 0)$ then the aggregated result is $(0, 0)$.

---

[3] The only exception is when $W_{t_1} = W_{d_1} = 1$, i.e., only the highest trust and distrust values are taken into account.

The following example illustrates the knowledge-based approach:

Example 4.12 (Knowledge-dependent weights). In the case of Example 4.11 with knowledge reward 1,

$$W^{kd} = \left(\frac{1}{1+3\delta}, \frac{\delta}{1+3\delta}, \frac{\delta}{1+3\delta}, \frac{\delta}{1+3\delta} \right)$$

$$W_T = \left(\frac{2}{2+\delta}, \frac{\delta}{2+\delta}, 0, 0 \right)$$

The final aggregation result will be $\left(\frac{2+\delta^2}{2+\delta}, 0 \right) \approx (1,0)$, which corresponds to our intuition.

Note that the procedure for obtaining the weights does not only differ from the fixed weight approach in Definition 4.20 because of the inclusion of knowledge defects, but also because of the treatment of the neutral elements: for K-OWA the $(0,0)$ trust scores are left out of the computation, while this is no longer the case for KK-OWA (they are taken into account, but receive weight 0), leading to a more elegant approach. Hence $(0,0)$ scores influence the construction of the K-OWA weight vector, whereas the length of the weight vector in KK-OWA is independent of the aggregates. In a way, one can say that the neutral elements for KK-OWA are more neutral than for K-OWA.

Proposition 4.10. *KK-OWA fulfills Definitions 4.4, 4.5, 4.6, 4.12, and 4.14. Definition 4.15 holds whenever $w_{T_i} = 0$ and $w_{D_i} = 0$ as soon as $i > \frac{n}{2}$.*

The application of knowledge-dependent OWA weights does not affect the conditions that do not pertain to monotonicity, but Definitions 4.8–4.11 cannot be maintained, not even in the weakened version which holds for fixed weights.

Example 4.13. Consider the following trust score sequences:

$$A = \langle (1,0), (0.9,0.2), (0,1) \rangle$$
$$B = \langle (1,0), (0.9,0.1), (0,1) \rangle$$
$$C = \langle (1,0.9), (0.9,0.2), (0,1) \rangle$$

Constructing the weight vectors as in Example 4.12, we obtain the aggregated trust scores $\left(\frac{281}{290}, 1 \right)$ for A, $\left(\frac{29}{30}, 1 \right)$ for B and $\left(\frac{101}{110}, 1 \right)$ for C. However, while $(0.9, 0.2) \leqslant_{td} (0.9, 0.1)$, $\left(\frac{281}{290}, 1 \right) \nleqslant_{td} \left(\frac{29}{30}, 1 \right)$ (comparing sequence A with B). Similarly, while $(1, 0) \leqslant_k (1, 0.9)$, $\left(\frac{281}{290}, 1 \right) \nleqslant_k \left(\frac{101}{110}, 1 \right)$ (comparing sequence A with C). Analogous for $\leqslant_t$ and $\leqslant_d$.

In this case, the failure of monotonicity is due to the change of the knowledge-dependent weight vector W^{kd}. Again, it can be argued that any attempt to penalize trust scores for their knowledge defects is incompatible with maintaining monotonicity. In fact, this is already evident in the fixed-weight approach of Sec. 4.3.2.1: to guarantee that $(0,0)$ can play its role as neutral element, it needs to be handled separately.

4.3.2.4   IOWA Trust Score Aggregation

An alternative knowledge-enhanced OWA strategy can be obtained by using IOWA operators (Definition 4.3). In order to use the IOWA approach, we require an order inducing variable that takes values drawn from a linearly ordered space. Since the bilattice orderings $\leqslant_{td}$ and $\leqslant_k$ are only partial rather than linear, they do not qualify to construct the required linearly ordered space. However, meaningful linear orderings over trust scores do exist; we will consider a combination of trust/distrust degrees and knowledge defect for this purpose. In particular, for the trust degrees vector $T = \langle t_i \rangle$ and distrust degrees vector $D = \langle d_i \rangle$, we define the value of the order inducing variables $U = \langle u_i \rangle$ and $U' = \langle u_i' \rangle$ respectively as

$$u_i = (kd(t_i,d_i),t_i) \text{ and } u_i' = (kd(t_i,d_i),d_i) \tag{4.1}$$

and order these values decreasingly according to the linear order $\leqslant_{kd}$ on $[0,1]^2$ defined by, for $(k_1,r_1),(k_2,r_2)$ in $[0,1]^2$,

$$(k_1,r_1) \leqslant_{kd} (k_2,r_2) \Leftrightarrow (k_1 > k_2) \vee (k_1 = k_2 \wedge r_1 \leqslant r_2) \tag{4.2}$$

In other words, trust scores with lower knowledge defects are ordered first, and in case of equal knowledge defect, the higher trust (resp., distrust) value prevails. It can be verified that $([0,1]^2, \leqslant_{kd})$ is a linearly ordered space.

The corresponding IOWA aggregation procedure is largely analogous to that for standard OWA:

(1) Determine n, the number of trust score arguments distinct from $(0,0)$. Trust scores that represent complete ignorance do not take part in the aggregation process[4].
(2) Construct the sequences T, D; U and U'; T and D contain the corresponding n trust values (resp., the n distrust values), while U and U' contain the order inducing values as in (4.1).
(3) Construct n-dimensional weight vectors W_T and W_D.
(4) Compute the aggregated trust score as

$$(IOWA_{W_T}(T,U,\leqslant_{kd}),IOWA_{W_D}(D,U',\leqslant_{kd})).$$

---

[4]If all trust scores equal $(0,0)$, the final result is also set to $(0,0)$ and the aggregation process terminates at this step.

This procedure gives rise to a second aggregation operator family that combines the OWA strategy with knowledge incorporation:

Definition 4.23 (K-IOWA).
We define the induced trust score OWA operator $K\text{-}IOWA_{W_T,W_D}$ associated with the trust weight vector W_T and distrust weight vector W_D as

$$K\text{-}IOWA_{W_T,W_D}\left((t_1,d_1),\ldots,(t_n,d_n)\right) =$$

$$\left(IOWA_{W_T}\left(\langle t_1,\ldots,t_n\rangle,U,\leqslant_{kd}\right),IOWA_{W_D}\left(\langle d_1,\ldots,d_n\rangle,U',\leqslant_{kd}\right)\right),$$

with W_T and W_D denoting the weight vectors obtained according to Definition 4.20. The order inducing variables for $IOWA_{W_T}$ and $IOWA_{W_D}$ are constructed according to (Eq. (4.1)), with associated ordering $\leqslant_{kd}$ as in (Eq. (4.2)).

Note that while the K-IOWA approach allows to take into account knowledge defects by using $\leqslant_{kd}$, it still makes sense to use knowledge-dependent weights. This becomes evident when we apply the approach to the data in Example 4.11, which gives the same outcome as in the standard OWA case. On the other hand, the monotonicity properties are not guaranteed for the K-IOWA approach, even if fixed weights are used. The following example illustrates this.

Example 4.14. Consider the following trust score sequences:

$$A = \langle (0.95,0.05),(0.8,0.2),(0,0.5)\rangle$$
$$B = \langle (1,0.05),(0.8,0.2),(0,0.5)\rangle,$$

with associated induced ordering vectors

$$U_A = \langle (0,0.95),(0,0.8),(0.5,0)\rangle$$
$$U'_A = \langle (0,0.05),(0,0.2),(0.5,0.5)\rangle$$
$$U_B = \langle (0.05,1),(0,0.8),(0.5,0)\rangle$$
$$U'_B = \langle (0.05,0.05),(0,0.2),(0.5,0.5)\rangle$$

For sequence U_A it holds that $(0,0.95) \geqslant_{kd} (0,0.8) \geqslant_{kd} (0.5,0)$, and for U'_A, $(0,0.2) \geqslant_{kd}$ $(0,0.05) \geqslant_{kd} (0.5,0.5)$, while for sequence U_B, $(0,0.8) \geqslant_{kd} (0.05,1) \geqslant_{kd} (0.5,0)$ and for U'_B, $(0,0.2) \geqslant_{kd} (0.05,0.05) \geqslant_{kd} (0.5,0.5)$. Constructing the weight vectors as in Example 4.7, we obtain the aggregated trust scores $(0.9,0.8)$ for A and $\left(\frac{13}{15},0.8\right)$ for B. However, while $(0.95,0.05) \leqslant_{td} (1,0.05)$ and $(0.95,0.05) \leqslant_k (1,0.05)$, $(0.9,0.8) \nleqslant_{td} \left(\frac{13}{15},0.8\right)$ and $(0.9,0.8) \nleqslant_k \left(\frac{13}{15},0.8\right)$.

Proposition 4.11. *The K-IOWA approach satisfies Definitions 4.4, 4.5, 4.6, 4.12, 4.14, 4.15 (if $w_{T_i} = 0$ and $w_{D_i} = 0$ as soon as $i > \frac{n}{2}$), and this regardless of whether fixed or variable weight vectors are used.*

4.4 Experimental Results

In this section, we will investigate the performance in practice of the aggregation operators introduced in the previous section. For our experiments, we use the same data sets and methodology as in Sec. 3.4.1 and 3.4.2. To measure the accuracy of the predictions, besides T-MAE, we also take into account a variation of the classical root mean squared error:

Definition 4.24 (T-RMSE). We define the trust score RMSE in a leave-one-out experiment with n trust score predictions as

$$\text{T-RMSE} = \sqrt{\left(\sum_{i=1}^{n} (t_{r_i} - t_{p_i})^2 + (d_{r_i} - d_{p_i})^2 \right) \Big/ n}$$

with (t_{r_i}, d_{r_i}) the real trust trust score and (t_{p_i}, d_{p_i}) the predicted trust score.

Note that the T-RMSE, like the classical RMSE, emphasizes larger errors. The extreme values that T-RMSE can reach are 0 and $\sqrt{2}$.

In the following experiments, we take into account propagation paths of exactly length 2 and use the P_1 propagation operator of Definition 3.10 (because it is at the basis of all other propagation operators) with $\mathscr{T} = \min$. In this way, we can ensure that every aggregate is the result of the same propagation process and that there is no variable path length which might introduce extra errors, making it harder to study the actual impact of the aggregation operators. In this configuration, the CouchSurfing data set consists of 1 298 170 distinct a-x trust scores with at least one a-b-x trust path between them (see Fig. 3.8). In the Epinions data set, we can perform 589 689 such leave-one-out experiments. Note that we do not include $(0,0)$ values in the data set, since we interpret them as no link. We do retain $(0,0)$ values which are the result of propagation.

In Sec. 4.4.1–4.4.4, we only consider results for the CouchSurfing data since we focus on the mutual relations between the operators. In Section 4.4.5, we then investigate the adaptability of the operators by comparing the CouchSurfing results with their performance on the Epinions data. The impact of the propagation operator choice is discussed in Sec. 4.4.6, including a comparison between P_1 and the distrust-enhanced P_3.

Table 4.1 Overall performance of bilattice-based aggregation strategies on the CouchSurfing data set, with propagation operator P_1 and $\mathcal{T} = \min$ for paths of length 2; T-MAE $\in [0, 2]$ and T-RMSE $\in [0, \sqrt{2}]$.

Aggregation operator		Fig. 4.5	T-MAE	T-RMSE
Trust maximizing	TMAX	A	0.316	0.321
Distrust maximizing	DMAX	B	0.325	0.324
Knowledge preference averaging	KAV	C	0.318	0.321
Knowledge maximizing	KMAX	D	0.322	0.324
Knowledge minimizing	KMIN	E	0.389	0.389
Fixed values	FIX	F	0.340	0.311

4.4.1 Comparative Analysis of the Bilattice-Based Approaches

In this section, we will discuss the performance of the aggregation operators introduced in Sec. 4.3.1, and compare them with two additional baseline strategies (the squares E and F in Fig. 4.5): KMIN (E) computes the aggregated trust score as $(t, d) = (\min(t_1, \ldots, t_n), \min(d_1, \ldots, d_n))$, and 'Fixed values' (F) is a strategy that always yields $(0.431, 0.206)$, which represents the average trust and distrust degree in the translated data set. Remark that, unlike TMAX, DMAX, KMAX and KAV, the results of the last two operators do not always reside in the gray area of Fig. 4.5. Table 4.1 contains the results.

The trust score aggregation operators (upper part of the table) perform more or less the same when considering T-RMSE; however, an inspection of the T-MAE values shows that TMAX and KAV achieve slightly better results than DMAX and KMAX. The baselines (lower part of the table) clearly produce the highest MAE errors, but the RMSE's are the opposite way round for the fixed values baseline, which means that it makes less large prediction errors than the others. At first glance, it looks as if there is no clear winner among TMAX, DMAX, KMAX and KAV. In the remainder of the discussion, we will show that overall T-MAE's and T-RMSE's do not give a complete picture of an operator's performance, and that sacrificing the knowledge condition allows for other operators that can produce more accurate trust estimations.

Figure 4.6 shows the evolution of T-MAE over the number n of trust scores that need to be aggregated. The split-up of the results gives us a clearer image than overall MAE errors. Notice that all operators perform more or less equally for small n, but that these classes are exactly the ones that are overrepresented in our experiment. The latter is depicted by the bars, their scale can be found on the right side of the graph. The bars illustrate for example that in more than 500 000 leave-one-out experiments there was only one propagation path and in almost 300 000 cases exactly two, as opposed to about 1 000 leave-one-out experiments which have to aggregate between 50 and 75 trust scores. These numbers explain why we get very similar average errors in Table 4.1.

On average, one can see that it becomes more difficult to produce accurate predictions as the number of inputs starts to increase, and that there is clearly a performance difference between the operators: DMAX and KMAX make a very bad showing from the moment they have to deal with more than 20 inputs; their T-MAE is often almost twice as high as TMAX's. Obviously, these two operators are too extreme for the CouchSurfing application. This tells us that distrust, as opposed to trust, is not easily established in CouchSurfing: one, or a few agents telling that another one should be distrusted is not sufficient for the inquiring agent to conclude that the agent should be distrusted, whereas the decision will be made much quicker if those agents indicate to trust him.

TMAX and KAV adapt themselves much better to changing aggregation conditions. Note that TMAX achieves somewhat lower errors in cases with more than 75 inputs, which can be explained by the fact that the average trust degree t_{r_i} for $n > 75$ is significantly higher than for $n \leqslant 75$ (viz. 0.594 vs. 0.423).

Figure 4.7 shows the evolution of the T-RMSE. Remark that the operators more or less relate to each other to the same extent. The reason for the lower global T-RMSE for the fixed values baseline can mainly be found in the good performance for the leave-one-out experiments that only contain one path (the largest class): FIX yields the average trust and distrust degree in the data set, whereas the other algorithms just copy the input. Note again that KAV and TMAX are well matched. This time, however, KAV is the winner in many scenarios; the moderating KAV producessmaller prediction errors (T-RMSE) than the more extreme TMAX: while no distinction could be made w.r.t. T-MAE for $n \leqslant 75$, for T-RMSE we can now clearly see that KAV achieves better results. Furthermore, the headstart of TMAX for higher n has melted away, and in some cases KAV even wins the battle.

4.4.2 *Effect of Orness Weights*

Table 4.1 and Fig. 4.6 demonstrated that KMAX's attitude is too explicit. As we discussed in Sec. 4.3.2.1, a possible solution is the introduction of or-like weights. We will illustrate the effect of tuning the weight vectors for K-OWA and show that they can indeed have a positive impact on the T-MAE. The goal of this experiment is to illustrate the importance of choosing the right trust and distrust weights, and not to compute the ideal weighting

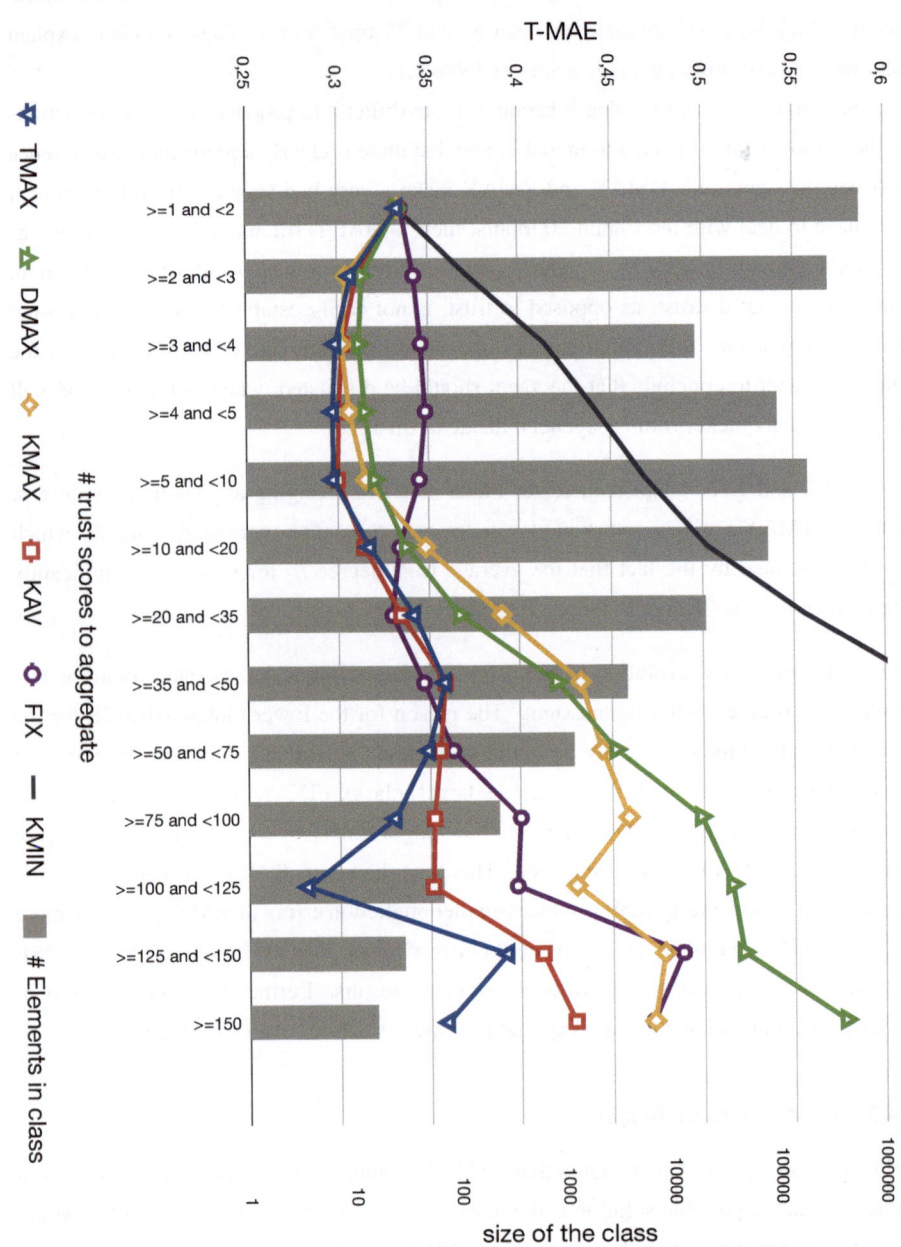

Fig. 4.6   T-MAE for the trust score aggregation operators on the CouchSurfing data set. Split-up according to the number n of aggregates; the bars depict the number of leave-one-out experiments in each class.

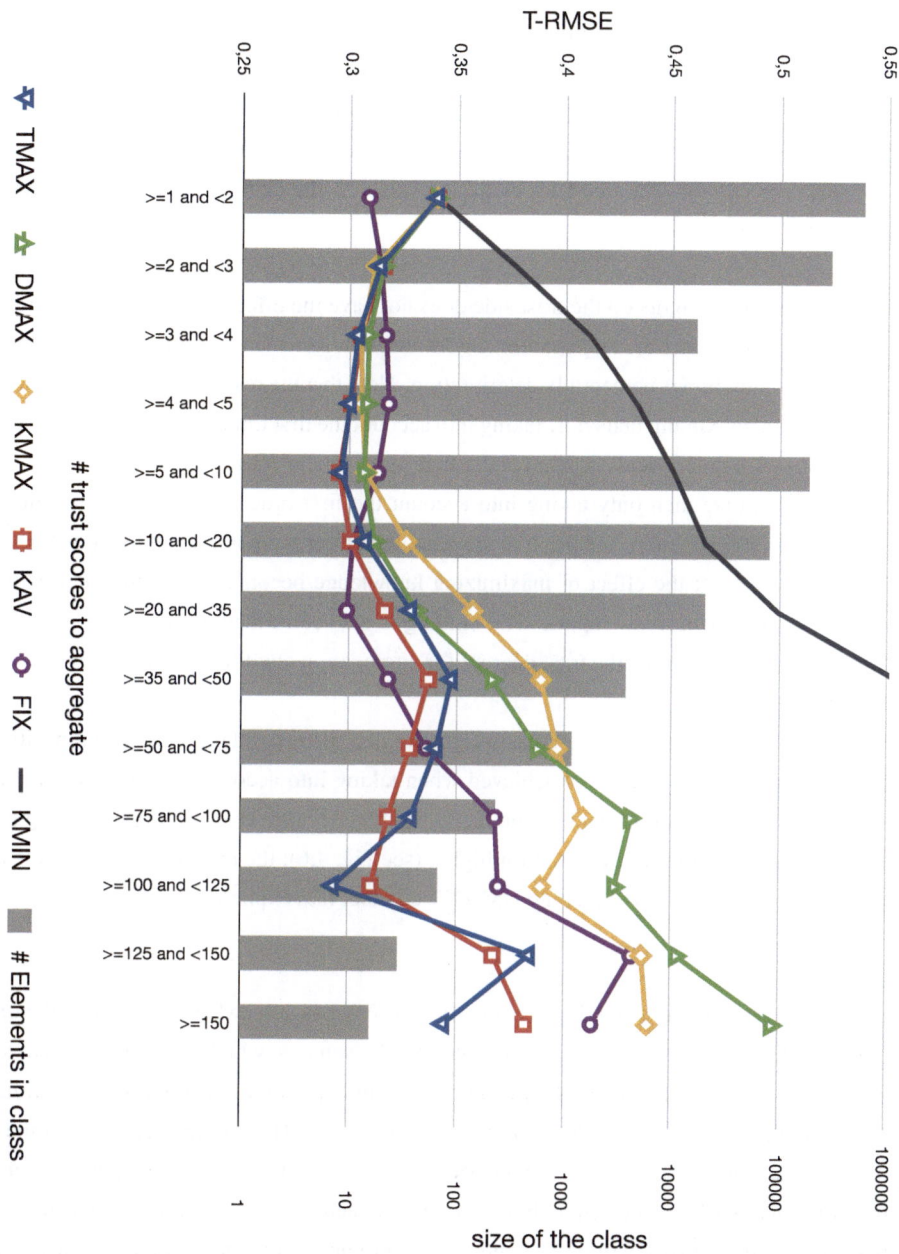

Fig. 4.7 T-RMSE for the trust score aggregation operators on the CouchSurfing data set. Split-up according to the number *n* of aggregates; the bars depict the number of leave-one-out experiments in each class.

strategy (the latter can for instance be achieved by automatic methods such as machine learning techniques). To this aim, we use the proposals in Example 4.8.

In Fig. 4.8, we compare KMAX's performance with some of the operators of the K-OWA family. KMAX is represented by the circles, while the mitigation on the trust and distrust side (tuning of α and β resp.) is represented by the triangles and the inverse triangles respectively. The line with the squares depicts the course of a K-OWA operator with $\alpha \neq n \neq \beta$.

Only introducing weights on the trust side does not have the effect we wished for: there is a small positive impact for aggregation conditions with less than 50 inputs, but for higher numbers the situation is perceptibly deteriorating. Note that the results are worse the further away from the maximum behavior: taking into account the first three quarters of the ordered arguments ($\alpha = 4/3$) yields worse results than only taking into account a quarter ($\alpha = 4$), which is worse than only taking into account the first ordered argument (maximum, KMAX, $\alpha = n$). The more sources to aggregate, the larger the possible effect of orderings and weight vectors; the effect of maximizing knowledge becomes more important when we have to deal with many inputs. This finding is also confirmed by the good results of TMAX (which maximizes the trust degree) for aggregation conditions with a high number of inputs.

It is clear that changing the orness-weights on the distrust side has an overall positive effect, and that better results are achieved when taking into account opinions from many sources, for conditions for both low and high n values. Recall that DMAX (maximizing the distrust degree) performed very bad for high n (see Fig. 4.6); the inverse triangle results in Fig. 4.8 show the benefits of making DMAX's conduct less explicit.

Obviously, the optimal weighting scheme for K-OWA lies somewhere in between the extremes TMAX and DMAX. This is illustrated by the squares, which embody the behavior of K-OWA with $\alpha = 4$ and $\beta = 4/3$, i.e., using the first quarter of the highest trust estimations and three quarters of the highest distrust estimations. This means that, in the context of CouchSurfing, trust is easier established than distrust; it is an open, voluntary, community of users who want to (and have to) rely on each other. Note in particular that the benefit of using K-OWA with $\alpha = 4$ and $\beta = 4/3$ to determine the trust and distrust level is especially high for intermediate aggregation conditions (> 10 and $\leqslant 50$), with T-MAE decreases of 25% compared to KMAX.

4.4.3 *Impact of Knowledge Incorporation*

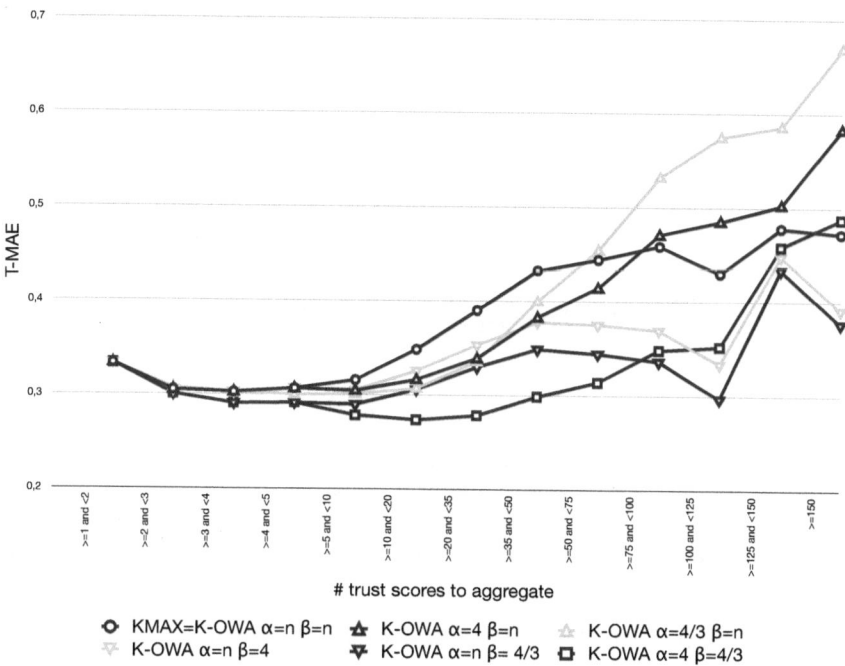

Fig. 4.8 Tuning the weights for K-OWA according to Example 4.8 for the CouchSurfing data set; $\alpha = \beta = n$ yields KMAX.

The knowledge preference averaging operator KAV only takes into account the opinions of the most knowledgeable users. In Sec. 4.3.2.2 we conjectured that its performance might be improved if we incorporate additional opinions, by rewarding those that are more certain (the KAAV operator). In this section, we show that this is indeed the case. Again, the goal of the experiment is not to compute the most optimal implementation of KAAV, but to illustrate its advantages over the KAV operator. In Fig. 4.9 we compare the results achieved for the arithmetic mean (all opinions are equally important, KAAV with $\gamma = 0$, solid line), three implementations of KAAV with increasing knowledge reward γ, and KAV (only the most knowledgeable opinions matter, diamonds). Note that for a very large γ, KAAV reduces to KAV. In other words, the line that is determined by the knowledge defect of the trust score resulting from the KAAV aggregation will approximate the corresponding KAV line for increasing knowledge rewards.

First note that this graph again illustrates that it becomes more difficult to accurately pre-

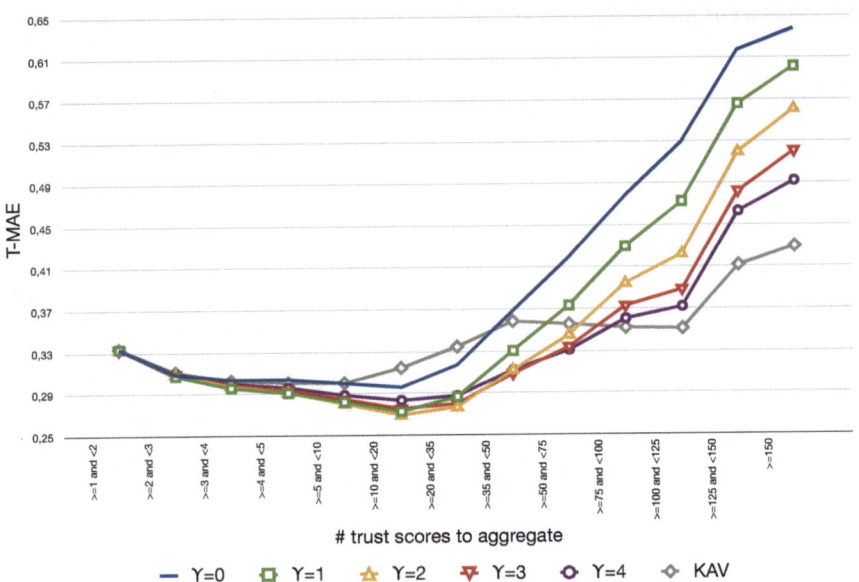

Fig. 4.9   Tuning the knowledge reward γ for KAAV for the CouchSurfing data set; $\gamma = 0$ results in the arithmetic mean, and $\gamma \rightarrow \infty$ yields KAV.

dict a trust score when a lot of opinions are available. Let us now compare the classical average with the knowledge preference average KAV. For only few inputs, the average performs better than KAV. However, for larger numbers n of aggregates, the average fails completely, with T-MAE increases up to 50% compared to KAV. This demonstrates that knowledge-enhanced aggregation strategies become more useful when many inputs have to be aggregated. The trend is also apparent when focusing on the KAAV implementations, with $\gamma = 1, \ldots, 4$: as the number of inputs increases, KAAV's with larger knowledge rewards achieve better results and come closer to KAV's trust score MAE. On the other hand, remark that mitigating KAV's behavior produces better results for smaller n's, even lower than those of the arithmetic mean.

The results show that, when choosing between the average, KAV and KAAV, a trade-off should be made between lower errors for lower n and lower T-MAE's for aggregation conditions with many inputs; an application with a well connected trust network (many available opinions) may benefit the most from KAV, while the average or KAAV might be more suited for applications for which not much trust scores are available. Another option is a combination of different aggregation operators depending on the number of inputs that need to be aggregated. The best configuration (combination, parameters) for a particular application can then for example be estimated during a training phase.

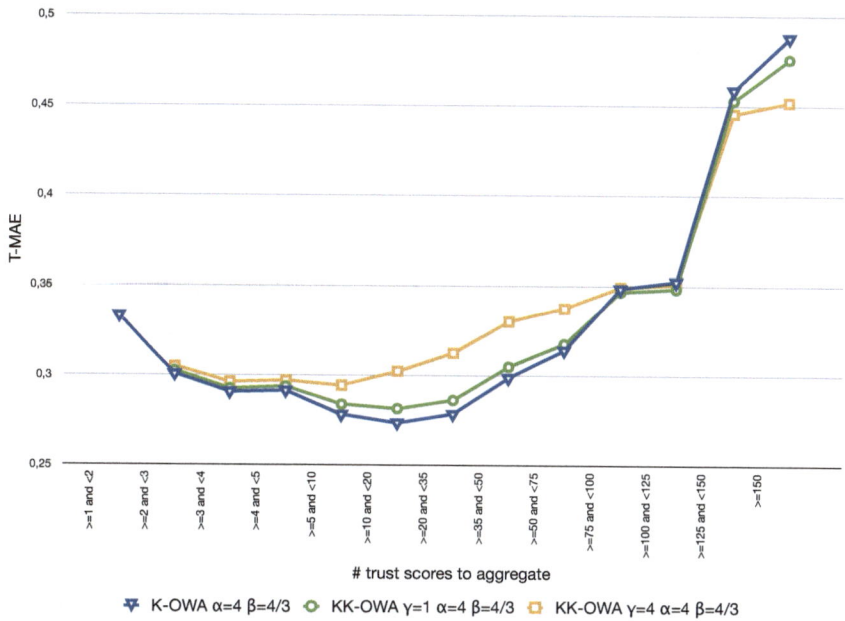

Fig. 4.10 Knowledge-enhanced OWA trust score aggregation for the CouchSurfing data set: K-OWA versus KK-OWA; according to Example 4.8.

4.4.4 Combining Orness Weights and Knowledge Information

In Sec. 4.3.2.3 and 4.3.2.4, we presented the knowledge-based OWA operator and the induced OWA operator, two trust score aggregation operators that combine the orness weight strategy (as in K-OWA) with the incorporation of knowledge defects (as in KAAV). Figure 4.10 and 4.11 depict the results for KK-OWA and K-IOWA respectively.

Let us first focus on the combination by altering the weights in the K-OWA strategy, i.e., the introduction of an extra weight vector which reflects the knowledge defect of each input. In Fig. 4.10, we include the best overall performing K-OWA strategy and two corresponding KK-OWA operators with knowledge reward 1 and 4. It is immediately clear that these particular weight combinations do not produce the desired effect; it is only for a large number n of inputs ($n \geqslant 75$) that the benefit starts to reveal itself (albeit a low positive impact). Note that this observation does support the claim we made in our discussion about KAAV and KAV, namely that the incorporation of knowledge defects becomes more

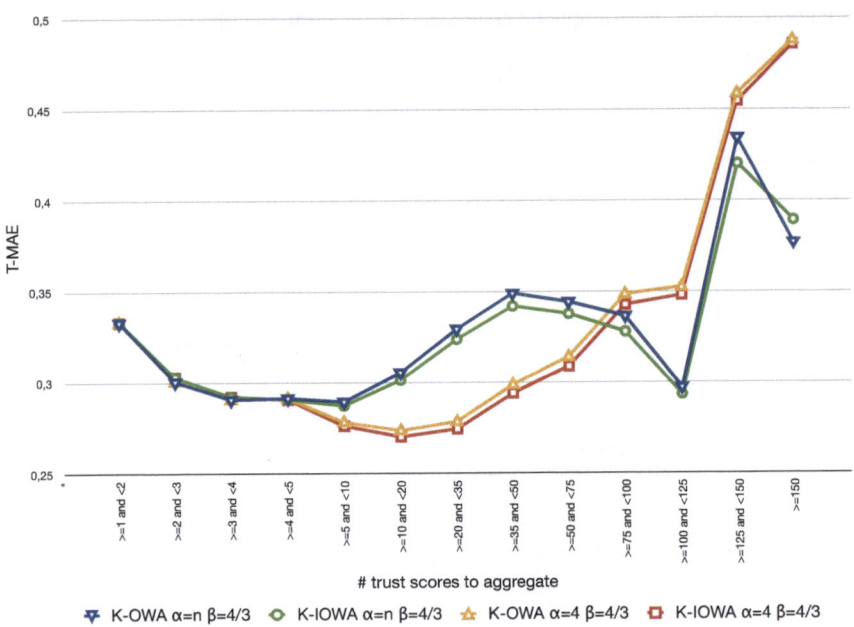

Fig. 4.11   Knowledge-enhanced OWA trust score aggregation for the CouchSurfing data set: K-OWA versus K-IOWA, according to Example 4.8.

important as the number of inputs grows: Fig. 4.9 showed that for small n, the average (which does not take into account knowledge) performs better than KAAV, and that KAV (large knowledge reward) achieves the best accuracy among the KAAV's for large n. The results for KK-OWA also show that the incorporation of knowledge defects is beneficial for large n compared to the K-OWA operator (which does not take into account any knowledge information), and that the latter scores better for small n.

In Fig. 4.11 we present the results of the second combination strategy, viz. K-IOWA. The difference with KK-OWA is that the knowledge information is not reflected in the weight vectors, but in the ordering of the inputs. We include two of the best performing K-OWA implementations and their induced counterparts. Remark that the induced operators achieve lower T-MAE's on every occasion but one. Notice that this is a small improvement, in general they are closely matched with the original results. The reason can partially be found in the definition of the induced variables (4.1) and ordering (4.2): a lot of the inputs that are first in the row for K-IOWA$_{W_T}$ and K-IOWA$_{W_D}$ will also be ordered first for K-OWA$_{W_T}$ and K-OWA$_{W_D}$, since inputs with a high trust (distrust) degree will often contain more perfect information (recall that we assume consistent agents). Furthermore, the inputs for which the induced and regular OWA ordering might differ the most are very often at the end of the order, thus receiving low weights (or even 0), which reduces the impact on the final aggregated trust score. Hence, for different weight strategies and/or different knowledge-enhanced orderings, the effect of K-IOWA can possibly be more significant.

4.4.5 Adaptability of the Operators

In the previous sections, we discussed the performance of the operators on one particular data set. However, practical trust score aggregation operators should also achieve good accuracy on other types of data. Hence, in this section, we focus on the adaptability of the operators by testing them on the Epinions data set. Note that its characteristics are very different than those of CouchSurfing: it contains bivalent data and no knowledge information (hence only full trust and full distrust statements are available), and consists of about 85% trust relations. Consequently, each trust score in the data set has perfect knowledge, and hence K-OWA, K-IOWA and KK-OWA will yield the same results. Analogously, KAV and KAAV coincide with the arithmetic mean. This means that we cannot discuss the performance of knowledge-enhanced strategies, but we can investigate whether the observations for the CouchSurfing application are also valid for Epinions, or, in other words, whether the operators can adjust themselves to changing data types.

Figure 4.12 depicts the situation for the bilattice-based approaches on the Epinions data set. Note that there is much more variation in the T-MAE's compared to those in Fig. 4.6. This is due to the average trust and distrust degrees in the data sets: for CouchSurfing they were resp. 0.431 and 0.206, while for Epinions 0.853 and 0.147. Hence, it is only natural that TMAX will achieve lower errors, and DMAX higher T-MAE's. Remark that KMAX and DMAX are again too extreme to be used in trust-enhanced applications; TMAX and KAV achieve much better results. As the average trust degree in the data set is very high, TMAX is the logical winner.

The 'peaks' of KMAX and DMAX can be explained by the nature of the data in the separate classes: of all leave-one-out experiments where the real value is full trust but the predicted value is complete distrust, the highest number is reached in the 35-50 group, secondly in the 50-75 group, and so on. DMAX maximizes distrust and hence minimizes trust, or, in other words, full distrust (zero trust) is predicted from the moment that one of the inputs is full distrust. However, most of the values in the data set denote full trust (zero distrust); hence, the T-MAE will be higher in the aforementioned classes. A similar effect is visible for KMAX, but in a somewhat mitigated form because KMAX maximizes the trust value too.

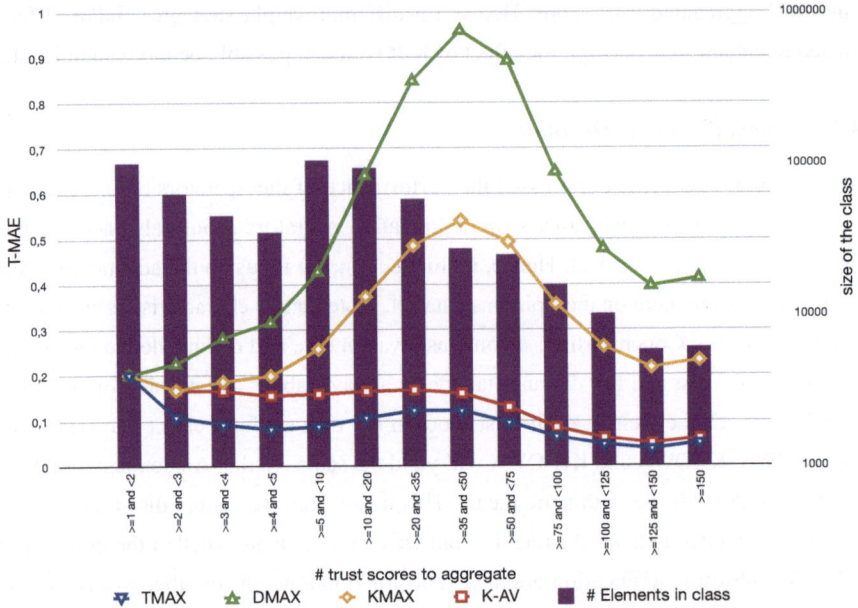

Fig. 4.12   T-MAE for the bilattice-based trust score aggregation operators on the Epinions data set. Split-up according to the number *n* of aggregates; the bars depict the number of leave-one-out experiments in each class.

Similar to the CouchSurfing experiment, K-OWA can also be used to improve KMAX's behavior for the Epinions application. The results of tuning K-OWA can be found in Fig. 4.13. First of all, the graph shows us that tuning on the trust side has no visible effect, which again can be explained by the omnipresence of trust in the data set. However, changing the orness weights on the distrust side does have a major positive impact on the T-MAE (as was the case for CouchSurfing too). Remark that the tuned versions adapt themselves much better to changing aggregation conditions; the peaks have almost disappeared.

Although the Epinions and CouchSurfing applications clearly have different characteristics, the performance of the operators on both data sets supports our claim that approaches which focus on maximizing distrust are not very suitable for social web applications, that TMAX, KAV and T-OWA adapt themselves much better to changing aggregation conditions, and that the tuning of the (distrust) weight vectors in maximum-like operators can have a significant positive impact on the accuracy of the aggregation process.

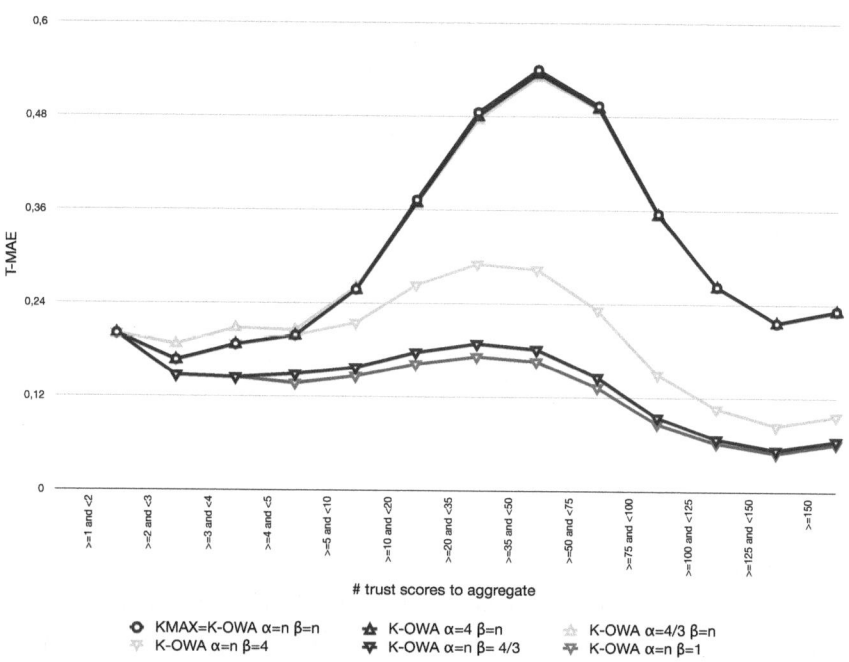

Fig. 4.13 Tuning the weights for K-OWA according to Example 4.8 for the Epinions data set; $\alpha = \beta = n$ yields KMAX.

4.4.6 *Discussion*

Although from a theoretical perspective, not satisfying the knowledge boundary can be regarded as a serious drawback for any trust score aggregation operator, our experiments demonstrate that dropping this condition opens the door for new, more practical, aggregation operators. The results on large real-world data sets from CouchSurfing and Epinions showed that this kind of operators can significantly improve the performance of the less sophisticated bilattice-based aggregation operators.

These findings may be explained by the imperfect, noisy nature of the data, a problem inherent in the larger part of social network applications. Some users might not fully understand the meaning of each trust/knowledge statement, others make an unintentional mistake (for example checked the wrong trust box, forgot to indicate the knowledge level, ...), and so on. Furthermore, the data in trust-enhanced applications must be mapped to a practical model, and the trust estimation mechanisms must be captured as precisely as possible. However, the resulting trust model and propagation operators remain approximations, and hence will

Table 4.2   Overall performance of bilattice-based aggregation strategies on the CouchSurfing data set, propagation operator P_3 versus P_1 with $\mathcal{T} = \min$ for paths of length 2; T-MAE $\in [0, 2]$ and T-RMSE $\in [0, \sqrt{2}]$.

Aggregation operator	Propagation P_3		Propagation P_1	
	T-MAE	T-RMSE	T-MAE	T-RMSE
TMAX	0.298	0.309	0.316	0.321
DMAX	0.312	0.314	0.325	0.324
KAV	0.301	0.309	0.318	0.321
KMAX	0.313	0.318	0.322	0.324
K-OWA with $\alpha = 4$ and $\beta = 4/3$	0.293	0.301	0.308	0.311
KAAV with $\gamma = 2$	0.289	0.297	0.310	0.311
KK-OWA with $\alpha = 4$, $\beta = 4/3$ and $\gamma = 1$	0.354	0.343	0.310	0.312
K-IOWA with $\alpha = 4$ and $\beta = 4/3$	0.359	0.345	0.308	0.311
KMIN	0.333	0.356	0.389	0.389
FIX	0.340	0.311	0.340	0.311

always introduce some extra noise.

One way of reducing the noise in the data is by making the aggregation operators less extreme, e.g. by using knowledge-enhanced strategies that give priority to better informed opinions, or by introducing weights that soften the standard behavior of the operators. This explains the good performance of the KAAV and K-OWA families, compared to the classical operators.

Moreover, one might also argue that the bilattice-based operators perform less well because the properties we enforced do not align well with the CouchSurfing data. It turns out that the knowledge boundary is not as vital as we thought, compared to the trust and distrust boundaries, the neutrality and opposite arguments condition. The former property is exactly the one that is only fulfilled for the bilattice-based approaches, whereas the KAAV and K-OWA families do satisfy the latter.

The choice as to which approach (TMAX, KAV, KAAV, K-OWA, ...) is most suitable also depends on the application at hand. In applications where prudence is in order, one can e.g. opt for a K-OWA operator with a large β-parameter (which results in a higher orness degree and hence will sooner yield a high aggregated distrust degree). Or, in large user networks where (partial) ignorance is the rule rather than the exception, KMAX or KAAV might be preferred over TMAX or K-OWA.

Obviously, the reported performances do not only depend on the choice of aggregation operator, but also on the combination with propagation, which inherently introduces errors in the computation too. Hence, the synergy between the two operator types and their separate influence on the accuracy are two factors that should also be taken into account. As an illustration, consider Table 4.2 which contains the results for the aggregation operators with P_1 and P_3; recall that the latter is the operator that achieved the best propagation results for the CouchSurfing data (see Sec. 3.4.2). As can be seen from the T-MAE and T-RMSE, all bilattice-based approaches and K-OWA and KAAV perform better with the distrust-enhanced propagation strategy. Hence, one could say that a more accurate propagation operator also yields more accurate aggregation results. However, the comparisons for KK-OWA and K-IOWA show that this will not always be the case, and that it is necessary to define the most optimal combination of the aggregation operator, the aggregation weights, and the propagation operator.

An important goal of our aggregation operators is to accurately represent a consensus about the trust estimation, which implies a good representation of the degree of inconsistency and neutrality in the final aggregated trust score (e.g. reflected in Definitions 4.14 and 4.15). Consequently, the operators that we have proposed are more suitable for environments with a central authority, in which aggregation is applied at the end of the process (first propagate then aggregate, FPTA). On the other hand, in a privacy-preserving setting (FATP), the aggregated scores are used as intermediate estimations in a propagation chain, and hence the focus is not necessarily on representation of the consensus. It is therefore reasonable to assume that the latter environments require an adapted set of aggregation conditions (more or less, or other properties) and corresponding trust score aggregation operators.

4.5 Conclusions and Future Work

Research in trust networks is still in its infancy, in particular when it comes down to the representation, propagation and aggregation of distrust. In this chapter, we focused on the trust and distrust aggregation problem, and investigated which requirements a good trust score aggregator should fulfill. Based on these aggregation conditions, we proposed four trust score aggregation strategies, each with their own distinct behavior: the trust maximizing operator TMAX which is the most optimistic choice (maximum trust degree for the lowest possible knowledge level), distrust maximizing DMAX which is the most pessimistic one (maximum distrust degree), knowledge preference averaging KAV which is the most moderating approach (average of the most knowledgeable trust scores), and the knowledge maximizing operator KMAX (maximum trust and distrust degree), the boldest aggregation option.

Besides, we also introduced several other families of operators: the (induced) OWA-based K-OWA and K-IOWA operators, the knowledge awarding averaging trust score operator KAAV and the knowledge-based trust score OWA operator, mitigating the behavior of KMAX, KAV and their combination respectively. Although these families have less desirable properties from a theoretical perspective, our experiments on large data sets from CouchSurfing and Epinions demonstrated that they achieve more accurate results in real-world social applications, which are inherently noisy.

A lot of interesting research directions remain unexplored so far, e.g. the determination of the most suitable propagation/aggregation combination for a particular application at hand, the study of aggregation conditions and corresponding operators for privacy-preserving environments, the investigation of the best performing aggregation and propagation order (i.e., FPTA versus FATP), etc. Another research area involves the further exploration of the role of knowledge defects, e.g. by extending well-known other weighted strategies such as the Choquet Integral [18] or the weighted ordered weighted averaging operator [136]. Finally, one can also take into account certain aspects of the virtual trust network's topology. In particular, the current approaches are indifferent as to the length of the paths that generated the individual trust scores, and also do not consider how many times the same user appears on a path; see e.g. [140].

Chapter 5

Social Recommender Systems

The wealth of information available on the web has made it increasingly difficult to find what one is really looking for. This is particularly true for exploratory queries where one is searching for opinions and views. Think e.g. of the many information channels you can try to find out whether you will love or hate the first Harry Potter movie: you may read the user opinions on Epinions.com or Amazon.com, investigate the Internet Movie Database[1], check the opinion of your favorite reviewers on Rotten Tomatoes[1], read the discussions on a Science Fiction & Fantasy forum[2], and you can probably add some more possibilities to the list yourself. Although today it has become very easy to look up information, at the same time we experience more and more difficulties coping with this information overload. Hence, it comes as no surprise that personalization applications to guide the search process are gaining tremendous importance. One particular interesting set of applications that address this problem are online recommender sytems [2, 15, 121, 125, 138].

In this chapter, we deal with the basics of recommender systems, so that we can lay the foundation for an easy understanding of the motives and techniques for trust-enhanced recommendation in Chap. 6 and 7. While the first part of this thesis focused on the modeling and processing of computational trust and distrust, this part is all about their practical use in recommender systems. Such trust-based recommenders are a specific type of social recommendation systems, which generate predictions (recommendations) that are based on information about their users' profiles and relationships between the users.

Social recommenders can come in many flavors and can be classified in several ways, depending on the type of information that is used [15], the way the recommendations are

---

[1]See www.imdb.com and www.rottentomatoes.com
[2]Such as www.sf-fandom.com

91

computed [2], how automated the process is [125], etc. In Sec. 5.1 and 5.2, we give a global overview of the recommender research area and position the trust-enhanced approaches. In Sec. 5.3 we zoom in on the shortcomings of classical recommendation approaches, and in particular collaborative filtering. In Sec. 5.4, we concentrate on evaluation methods and measures we will need for the reported experiments in the next chapters.

5.1 Classification of Recommendation Methods

Recommender systems can be used for several purposes, such as generating a ranking of items, recommending a sequence of items (think e.g. of the personalized radio stations on Last.fm), or predicting the score of an item [54]. In this book, we focus on the latter type of systems, i.e., recommenders that are used to accurately estimate the degree to which a particular user (the *target user*) will like a particular item (the *target item*). In [15], Burke classified recommender approaches based on the kind of data that is needed to generate recommendations. Given a set of users U and a set of items I, he distinguished five basic types, viz. demographic, utility-based, knowledge-based, content-based and collaborative recommender systems.

Demographic systems gather personal data such as age, gender, residence, profession, etc., and try to categorize a target user $a \in U$ based on this information. Recommendations for a are then generated based on the items $i \in I$ that demographically similar users like (i.e., i's they have rated highly). Examples of this approach can be found in, among others, [110, 122] in which respectively a web page and book recommendation algorithm is presented.

Utility-based recommenders do not ask for ratings of items, but need a description of the features of the items in I, apply a utility function to the items, and determine their rank (and hence are more suitable for ranking problems than for predicting accurate scores). Their chief benefit is that they allow to take into account factors that are not related to the description of i, such as the availability of the item, its delivery schedule, etc., but their main difficulty is how to create a utility function for each target user a. Several utility-based recommenders are presented in [51].

Knowledge-based systems are similar to utility-based recommenders in the sense that they also require features of the items and do not need ratings. Instead of a utility function however, their recommendations are inferred from the users' needs and preferences; knowledge-based recommenders can reason about the relationship between a need and the target item i. For example, the restaurant recommender application Entree [15] knows that the Pacific New Wave cuisine consists of a French and an Asian component (and that Chinese is a subtype of Asian); hence, when a user asks for a recommendation in the style of a particular Chinese restaurant, Entree might suggest the Pacific one.

The two most mature and most often used recommendation types are content-based and collaborative, or a combination of two or more types (the so-called hybrid recommenders [13, 15, 21, 75]). A content-based system generates recommendations based on the ratings of the target user; it suggests items that are similar to the ones that the user has liked in the past. To this aim, content-based recommenders require a feature description of the items, for example actors, genre, director and language in the case of a movie recommender. Examples can be found in [98, 111]; more details and further references on content-based recommender systems can be found in the overview paper of Adomavicius and Tuzhilin [2].

Content-based systems have their roots in information retrieval and information filtering research, which manifests itself in the determination of similar items. E.g., the term frequency/inverse document frequency (TF/IDF) measure is a well-known method in information retrieval to compute the weights of keywords in a document. As another example, the cosine similarity is often used to measure the distance between two feature vectors. For more information on TF/IDF and cosine similarity, we refer to [84]. These techniques can not only be used to determine the similarity between web pages or documents, but also for other item types (such as movies), as long as feature descriptions are available.

At the same time, however, this is also one of the main weaknesses of content-based systems: items for which no description is available cannot be recommended, and the accuracy of the recommendations heavily relies on the quality of the annotations. Furthermore, these systems tend not to explore interests of the user besides those expressed in his rating record. In this sense, they can be improved significantly by (additionally) using collaborative methods, which do not require annotated items. In essence, collaborative (filtering) systems suggest items i to target user a that are liked by users that are similar to a. Note the difference with content-based systems which suggest items similar to items that a liked. Well-known collaborative examples are the Grouplens recommender for news articles [120] and the music recommendation system Ringo [127].

In the following section, we go more deeply into collaborative recommenders, since the the trust-enhanced techniques that we will discuss in the following chapters are based on the same rationale; they do not need any description of the data, but rely on the ratings of other users in the system.

5.2   Collaborative Filtering Algorithms

Collaborative filtering (CF) recommenders can be classified as either memory-based (heuristic-based) or model-based. The former generate recommendations that are based on the entire set of ratings that is available, from the target user but also from all other users in U. On the other hand, the latter only use the ratings to learn a model and then suggest items based on that model; think e.g. of clustering or matrix reconstruction techniques. For a discussion on model-based approaches, we refer to [2]; in this chapter we focus on memory-based approaches, since they are more relevant to the trust-enhanced algorithms in the following chapters.

In a memory-based setting, the unknown rating $p_{a,i}$ for target item i and target user a can be predicted by using a combination of the ratings of *neighbors* (similar users) $u \in U$ that are already familiar with item i, i.e., who rated i as $r_{u,i}$. We denote the set of users who have evaluated the target item by R. In Def. 5.1 and 5.2, we show two possibilities for combining the ratings [2]. The first formula represents the classical weighted average, in which the ratings of neighbors that are more similar to the target user receive larger weights $w_{a,u}$.

Definition 5.1 (Weighted sum). The unknown rating for target item i and target user a can be computed as

$$p_{a,i} = \frac{\sum\limits_{u \in R} w_{a,u} r_{u,i}}{\sum\limits_{u \in R} w_{a,u}}$$

However, this approach does not take into account the fact that not every user exhibits the same rating behavior; e.g., user x might be easy to please and hence regularly issues high ratings, while user y has a more pronounced taste, revealing itself in lower ratings. As a consequence, the average rating by x will be much higher than the average rating by y. This limitation can be overcome by the following approach:

Definition 5.2 (Classic collaborative filtering). The unknown rating for target item i and target user a can be computed as

$$p_{a,i} = \bar{r}_a + \frac{\sum\limits_{u \in R} w_{a,u}(r_{u,i} - \bar{r}_u)}{\sum\limits_{u \in R} w_{a,u}}$$

The unknown rating $p_{a,i}$ is predicted based on the mean $\bar{r}_a$ of ratings by target user a for other items than the target item i, as well as on the ratings $r_{u,i}$ by a's neighbors u for the target item. The deviation between the ratings for a particular neighbor u $(r_{u,i} - \bar{r}_u)$ measures how much u likes or dislikes the target item: a large positive deviation means the user really enjoyed the item, whereas a negative deviation tells us that the target item was not (at all) to his taste.

Both formulas take into account the similarity $w_{a,u}$ between the target user a and a neighbor u. Several methods exist to compute similarity, one of the most popular being the Pearson's Correlation Coefficient (PCC) [54]:

Definition 5.3 (Pearson's correlation coefficient). The PCC of users a and u is computed as (with n the number of items j rated in common)

$$w_{a,u} = \frac{\sum_{j=1}^{n} (r_{u,j} - \bar{r}_u) \cdot (r_{a,j} - \bar{r}_a)}{\sqrt{\left(\sum_{j=1}^{n} (r_{u,j} - \bar{r}_u)^2\right) \cdot \left(\sum_{j=1}^{n} (r_{a,j} - \bar{r}_a)^2\right)}}$$

The PCC measures the extent to which there is a linear relationship between the rating behaviors of the two users, the extreme values being -1 and 1. A positive correlation coefficient reflects the fact that both users have similar taste in the sense that, when one of them rates an item above/below average, the other one does so too. The more negative the coefficient, the more the rating behaviors are opposites; e.g., $w_{a,u} = -1$ means that whenever user a rates an item highly, u does the exact reverse, and vice versa. Analogously, $w_{a,u} = 1$ denotes identical rating behavior. A correlation coefficient of 0 means that there is no relationship between the two sets of ratings. In practice, most often only users with a positive correlation (> 0) are considered in the recommendation process. We denote this set by R^+.

As mentioned in Sec. 5.1, the trust-enhanced recommendation techniques of the following chapters adhere most closely to the collaborative filtering paradigm, since they also rely on the ratings of the other users. The neighbors (resp. the corresponding weights) will be defined as similar users (resp. the PCC), as trusted users (resp. propagated and aggregated trust scores), or as a combination of both.

5.3 Limitations of Recommender Systems

As discussed in the previous section, one of the strengths of collaborative filtering is that
it does not require any description about the data, and hence can deal with any kind
of items; it is sufficient to have enough ratings from users in the system to make good
recommendations. Obviously, the more ratings become available, the more recommendations can be generated and the more accurate they become. Hence, another advantage of using such an approach is that it is adaptive, i.e., the quality of the system improves over time (which is also the case with content-based systems). Since collaborative filtering takes into account the opinion of neighbors that are selected based on their
similarity with the target user (and not items that are based on their similarity with the
target item), it can add a serendipitous factor into the recommendation process, which
content-based systems cannot. E.g., suppose that you have never seen a western before, but that it turns out that all your neighbors really liked 'Once Upon a Time in
the West', then there is a good chance that you will also enjoy the movie, even though
you would never have thought of choosing a western yourself.

However, despite significant improvements on recommendation approaches, some important problems still remain. In this section, we briefly discuss the main drawbacks and take
collaborative filtering as a particular example. We will explain in Sec. 6.1, on a global level,
how the incorporation of trust and distrust can alleviate these weaknesses, and address them
in detail in further sections of Chap. 6 and 7.

A first problem is that users typically rate or experience only a small fraction of the
available items, which makes the rating matrix (the matrix which consists of rows for each
user and columns for each item) very sparse, since a recommender system often deals with
millions of items. For instance, Guha *et al.*'s data set from Epinions contains over 1 500 000
reviews that received about 25 000 000 ratings by more than 160 000 different users (also
see Sec. 5.4.1). Due to this *data sparsity*, a collaborative filtering algorithm experiences
a lot of difficulties when trying to identify good neighbors in the system: it is hard to
find users that have rated enough items in common, let alone to find those that also have a
similar rating behavior. Consequently, the quality of the generated recommendations might
suffer from this.

Moreover, it is also very challenging to generate good recommendations for users that
are new to the system, as they have not rated a significant number of items and hence
cannot properly be linked with similar users. This is the so-called *user cold start problem*,

a major issue that is high on the agenda, especially in e-commerce environments, because it is important that new users are satisfied with the system so that they keep coming back (continue purchasing).

A related drawback is the item cold start problem: new items have only been rated by a few users, which makes it hard to find similar users that rated such an item (due to the sparsity of the rating matrix). Another issue with respect to target items are the *controversial items*. These are very challenging items for a recommender system, since it is much harder to predict a score for an item that has received a variety of high and low ratings, than for an all-time favorite. More than in any other case, a recommendation for a user needs to be truly personalized when the target item under consideration is controversial; i.e., when an item has both 'ardent supporters' and 'motivated adversaries', with no clear majority in either group.

Fourthly, recommendation systems have to cope with *malicious users*. As recommenders are widely used in the realm of e-commerce, there is a natural motivation for producers of items (manufacturers, publishers, etc.) to abuse them so that their items are recommended to users more often (see e.g. [71, 106, 154]). For example, a common 'copy-profile' attack consists in copying the ratings of the target user, which results in the system thinking that the adversary is most similar to the target.

Finally, one of the main reasons why recommender systems are only being used in low risk domains (think of a buying a book vs. a car) is that most users still perceive a recommender as a 'black box', meaning that they lack *transparency*. Sinha and Swearingen [128, 133] have shown that users prefer more transparent systems, and that people tend to rely more on recommendations from people they trust ('friends') than on online recommender systems which generate recommendations based on anonymous people similar to them.

5.4 Evaluation of Recommender Systems

Recommender systems can be evaluated in several ways, depending on the type of data at hand, the goal of the system, etc. A comprehensive overview of collaborative filtering evaluation issues can be found in [54]. In this section, we focus on the problem of selecting and finding suitable data sets, and explain which methods we will use to evaluate the trust-enhanced techniques in the next chapters.

5.4.1 *Obtaining Data*

Evaluating the performance of recommendation systems can be done live (which involves user studies), offline (i.e., automated experiments) or by a combination of both. The advantage of offline analyses is that they are quick and economical for large evaluations, they can be conducted on several data sets or algorithms at once and they are repeatable. The downside is that, due to the sparsity of most applications and data sets, only a limited set of items can be evaluated, and not in a subjective way. Live user experiments, on the other hand, are capable of measuring subjective matters such as participation, user satisfaction, or perceived transparency. The latter issues are out of the scope of this book; instead, we focus on offline experiments and objective performance measures (see Sec. 5.4.2).

Two options arise when choosing offline evaluations, namely to evaluate on synthesized or natural data sets. Using synthesized data is an easy way to test for obvious flaws, but can only be used in the early steps, because it does not accurately model the nature of real users and real data. Besides, one must be careful not to fit the data too well to the algorithm to be tested. Hence, it is fairer and more objective to use natural data sets in the evaluation, but these are also more difficult to obtain; the task that the algorithm is designed for must correspond to the tasks supported by the system of the data set. E.g., if an algorithm is designed to accurately predict ratings for movies on a scale from 1 to 5, then a data set with only bivalent ratings is far from ideal. As another example, the data set of an application in which ratings are gathered implicitly (e.g. by keeping track of how many times a user clicked a particular topic, how long a user listened to a particular song, ...) does not align well with an algorithm that requires explicit input from its users, for example in the form of a continuous rating scale. In this work, we focus on recommendation algorithms that need the latter type of data, i.e., applications that gather explicit ratings and explicitly stated trust and distrust statements.

In the recommendation research area, several data sets are publicly available for testing purposes. Most often used are the MovieLens[3] data sets which contain annotations about movies, demographic information about the users, time stamps, and explicit ratings on a 5 star scale. The largest Movielens data set contains 10 million ratings for around 10 000 movies and 71 500 users. Other possibilities that are available for the recommender community are e.g. the Book-Crossing data set [159], the Jester Joke data set[4], and more recently the Netflix data set from the competition. A few other data sets have also been

---

[3] Available at www.grouplens.org/taxonomy/term/14
[4] See www.ieor.berkeley.edu/~goldberg/jester-data/ for more information.

used, but the majority of them are not publicly available.

Social network data sets are not very hard to find, think e.g. of the Enron email data set[5], the scrapes of Twitter's API[5], the many studies using Facebook data (among others [65, 132]), the research on links between blogs [47], ... However, it becomes more difficult if one needs weighted relational data, i.e., data sets that do not just consist of 'friend' or 'fan' links, but distinguish between different levels or tie strengths. There are even fewer data sets available with explicit trust statements. An important example is the CouchSurfing data set containing gradual trust and distrust levels (see Sec. 3.4.1), or Golbeck's FilmTrust data set with trust statements on a scale from 1 to 10 [41].

If we want to evaluate the performance of *trust-enhanced recommenders* which aim to accurately estimate the degree to which a target user will like a target item based on ratings of users in their trust network, we need data sets that consist of a significant number of item ratings *and* trust statements. However, the lack of such data sets remains a significant challenge in the trust-based recommendation domain: most data sets contain either only ratings or only trust statements; there exist a few containing both, but not all of them can be obtained for research purposes[6], and the ones that are available have other shortcomings. E.g., the CouchSurfing data set consists of a large collection of gradual trust statements, but the ratings ('experiences') are either 'positive', 'negative' or 'neutral', and merely 0.03% of them are negative. Hence, this is more of a classification problem, while our focus is on algorithms to accurately predict ratings on a (continuous) scale. On the other hand, the Epinions data from Guha *et al.* [50] (Sec. 3.4.1) contains a variety of ratings (helpfulness scores for reviews) on a scale from 1 to 5, but only has bivalent trust and distrust statements. Yet another Epinions data set, crawled by Massa *et al.* [91], consists of consumer product ratings (also on a scale from 1 to 5) and only trust relations (no distrust statements).

In the remainder of this book, we call Guha *et al.*'s and Massa *et al.*'s data sets respectively the *Epinions-reviews* and *Epinions-products* data sets. The large Epinions-reviews data set contains 1 560 144 reviews that received 25 170 637 ratings by 163 634 different users. The reviews are evaluated by assigning a helpfulness rating which ranges from 'not helpful' (1/5) to 'most helpful' (5/5). The trust evaluations make up a web of trust graph consisting of 131 829 users and 840 799 non self-referring trust or distrust relations. The Epinions-products data set was collected by Massa and Bhattacharjee in a 5-week crawl

---

[5]See   blog.infochimps.org/2009/11/11/twitter-census-publishing-the-first-of-many-datasets and www.cs.cmu.edu/~enron

[6]As an example, the trust network of Golbeck's FilmTrust application cannot be released because of privacy concerns.

and contains 139 738 products that are rated (on a scale from 1 to 5) by 49 290 users in total; the users issued or received 487 003 trust statements in total. Hence, an item (rating) denotes a review (helpfulness score) in the context of the Epinions-reviews data set and a consumer product (product rating) in the context of the Epinions-products data set.

Despite their shortcomings, a big benefit of the Epinions data sets is that they are extensive. Hence, they can give us a good realistic image of their users' rating behavior and the way trust networks are formed, and enable us to safely interpret the results of our trust-enhanced experiments. In the following chapters, we will use one or both of the data sets to evaluate our approaches, depending on the problem at hand. For example, both data sets are suitable to discuss the role of controversial items in trust-enhanced recommender systems (Sec. 6.2), whereas the role of distrust can only be analyzed on the Epinions-reviews data set (Sec. 6.3). The cold start issue in Chap. 7 is analyzed by means of the largest of the Epinions data sets, namely Epinions-reviews (Sec. 7.4).

5.4.2 *Evaluation Measures for Rating Prediction*

Recall that we will not perform live user experiments, and are hence not able to measure e.g. user satisfaction. Offline experiments, however, do give us the opportunity to focus on the quality of the recommendations. There exist several ways to measure the accuracy of a particular recommendation algorithm, a nice overview is given in [54]. Since we concentrate on recommender systems that are designed to accurately predict the rating for a (target user, target item) pair, we do not consider precision/recall, ROC-curves, or other measures related to binary classification problems [54], and also no correlations such as Spearman's ρ and Kendall's τ which are used in ranking problems [54]. Instead, we use the leave-one-out method in combination with the mean absolute error (MAE) and root mean squared error (RMSE) [54]:

Definition 5.4 (Mean absolute error, Root mean squared error). The MAE and RMSE in a leave-one-out setting with n leave-one-out experiments is defined as

$$\text{MAE} = \frac{\sum_{i=1}^{n} |r_i - p_i|}{n}$$

$$\text{RMSE} = \sqrt{\left(\sum_{i=1}^{n} (r_i - p_i)^2 \right) \Big/ n},$$

with r_i the real rating and p_i the predicted rating for a particular (target user, target item) pair.

Remark that the leave-one-out setting for item recommendations is different than the one in Sec. 3.4.2: instead of hiding a trust relation, we now hide a rating and try to predict its value based on other ratings and trust relations in the system. The MAE and RMSE are classical accuracy measures that are often used in the recommender area; MAE considers every error of equal value, while the RMSE emphasizes larger errors. Note that the MAE and RMSE are on the same scale, which depends on the rating scale in the system. Suppose e.g. that the items are rated on a scale from 1 to 5 (as is the case for both Epinions data sets), then the extreme values that MAE and RMSE can reach are 0 and 4.

Of course, accuracy is not the only factor that makes a good recommendation. We may also take into account the novelty, serendipity, learning rate of the system, and so on; [54] contains an overview of such measures that go beyond accuracy. We are particularly interested in one of these measures, a factor that can easily be evaluated in offline experiments, namely coverage. The coverage of a recommender system refers to the number of (target user, target item) pairs for which a prediction can be generated; it may not always be possible to predict a rating w.r.t. a user or an item, e.g. when a user has no neighbors or the item has not been evaluated.

A classical way to measure the coverage is by using the leave-one-out method. The coverage of a specific algorithm then refers to the amount of computable predictions p_i versus the number of leave-one-out experiments to perform (i.e., the number of ratings available in the data set). For Def. 5.1 and 5.2 we call $p_{a,i}$ computable if there is at least one user u for whom $w_{a,u}$ can be calculated and who rated item i.

Definition 5.5 (Coverage). The coverage in a leave-one-out setting with n leave-one-out experiments are defined as

$$\left(\sum_{i=1}^{n} comp(p_i) \right) / n,$$

with $comp(p_i) = 1$ if p_i is computable, and 0 otherwise.

Accuracy and coverage are two measures that must be considered together; a recommender system can only be useful if both accuracy and coverage are high. As a simple example, consider a system with 1000 ratings for 1000 items which can perfectly predict the score of 10 items (yielding a very good accuracy of MAE=RMSE=0), but nothing else (yielding a coverage of 1%). Analogously, one can create a recommender that always generates the maximum score for an item; hence, coverage will be 100%, but possibly with a very high MAE and RMSE. Obviously, in the design phase of a recommendation algorithm, one should always consider the trade-off between the quality and the amount of the recommendations, or, in other words, between the desired level of accuracy and coverage for the application.

5.4.3 *Evaluation Measures for Item Controversiality*

When evaluating the accuracy of a recommendation algorithm, the MAE and RMSE are often computed on the entire data set, but this does not always give us a complete picture of its performance. For example, a recommender system may produce very different results for cold start users compared to regular users (see Chap. 7). In a similar way, one can also focus on different kinds of items, e.g. controversial items compared to favorites which score well for almost all users. Obviously, ratings for the former will be much harder to predict (see Chapter 6). In this section, we propose a new technique to appropriately identify whether a target item is controversial or not, leading to an operational definition of the concept of controversial items that is applicable to a wide variety of recommender systems. method, will lead to effective as well as efficient recommender systems. Our first step in this direction is the proposition of an operational definition of the concept of controversial items that is applicable to a wide variety of recommender systems.

Throughout the section, we will use the Epinions-reviews data set (see Sec. 3.4.1 and 5.4.1) to illustrate the rationale that will lead to our definition of a controversial item; a similar argumentation can be obtained when using the Epinions-products data set (see page 107). Most items in the Epinions-reviews data set receive very high scores, in fact, over 75% of all reviews received the highest possible evaluation. This means that a trivial algorithm that always predicts 5, or that uses the average score for the item as its prediction, can achieve high accuracy. However, such recommendation strategies have difficulties coping with controversial items.

A straightforward way to detect a controversial item in a data set is to inspect the standard deviation of the ratings for each item i (see e.g. [86]). The higher the standard deviation of the ratings for an item, the more controversial the item is. We denote this by $\sigma(i)$. The standard deviation of the ratings of items in the Epinions data sets ranges between 0 (full agreement on the score for an item) and 2 (the maximum standard deviation given the score range from 1 to 5). Figure 5.1 depicts the cumulative distribution function of σ over all the items in the Epinions-reviews data set. A little under 10% of the items have a σ of at least 0.9; there are 103 495 such items in total. About 70% of all items have a σ that is lower than 0.5. This comes as no surprise, since the low values are due to the abundance of 5-ratings. Hence, it is only natural that the more times an item is evaluated, the more 5-ratings it receives, and hence the lower the standard deviation will be. This is illustrated in Fig. 5.2.

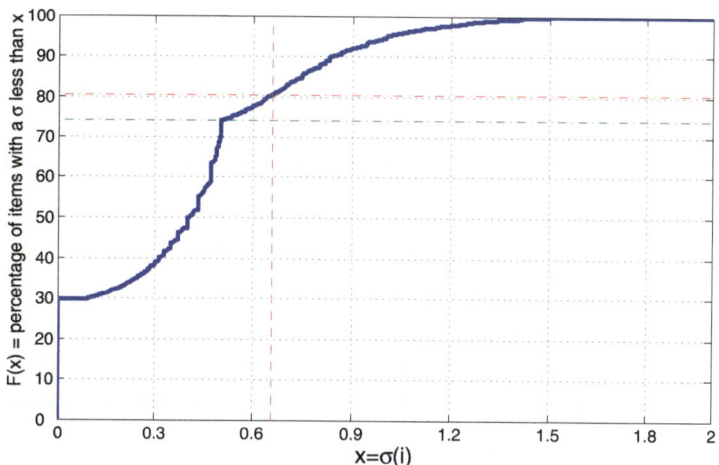

Fig. 5.1   Cumulative distribution function for σ in the Epinions-reviews data set.

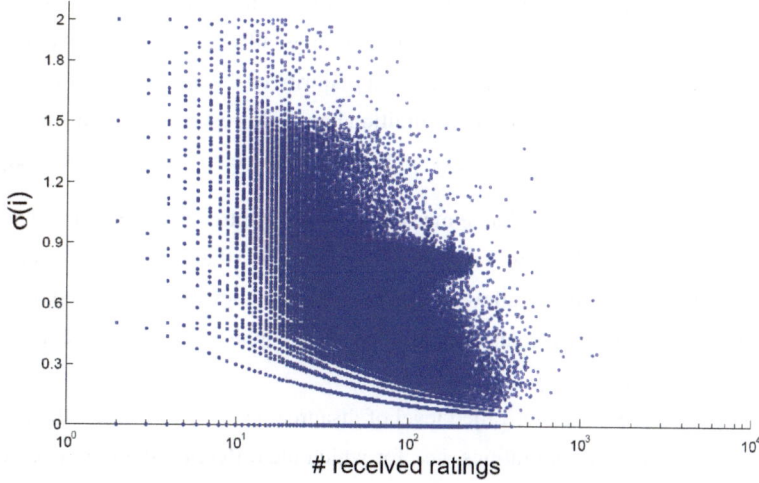

Fig. 5.2   The standard deviation $\sigma(i)$ vs. number of received ratings for item i in the Epinions-reviews data set.

Table 5.1   Example of three items and their ratings; $f_k(i)$ denotes the number of times item i received rating k, $\sigma(i)$ the standard deviation and $(\alpha@2)(i)$ the 2-level of disagreement of item i.

	$f_1(i)$	$f_2(i)$	$f_3(i)$	$f_4(i)$	$f_5(i)$	$\sigma(i)$	$(\alpha@2)(i)$
i_1	1	1	0	3	5	1.34	0.20
i_2	1	2	3	2	1	1.15	0.44
i_3	1	0	0	4	4	1.20	0.11

Another possibility for estimating the controversiality of an item is by computing the entropy of its ratings (see e.g. [71]). However, for our purposes, this measure has certain drawbacks; for example, let $f_k(i)$ denote the number of times item i received rating k. The entropy of an item i with $f_1(i) = 10$ and $f_5(i) = 15$ will be the same as an item with $f_2(i) = 15$ and $f_3(i) = 10$, although it is clear that the former is more controversial than the latter. This is due to the fact that the entropy considers every rating individually. The entropy measure tries to determine how difficult it is to exactly predict the real score, while the standard deviation tries to assess how difficult it is to estimate the real score as closely as possible. Since we will evaluate the recommendation algorithms with MAE and RMSE (which do not merely measure whether a prediction is good or bad, but also take into account the deviation from the actual rating), it is more appropriate to use standard deviation for this type of problem.

However, standard deviation does not convey the full picture of controversiality. As an example, consider the ratings for items i_1, i_2 and i_3 in Table 5.1. Intuitively, item i_2 seems the most controversial since it received ratings all over the range, while there is more agreement on i_1 and i_3 that are liked by a majority of the users. Still, in this example the most controversial item according to intuition has the lowest σ, which illustrates that by itself standard deviation does not always reflect the controversiality of an item adequately.

Important characteristics of a suitable measure to detect controversal items are (1) that it is mathematically precise, allowing for an implementation, (2) that it appeals to intuition, and even more important, (3) that it allows to improve the accuracy of personalized recommendations by singling out those items that call for a more sophisticated recommender strategy than a default (trivial) strategy.

We propose a new measure, called level of disagreement, that considers the likelihood that an item receives adjacent ratings, i.e., for which the difference does not exceed a predetermined window size Δ. The underlying intuition is that different scores that are close to each other reflect less disagreement than different scores that are on opposite ends of the scale. In a system with discrete ratings on a scale from 1 to M, the size of the window in which adjacent scores are being considered can vary from 1 to M. In the definition below, the granularity of the window is controlled by a parameter Δ.

Definition 5.6 (Level of disagreement). For a system with discrete ratings on a scale from 1 to M, let $\Delta \in \{1, \ldots, M\}$. We define the Δ-level of disagreement for an item i as

$$(\alpha @ \Delta)(i) = 1 - \max_{a \in \{1, \ldots, M - \Delta + 1\}} \left(\frac{\sum_{k=a}^{a+\Delta-1} f_k(i)}{\sum_{k=1}^{M} f_k(i)} \right)$$

with $f_k(i)$ the number of times that item i received rating k.

A window size of $\Delta = 1$ means that scores are considered in isolation. A window size of $\Delta = 2$ means each score is considered with a neighboring score, i.e. scores are considered in groups of 2. If $\Delta = M$, then $(\alpha @ \Delta) = 0$, since there can be no disagreement when all ratings are considered together. The last column of Table 5.1 displays the 2-level of disagreement for items i_1, i_2 and i_3, indicating that there is more disagreement on i_2 than on i_1 and i_3.

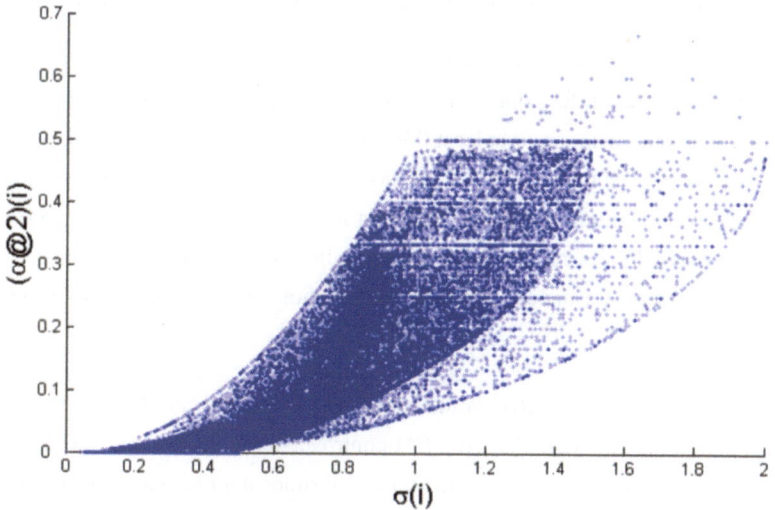

Fig. 5.3 $\alpha @ 2(i)$ vs. $\sigma(i)$ in the Epinions-reviews data set.

Figure 5.3 depicts the standard deviation (horizontal axis) and the 2-level of disagreement (vertical axis) of items in the Epinions-reviews data set. While a small standard deviation typically entails a small level of disagreement, there is considerable variation for high

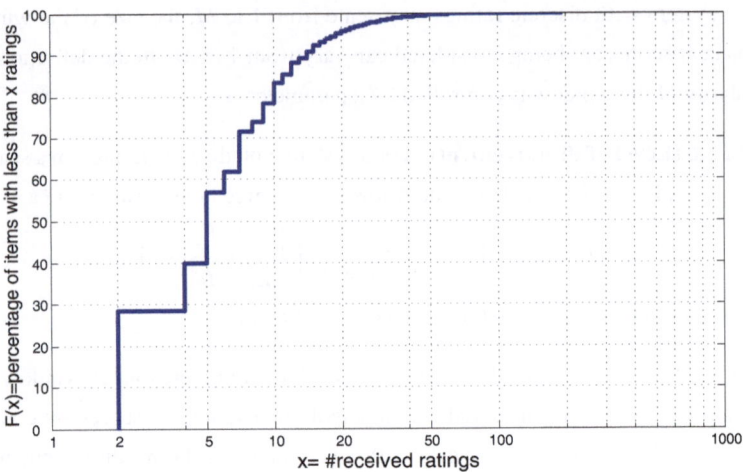

Fig. 5.4   Number of received ratings per controversial item in the Epinions-reviews data set.

values of σ (and vice versa). This highlights that σ and $\alpha @ \Delta$ are significantly different measures that can be used together to define the concept of a controversial item.

In systems with a large item set, typically a lot of the items will receive few ratings. Figure 5.4 shows the situation for controversial items in the Epinions-reviews data set: of all items with a standard deviation of at least 0.9 and a 2-level of disagreement of at least 0.4 (yielding a set of 28 710 items), about 57% has only been evaluated 5 times or less, and an additional 25% maximum 10 times. Since an item can appear to be controversial because it only received a few ratings so far (the so-called cold start items) and those ratings happen to be different, we include a popularity threshold in our definition to ensure real controversiality:

Definition 5.7 ($(\sigma^\star, \alpha^\star, \beta^\star)$-controversial item). For a system with discrete ratings on a scale from 1 to M, we call item i $(\sigma^\star, \alpha^\star, \beta^\star)$-controversial iff $\sigma(i) \geqslant \sigma^\star$, $(\alpha @ 2)(i) \geqslant \alpha^\star$ and $f(i) \geqslant \beta^\star$, in which $f(i)$ denotes the number of times item i has been evaluated, i.e., $f(i) = \sum_{k=1}^{M} f_k(i)$.

Applying this definition to the Epinions-reviews data set requires a parameter selection that is adapted to its characteristics, e.g., the predominance of rating value 5. To ensure this, we choose a $\sigma^\star$ value of 0.9 and an $\alpha^\star$ value of 0.4, obtaining a subset of 28 710 items for which a recommendation algorithm might experience high prediction difficulties. For the level of disagreement, we choose $\Delta = 2$ because this window yields a sufficiently refined item set (of course, other windows can be used for other kinds of data/applications). We can further restrict the item set to contain only the 1 416 controversial reviews that have been rated at least $\beta^\star = 20$ times. The same rationale can be followed for the Epinions-products data set. For this data set, we impose $\sigma^\star = 1.4$ (yielding about 10% of all items, as was also the case for the Epinions-reviews data set), $\alpha^\star = 0.4$ and $\beta^\star = 20$, yielding 266 controversial products that have been rated at least 20 times. Note that the σ-threshold is higher than for the other data set, which is due to the higher inherent controversiality level of the Epinions-products data set.

In the following chapter, whenever we focus on controversial items, we will use subsets from the Epinions-reviews and Epinions-products data sets that are obtained by applying the above procedure.

5.5 Conclusions

Systems that guide users through the vast amounts of online information are gaining tremendous importance. In this book, we focus on one particular set of such applications, namely recommender systems. In this chapter, we discussed several types of existing recommendation algorithms and focused specifically on collaborative filtering, the technique that is most closely related to the trust-enhanced approaches of the following chapters. We explained that collaborative filtering has some interesting benefits, but also some weaknesses, such as sparsity or susceptibility to attacks.

Throughout the following chapters, it will become clear how the incorporation of trust and distrust can alleviate these shortcomings. Two of the most significant problems are the controversial items and cold start users, which will be addressed in detail in Chap. 6 and 7 respectively. The corresponding experiments will be conducted on two data sets from Epinions.com. In this chapter, we investigated the controversiality level of items in Epinions, illustrated that classical controversiality measures are not sufficient, and proposed a new technique to detect Epinions' true controversial items.

Chapter 6

Trust & Distrust-Based Recommendations

When a web application with a built-in recommender offers a social networking component which enables its users to form a trust network, it can generate more personalized recommendations by combining content from the user profiles (ratings) with direct and/or propagated and aggregated information from the trust network. These are the so-called trust-enhanced recommendation systems. As we will explain later on, to be able to provide the users with enough accurate recommendations, the system requires a trust network that consists of a large number of users: the more connections a user has in the trust network, the more recommendations can be generated. Furthermore, more trust connections create more opportunity for qualitative or accurate recommendations. Hence, it is important to trust as many users as possible. However, at the same time, the trust connections you make should reflect your real opinion, otherwise the recommendations will become less accurate. In other words, on the one hand it is advisable to make many trust connections, but on the other hand you need to pay enough attention to which people you really want to trust; in some cases, even distrust can be beneficial for the quality of the recommendations you receive. Consequently, every user needs to find the right balance to get the best out of a trust-based recommendation system.

In the following section, we explain in an informal way how the incorporation of trust and distrust can alleviate some of the major issues in recommender systems. After our motivation, we continue the discussion in two parts: the first part covers the state of the art on trust-enhanced recommenders, a discussion of our new algorithm, and a head-to-head comparison of their performance (Sec. 6.2.1–6.2.4). In the second part, we explore the distrust-enhanced domain just out of the cradle; we experimentally investigate several possibilities for including distrust in the recommendation process (Sec. 6.3.1 and 6.3.2). We conclude the chapter with a discussion of related issues (Sec. 6.4).

6.1   Motivation

In real life, a person who wants to avoid a bad deal may ask a friend (i.e., someone he trusts) what he thinks about a certain item i. If this friend does not have an opinion about i, he can ask a friend of his, and so on until someone with an opinion about i (i.e., a recommender) has been found. Trust-enhanced recommender systems try to simulate this behavior, as depicted in Fig. 6.1: once a path to a recommender is found, the system can combine that recommender's judgment with available trust information (through trust propagation and aggregation) to obtain a personalized recommendation. In this way, a trust network allows to reach more users and more items.

In the collaborative filtering setting in Fig. 6.2, users a and b will be linked together because they have given similar ratings to certain items (among which i_1), and analogously, b and c can be linked together. Consequently, a prediction of a's interest in i_2 can be made. But in this scenario there is no link between a and i_3 or, in other words, there is no way to find out whether i_3 would be a good recommendation for agent a. This situation might change when a trust network has been established among the users of the recommender system. The solid lines in Fig. 6.2 denote trust relations between user a and user b, and between b and user c. While in a scenario without a trust network a collaborative filtering system is not able to generate a prediction about i_3 for user a, this could be solved in the trust-enhanced situation: if a expresses a certain level of trust in b, and b in c, by propagation an indication of a's trust in c can be obtained. If the outcome indicates that agent a should highly trust c, then i_3 might be a good recommendation for a, and will be highly ranked among the other recommended items.

This simple example illustrates that augmenting a recommender system by including trust relations can help in solving the sparsity problem. A trust-enhanced system also alleviates the cold start problem: it has been shown that by issuing a few trust statements, compared to a similar amount of rating information, the system can generate more, and more accurate, recommendations [88] (more on this topic in Chap. 7). Moreover, a web of trust can be used to produce an indication about the trustworthiness of users and as such make the system less vulnerable to malicious insiders: a simple copy-profile attack will only be possible when the target user, or someone who is trusted by the target user, has explicitly indicated that he trusts the adversary to a certain degree. Finally, the functioning of a trust-enhanced system (e.g. the concept of trust propagation) is intuitively more understandable for the users than the classical 'black box' approaches. A nice example

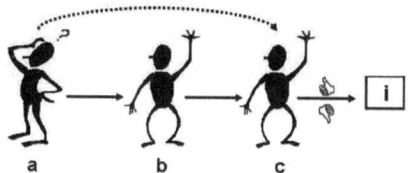
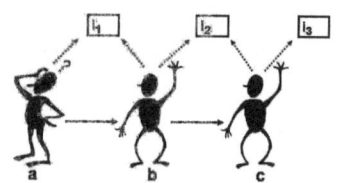

Fig. 6.1 Recommending target item i for target user a.

Fig. 6.2 Recommendation of items through trust relations.

is Golbeck's FilmTrust system [39] which asks its users to evaluate their acquaintances based on their movie taste, and accordingly uses that information to generate personalized predictions.

The reason why trust-based recommendations work can partially be explained by the effect of social influence and selection in social networks. The theory of social influence states that users will behave more alike to users they interact with (i.e., become more similar), while selection (or homophily) denotes the process of forming relationships to people who are already similar. In other words, there is an interaction between similarity and social (hence also trust) relations. The two factors have been widely studied in sociology; nice literature overviews can be found in, among others, [95] and [130].

Since nowadays more and more online social network data becomes available to researchers, also the web intelligence domain has started to investigate this phenomenon; e.g., Ziegler and Golbeck used data sets from a movie and book recommender system to show that there exists a positive correlation between trust relations and similarity [157]. However, they also claimed that trust and similarity are not the same, and can be used complementary. This is also illustrated by the study of Crandall *et al.* on data sets from Wikipedia and LiveJournal[1]: they showed that the similarity and social graphs often have not much overlap (and hence cannot be regarded as similar concepts), and that both types of data can be used as predictors of future behavior of a particular user [22]; in our context this means that both computed similarity and social ties can be used in the recommendation process, each adding a different dimension to the recommendation.

The trust- and distrust-enhanced algorithms that we will discuss in this chapter work in a personalized, or 'local' way. Instead of taking into account all available trust connections in the network when estimating the trust in a particular recommender (the 'global' way), they only rely on the part of the network that is formed by putting the target user at the

---

[1] A social network community with a focus on blogging, see www.livejournal.com

centre (also see Sec. 3.1). Let us explain this with an analogy from a classical movie rec-ommender system; in a collaborative filtering algorithm the target user is also at the centre of the network, since only the users that are similar to him take part in the recommendation process. If you want to find out if you will like 'The Godfather' (one of the best movies ever according to the users of the Internet Movie Database[2]), then the predicted score prob-ably will be the same whether the system just uses an average of all scores for that movie, or a collaborative filtering algorithm where only the scores of users similar to you are taken into account. However, for more controversial movies such as 'A Clockwork Orange' or 'Titanic', collaborative filtering will be able to give you a much more accurate estimation than a global average, because it is more tailored to your tastes.

Trust-enhanced recommenders work in a similar way as collaborative filtering, only this time it is not the ratings from users that are close to the target user in the similarity network that are used, but the ratings from the users that are in the neighborhood of the target user according to the trust network. This local and personalized approach is one of the main strengths of many trust-enhanced recommender applications.

In this chapter, we will evaluate the performance of the recommendation algorithms on both data sets from Epinions. A thorough description of the features of the Epinions-products data set can be found in [91], for more information also see Sec. 5.4.1. We refer to Sec. 3.4.1 and 5.4.1, or [50], for a discussion of the Epinions-reviews data set. Hence, besides a classical consumer goods recommender system, we will also evaluate a review recommender system.

The research on review recommender systems attracts increasing attention, since nowa-days reviews are not only written by a select group of experts anymore, but also by the customers themselves, and more prevalent, think of Epinions, Amazon, or the Internet Movie Database. A lot of applications try to help the users in finding the best reviews by computing one global score for the review, for example Amazon's 'x out of y people found the following review helpful'. Other applications generate the global score by combining techniques from the text classification area and opinion/sentiment analysis, see [34, 81] for some recent examples. All of them illustrate that review recommendation is becom-ing an important topic. However, a review that is helpful for one user is not necessarily equally useful for another user; recall our rationale from the last paragraph. In other words, trust-enhanced recommendation techniques can also be very useful in the domain of review recommendation.

---

[2]See www.imdb.com/chart/top

Table 6.1   Notations and abbreviations used in Sec. 6.2 and 6.3.

a	target user	u	user who takes part in the recommendation process
i	target item		
CI	controversial item	RI	randomly selected item
CF	collaborative filtering	PCC	Pearson's correlation coefficient
R	set of users who rated i	R^+	set of users who have a positive PCC w.r.t. a and who rated i
R^T	set of users trusted by a who rated i	R^{T+}	set of users trusted by and positively correlated with a and who rated i
R^D	set of users distrusted by a who rated i	R^{TD}	set of users who are either trusted or distrusted by a and who rated i

6.2   Trust-Enhanced Recommendations

All the aforementioned examples illustrate that establishing a trust network among the users of a recommender system may contribute to its success. Hence, unsurprisingly, some attempts in this direction have already been made, see for example [38, 55, 74, 90, 104, 108, 113]. Trust-enhanced recommender systems can roughly be divided into two classes, according to the way the trust values are obtained. In the following section, we give an overview of the state of the art in trust-based systems, while in Sec. 6.2.2 we investigate their applicability on real-world data sets. In Sec. 6.2.3 we compare them with a new approach that combines aspects of collaborative filtering and its trust-based variants, while in Sec. 6.2.4 we go more deeply into the effect of trust propagation. Table 6.1 gives an overview of the notations we will use in the remainder of this chapter.

6.2.1   *State of the Art*

The first group of trust-enhanced recommendation approaches uses information coming from a trust network that is generated by the direct input of the users, i.e., by explicitly issuing trust statements. Examples can be found in, among others, [39, 55, 90]. Such a strategy allows to use trust propagation and aggregation in the network to infer the final trust values that are needed in the recommender algorithm. On the other hand, the second group does not require the users to estimate the trust in their acquaintances. Instead, trust values are computed automatically. If no explicit trust information is given, one must rely on other information that is available, which are most often the ratings. Consequently similarity will usually play a role in the trust computation, but not completely determine the trust estimation process (other non-similarity factors also play a role). E.g., trust can be based on a user's history of making reliable recommendations [74], in which an extra dimension is added to the trust computation by taking into account the interpretation of a rating by the target user, or based on transitivity rules for user-to-user similarity (adding an extra dimension by including transitivity) [108].

In the behavioral literature, the concept of trust is well defined; see for example Mayer *et al.*'s framework in which ability, benevolence, integrity and propensity to trust are determined as its key factors [92], or McAllister's work that distinguishes between cognition-based and affect-based trust [93]. However, in the recommendation research area, trust is often used as an umbrella term for a wide range of relationships between people, especially when dealing with automatic computation of trust values. In these cases, trust is being used to denote a variety of concepts, ranging from perceived similarity of tastes, over reputation, to the assessment of a user's competence. In Sec. 6.4 we discuss this in more detail; in this section, we focus on the basics of both strategies (i.e., mining a trust network and automatic computation of trust values), and illustrate the techniques with representative work in each class.

6.2.1.1 *Mining a Trust Network*

The most common trust-enhanced recommender strategies ask their users to explicitly issue trust statements about other users. Take for instance Moleskiing [87], a ski mountaineering community site which uses Friend Of A Friend-files[3] that contain trust information on a scale from 1 to 9 [42], or the e-commerce site Epinions.com which ranks reviews based on a trust network that it maintains by asking its users to indicate which members they trust (i.e., their personal web of trust) or distrust (block list). Another well-known example is Golbeck's FilmTrust [39], an online social network combined with a movie rating and review system in which users are asked to evaluate their acquaintances' movie tastes on a scale from 1 to 10.

All these systems exploit the relations in the trust network to determine which opinions or ratings should weigh more or less in the recommendation process. In other words, this group of algorithms uses the trust estimates (obtained by propagation and aggregation) as weights in the decision process. This weighting can be done in several ways. In this section, we focus on the two most commonly used strategies, namely classical weighted average and adaptations of the collaborative filtering mechanism, and illustrate each of

---

[3]FOAF-files are machine readable documents describing basic properties of a person, including links between the person and objects/people they interact with.

them with one well-known state of the art implementation.

In a recommender system without a trust network, a simple recommendation algorithm that needs to estimate how well a target user will like a target item i can compute the average rating for i by taking into account the ratings $r_{u,i}$ from all the system's users u who are already familiar with i; see Definition 5.1. This baseline recommendation strategy can be refined by computing a *trust-based weighted mean*. In particular, by including trust values $t_{a,u}$ that reflect the degree to which the raters u are trusted, the algorithm allows to differentiate between the sources. In fact, it is only natural to assign more weight to ratings of highly trusted users; the formula is given in Definition 6.1.

Definition 6.1 (Trust-based weighted mean). The unknown rating for target item i and target user a can be computed as

$$p_{a,i} = \frac{\sum\limits_{u \in R^T} t_{a,u} r_{u,i}}{\sum\limits_{u \in R^T} t_{a,u}},$$

with R^T the set of users who evaluated i and for whom the trust value $t_{a,u}$ is greater than or equal to α.

Since there is not always direct trust information available for a particular couple of agents, we need trust metrics to compute a trust estimate for them.

The formula in Definition 6.1 is at the heart of Golbeck *et al.*'s recommendation algo- rithm [38]. The novelty of this algorithm mainly lies in the way the trust estimates $t_{a,u}$ are inferred, by means of a trust metric that they have called *TidalTrust*. In [41], the au- thors give an overview of the observations that have lead to the development of Tidal- Trust. In each experiment, they ignored an existing trust relation from a user a to a user u, and focused on all paths that connect a to u. In short, by comparing the prop- agated trust results from these paths with the original, hidden, trust value, they noticed that (1) shorter propagation paths yield more accurate trust estimates, and that (2) paths containing higher trust values yield better results too.

Hence, taking into account the first observation, only allowing shorter paths should yield the best results. However, in some cases only a few users will be reachable if a limit is set on the path length. This trade-off is incorporated through a variable path length limit: the shortest path length that is needed to connect the target user a with a user u that has rated the target item i (i.e., a rater) becomes the path depth of the algorithm. This can be achieved by performing a breadth-first search from a until the level is reached on which at least one user can be found who has rated i; the algorithm then knows all the shortest paths from a to users on that level who have rated i. Note that this process requires a central authority and that the depth of the breadth-first search varies from one computation to another.

One way of addressing the second observation (higher trust values on the path yield better trust estimates) is to limit the information such that only the most trusted users are taken into account. However, every user has his own behavior for issuing trust values (one user may give the maximum value quite often while another one never does), and in addition, it will often be the case that only a few paths contain the same high trust value. This is why it is difficult in practice to set a static threshold, so instead, thresholds are chosen dynamically: Golbeck *et al.* opted to incorporate a value that represents the path strength (i.e., the minimum trust rating on a path leading to the user who is connected with u), and to compute the maximum path strength over all paths leading to the raters. This maximum (*max*) is then chosen as the minimum trust threshold for participation in the process. In other words, TidalTrust only takes into account the shortest, strongest paths.

Definition 6.2 (TidalTrust). The trust value from target user a in user u is estimated recursively as

$$t_{a,u} = \frac{\displaystyle\sum_{v \in WOT^+(a)} t_{a,v} \cdot t_{v,u}}{\displaystyle\sum_{v \in WOT^+(a)} t_{a,v}},$$

with $WOT^+(a)$ the set of users in $WOT(a)$ for whom a's trust statement is greater than or equal to the given threshold max. If $WOT^+(a)$ is empty, then $t_{a,u} = 0$.

Algorithm 6.1.

1: for each user u do *PathStrength*$[u] = -1$, *PathStrength*$[a]=1$;

2: *maxDepth* $= \infty$, *depth*=1, add a to *queue*

3: **while** *queue* not empty and *depth* $\leqslant$ *maxDepth* **do**

4:     x=*queue*.dequeue, push x on *stack*

5:     **if** x and u are not adjacent **then**

6:         **for** each user i adjacent to x **do**

7:             add i to *next_level_queue* if i is not yet visited

8:             **if** *next_level_queue* contains i **then**

9:                 *strength* $= \min(PathStrength[x], t_{x,i})$

10:                 *PathStrength*$[i] = \max(PathStrength[i], strength)$

11:             **end if**

12:        **end for**

13:    **else**

14:        $maxDepth = depth, strength = PathStrength[x]$

15:        $PathStrength[u] = \max(PathStrength[u], strength)$

16:    **end if**

17:    **if** $queue$ is empty **then**

18:        $queue = next\_level\_queue, next\_level\_queue$=new queue, $depth$++

19:    **end if**

20: **end while**

21:

22: for each user u do $trust\_to\_sink[u] = -1$

23: **while** $maxDepth$!=MAX and $stack$ is not empty **do**

24:    v=$stack$.pop   ▷ if $maxDepth = \infty$ then $t_{a,u} = 0$

25:    **if** v is adjacent to u **then**

26:        $trust\_to\_sink[v] = t_{v,u}$

27:    **else**

28:        numerator=denominator=0

29:        **for** each user i adjacent to v **do**

30:            **if** $t_{v,i} \geqslant PathStrength[u]$ and $trust\_to\_sink[i]! = -1$ **then**

31:                $numerator+ = t_{v,i} * trust\_to\_sink[i], denumerator+ = t_{v,i}$

32:            **end if**

33:        **end for**

34:        **if** $denumerator > 0$ **then**

35:            $trust\_to\_sink[v] = numerator/denumerator$

36:        **end if**

37:    **end if**

38: **end while**

39: $t_{a,u} = trust\_to\_sink[a]$ ▷ if $trust\_to\_sink[a] = -1$ then $t_{a,u} = 0$

TidalTrust consists of two phases; the pseudocode is given in Algorithm 6.1. In the first phase (lines 1 to 20), as explained above, the central authority performs a breadth-first search to find all users v on the shortest paths leading to i; as it is breadth-first, the algorithm uses a queue (first in first out). During the search, the central authority computes the *max* threshold (represented in the code by $PathStrength[u]$; all other entries of the array contain intermediate results). In the second phase (lines 22-39), the actual trust estimate $t_{a,u}$ is computed recursively as the weighted mean of trust values $t_{v,u}$ for all users v that are a first link on a shortest path from a (the 'source') to u (the 'sink'), as in the formula in Definition 6.2. An additional restriction is that only trust information that is at least as high as max is taken into account. Remark that the algorithm uses a stack for the second algorithm (last in first out structure) to implement the linking from the sink back to the source.

Note that the first phase is a forward movement ('wave') which requires a central authority, while the second phase is implemented as a backward FATP (see Sec. 4.1) wave in which agents can have more autonomy. The name TidalTrust was chosen because calculations sweep forward from a to u in the trust network, and then pull back from u to return the final trust value to a [38].

Example 6.1. Figure 6.3 depicts an example of a trust network, in which one needs to compute a recommendation for target user a and target item i. The upper path will not take part in the computation because it is longer than the shortest path to item i (of length 3); consequently, $t_{a,u}$ need not be computed. Among the other three paths, only the two lowest will contribute to the final recommendation, because $max = \max(\min(0.8, 0.2), \min(0.5, 0.8), \min(0.5, 0.7)) = 0.5$ and the path strength of the second path is merely 0.2. The trust value $t_{a,w}$ is hence computed as

$$\frac{t_{a,h} \cdot t_{h,w} + t_{a,j} \cdot t_{j,w}}{t_{a,h} + t_{a,j}} = \frac{0.5 \cdot \left(\frac{0.8 \cdot t_{y,w}}{0.8}\right) + 0.5 \cdot \left(\frac{0.7 \cdot t_{k,w}}{0.7}\right)}{0.5 + 0.5}$$

$$= \frac{0.5 \cdot 0.5 + 0.5 \cdot 0.9}{1.0}$$

$$= 0.7$$

TidalTrust belongs to the class of gradual trust approaches and is an example of a local trust metric. Golbeck *et al.* have shown that using trust-based weighted mean in combination with TidalTrust does not necessarily offer a general benefit over computing the average or applying collaborative filtering, but that it does yield significantly more accurate recommendations for users who disagree with the average rating for a specific item (see for example [38, 41]).

Whereas Golbeck *et al.*'s approach is an example of a weighted average implementation, another class of trust-enhanced systems is tied more closely to the *collaborative filtering* algorithm; see Sec. 5.2 for the details of collaborative filtering. As in Definition 5.2, the

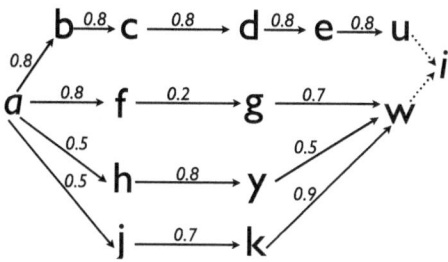

Fig. 6.3   Example of a trust network for generating a recommendation for target user *a* w.r.t. target item *i*.

weights for the neighbors are most often determined by Pearson's Correlation Coefficient. However, instead of a correlation-based computation of the weights, one can also infer the weights through the relations of the target user in the trust network (again through propagation and aggregation); see the formula in Definition 6.3 which adapts Definition 5.2 by replacing the similarity correlation weights $w_{a,u}$ by the trust values $t_{a,u}$. This strategy is also supported by the fact that trust and similarity are correlated, as shown in [157].

Definition 6.3 (Trust-based collaborative filtering). The unknown rating for target item *i* and target user *a* can be computed as

$$p_{a,i} = \overline{r_a} + \frac{\sum\limits_{u \in R^T} t_{a,u}(r_{u,i} - \overline{r_u})}{\sum\limits_{u \in R^T} t_{a,u}}.$$

We call this alternative *trust-based collaborative filtering*. Note that, because the weights are not equal to the PCC, this procedure can produce out of bounds results. When this is the case, $p_{a,i}$ is rounded to the nearest possible rating.

Algorithm 6.2.

1: *dist*=0, *users*[*dist*] = *a*
2: add *a* to *modified_trust_network*
3: **while** *dist* < *d* **do**
4:     *dist*++
5:     *users*[*dist*]=users adjacent to *users*[*dist* − 1] and not yet visited
6:     **for** each user *b* from *users*[*dist*] **do**
7:         add *b* to *modified_trust_network*
8:         add all edges from *users*[*dist* − 1] to *b* to *modified_trust_network*
9:     **end for**

10: **end while**

11:

12: $dist = 1, t_{a,a} = 1, \forall u \in users[1]: t_{a,u} =$ trust statement issued by a

13: **while** $dist < d$ **do**

14:     $dist$++

15:     **for** each user u in $users[dist]$ **do**

16:         $predecessors$=users v for whom $t_{v,u} \geqslant \alpha$ in $modified\_trust\_network$

17:         $t_{a,u} = \dfrac{\sum_{v\in predecessors} t_{a,v} \cdot t_{v,u}}{\sum_{v\in predecessors} t_{a,v}}$

18:     **end for**

19: **end while**

Definition 6.3 is at the basis of Massa *et al.*'s recommendation algorithm which incorporates a new trust metric, called *MoleTrust* [89]; see Algorithm 6.2 for its pseudocode. The trust metric consists of two phases. In the first stage (lines 1 to 10), cycles in the trust network are removed during a search in which all users are stored (in the array *users*) according to their distance *dist* from user a, while the second stage includes the actual trust computation (propagation and aggregation) based on the cycle free *modified_trust_network* (lines 12 to 19).

An example of a cycle is $t_{a,b}$, $t_{b,c}$ and $t_{c,a}$. In this case, the last trust statement should be removed, since the problem created by cycles is that, during a search in the network, a would be visited over and over again until the propagation horizon is reached, see below. Massa *et al.* acknowledge that this step removes trust statements that can be informative, but claim that the technique is acceptable because of time-efficiency. After the removal of the cycles, the prediction for a particular $t_{a,u}$ can then be obtained by performing a simple breadth-first search: first the users at distance 1 (i.e., users who are directly trusted by a) are looked up (see $users[1]$ in the pseudocode), while their trust value is fetched (i.e., direct trust information), then the users at distance 2 (users who are trusted by users who a trusts) who are not at distance 1 are looked up (in $users[2]$), etcetera. Note that like this, MoleTrust ensures that only the shortest paths from a to another user are taken into account.

While the first phase consists of the search and storage of the users, the second phase deals with the computation of the trust estimates in users on distances $m > 1$. The trust in the users at distance 2 or more is calculated in a way similar to TidalTrust, in the sense that it is also a weighted mean-based algorithm. However, the details of the implementation differ significantly. In TidalTrust, a user v is added to $WOT^+(a)$ only if he is on a shortest path from target user a to target item i. On the other hand, in MoleTrust, $WOT^+(a)$ includes all users who have rated the target item and who can be reached through a direct or propagated trust relation. But trust is not computed for all eternity: before the computation begins, one must assign a value d to the 'propagation horizon' parameter. Like this, only users who are reachable within distance d are taken into account (i.e., are stored and their trust estimate is computed). Another important input parameter of MoleTrust is the trust threshold α for participation in the process (unlike the dynamic *max* value in TidalTrust), which is e.g. set to 0.6 (on a scale from 0 to 1) in the experiments reported in [89]. These parameters lead to the following formula [87]:

Definition 6.4 (MoleTrust). The trust value from target user a in user u is estimated as

$$t_{a,u} = \frac{\sum\limits_{v \in WOT^+(a)} t_{a,v} \cdot t_{v,u}}{\sum\limits_{v \in WOT^+(a)} t_{a,v}},$$

with $WOT^+(a)$ the set of users for whom a's trust statement or previously computed trust estimate is greater than or equal to a given threshold α and who are within distance of trust horizon d. If there is no such path, then $t_{a,u} = 0$.

As explained above, MoleTrust works with a central authority and starts with a breadth-first search phase to find all shortest paths for every user u within the trust horizon d who has rated i. In the second phase, the trust values $t_{a,u}$ are computed as the weighted mean of trust values $t_{v,u}$ for all users v for whom the trust value $t_{a,v}$ is directly available, or, if not, the trust estimate $t_{a,v}$ has already been computed; only trust information that is at least as high as α is taken into account. In other words, the second phase in MoleTrust is implemented as a forward movement (as opposed to the backward, recursive, wave in TidalTrust): a trust estimation in a particular user on distance $m > 1$ must only be computed (and stored) once; this estimate is then used for the computation of trust estimations in users on distance $m + 1$.

Example 6.2. Let us again take a look at Fig. 6.3, and suppose that the trust horizon d is set to 5 and $\alpha = 0.5$. Then u is just within distance of the propagation horizon d, and hence $t_{a,u}$ will be computed: $t_{a,u} = (t_{a,e} \cdot 0.8)/t_{a,e} = \cdots = 0.8$. Of the three paths leading to w, only the bottom two will take part in the actual computation because on the upper path one of the trust relations is lower than α ($0.2 < 0.5$). The trust estimation $t_{a,w}$ is then computed as (assuming that $t_{a,h}$, $t_{a,j}$, $t_{a,y}$ and $t_{a,k}$ have already been computed) $t_{a,w} = \frac{0.8 \cdot 0.5 + 0.7 \cdot 0.9}{1.5} \approx 0.69$.

For environments where only bivalent trust ratings are available, Definition 6.4 always yields $t_{a,u} = 1$ if there is a path within distance of the trust horizon. Therefore, instead of the original MoleTrust implementation, Massa *et al.* propose to use a horizon-based technique to introduce gradual trust values into the algorithm [88]:

Definition 6.5 (Horizon-based MoleTrust). The trust value from target user a in user u at distance n is estimated as

$$t_{a,u} = \frac{d - n + 1}{d},$$

if $n \leqslant d$. If u is not reachable within distance d from a, then $t_{a,u} = 0$.

Note that, analogous to TidalTrust, MoleTrust and horizon-based MoleTrust belong to the class of gradual local trust metrics. In their experiments, Massa and Avesani have illustrated that MoleTrust provides better trust estimates than global trust metrics such as eBay's[4], especially when it comes down to estimating the trust in controversial users (who are trusted by one group and distrusted by another) [89]. They also showed that MoleTrust yields more accurate predictions for cold start users, compared to a classical collaborative filtering system [86, 88].

Golbeck *et al.*'s and Massa *et al.*'s approach are two typical examples of trust-enhanced recommender techniques that use explicit trust information. Table 6.2 summarizes their most prominent characteristics. Another recommendation approach that also mines a trust network can be found e.g. in [55] which presents a recommender system for research papers; it is similar to Golbeck *et al.*'s approach, but also takes into account a document reference network.

6.2.1.2 *Automatic Trust Generation*

The algorithms discussed in the previous section require explicit trust input from the users. As a consequence, the applications that use such an algorithm must provide a means to obtain the necessary information; think for example of FilmTrust or Moleskiing. However, this might not always be possible or feasible. In such cases, methods that automatically infer trust estimates, without needing explicit trust information, might be a better solution. An example of such a system can be found in [105].

Most commonly, these approaches base their trust generation mechanism on the past rating behavior of the users in the system. More specifically, deciding to what degree a particular user should participate in the recommendation process is influenced by his

---

[4] www.ebay.com

Table 6.2 Characteristic features of two state of the art recommendation approaches that mine a trust network to predict a rating for target user a and target item i, based on ratings of other users u for i.

	Golbeck et al.	Massa et al.
propagation	multiplication	multiplication
aggregation	trust-based weighted mean (6.2)	trust-based weighted mean (6.4)
max length of propagation path	dynamic (shortest path)	static (horizon)
trust threshold	dynamic (strongest chain)	static
entry requirement for path in propagation process	shortest path	path within the horizon
entry requirement for user v in recommendation process	v is on a path that exceeds the threshold max	v is on a path that exceeds a static threshold
prediction of rating	trust-based weighted mean	trust-based collaborative filtering

history of delivering accurate recommendations. Let us exemplify this with the well-known approach of O'Donovan *et al.* [104].

Our intuition tells us that a user who has made a lot of good recommendations in the past can be viewed as more trustworthy than other users who performed less well. To be able to select the most trustworthy users in the system, O'Donovan *et al.* introduced two trust metrics, viz. *profile-level* and *item-level trust*, reflecting the general trustworthiness of a particular user u, and the trustworthiness of a user u with respect to a particular item i, respectively. Both trust metrics consist of a computation of the correctness of u's recommendations. In particular, a prediction $p_{a,i}$ that is generated only by information coming from u (hence u is the sole recommender) is considered correct if $p_{a,i}$ is within ε of a's actual rating $r_{a,i}$.

The profile-level trust t_u^P for u is then defined as the percentage of correct recommendations that u contributed. Remark that this is a very general trust measure; in practice it will often occur that u performs better in recommending a set of specific items. To this aim, O'Donovan *et al.* also proposed the more fine-grained item-level trust t_u^i, which measures the percentage of recommendations for item i that were correct. Hence, in such automated approaches, trust values are not generated via trust propagation and aggregation, but are based on the ratings that were given in the past. Remark that O'Donovan *et al.*'s methods are global trust metrics; there is no personal bias w.r.t. target user a involved. The way the values are obtained can be seen as probabilistic, i.e., the trust value represents the probability that the recommendation will be correct (within ε).

Similar to other trust-enhanced techniques, the values that are obtained through the trust metric are used as weights in the recommendation process. Just like Massa *et al.*, O'Donovan *et al.* focus on trust-based adaptations of collaborative filtering. An alternative to Massa *et al.*'s scheme is to use trust values as a filter, so that only the most trustworthy neighbors participate in the recommendation process. This strategy is called *trust-based filtering* [104]:

Definition 6.6 (Trust-based filtering). The unknown rating for target item i and target user a can be computed as

$$p_{a,i} = \overline{r_a} + \frac{\displaystyle\sum_{u \in R^{T+}} w_{a,u}\left(r_{u,i} - \overline{r_u}\right)}{\displaystyle\sum_{u \in R^{T+}} w_{a,u}},$$

in which $w_{a,u}$ denotes the Pearson's Correlation Coefficient and $R^{T+} = R^T \cap R^+$, with R^+

the set of neighbors of a with a positive correlation coefficient, and R^T the set of users whose item/profile-level trust is greater than or equal to a given threshold α.

Note that this algorithm does not involve trust propagation or aggregation due to the global way of computing the trust values. In the next section, we will use the trust-based filtering framework (i.e., the formula in Definition 6.6), but experiment with another trust metric (i.e., another, local, implementation of R^T).

In [104], O'Donovan and Smyth showed that trust-based filtering achieves better accuracy than collaborative filtering in terms of average errors. The algorithm based on profile-level trust yields lower errors than collaborative filtering in nearly 70% of all prediction cases. O'Donovan et al.'s method is a representative example in the group of strategies that use automatic trust generation. A related approach can be found in [74], which works with an utilitarian measure instead of a binary correctness function.

6.2.2   Empirical Comparison

One question that stands out is which of the state of the art approaches discussed above performs best in practice. Basically, so far, researchers in the trust-based recommender field introduced their own new algorithms and evaluated these on their own applications and/or data sets, without including a comparison of other trust-enhanced approaches based on the same data set/application. Therefore, we provide a head-to-head comparison of the performance that the previously discussed trust-enhanced techniques can achieve on one and the same data set.

We focus on Golbeck et al.'s trust-based weighted mean with TidalTrust (Definitions 6.1 and 6.2), Massa's trust-based collaborative filtering with horizon-based MoleTrust (Definitions 6.3 and 6.5), and O'Donovan et al.'s trust-based filtering (Definition 6.6). Since our goal is to compare all techniques on the same data sets and to investigate the influence of trust propagation, we have chosen not to implement O'Donovan et al.'s automatic trust generation strategy, but to mine the same trust network as the other two strategies. Although O'Donovan et al. do not use trust propagation and aggregation in their experiments [104], it is of course possible to do so. Since there is no explicit use of trust values in Definition 6.6, we only need to specify how propagation and aggregation enlarge $R^{T+} = R^T \cap R^+$: we choose to add a user u to R^T if $t_{a,u}$ is greater than or equal to the threshold α, with $t_{a,u}$ computed as in Definition 6.4.

As discussed in Sec. 6.1, the data sets we use in our experiments are obtained from Epinions.com; in the context of the Epinions-reviews data set, an item denotes a review of consumer goods, whereas for the Epinons-products data set an item denotes a consumer product. Both reviews and products are rated on a scale from 1 to 5. We focus on the coverage and accuracy of the algorithms for controversial items, which are the most challenging for a recommender system. To this aim, we use the methodology described in Sec. 5.4.3. To compare the performance achieved for controversial items (CIs) with the performance that can be obtained in general, we also present the average coverage and accuracy for 1 416 and 266 randomly selected 'popular' items (RIs) (that have been evaluated at least 20 times, analogous to the controversial items).

Epinions also allows users to evaluate other users based on the quality of their reviews, and to provide trust and distrust evaluations in addition to ratings. The fact that both data sets contain explicit trust information from the users makes them very appropriate to study issues in trust-enhanced recommender systems. Users can evaluate other users by including them in their WOT (i.e. a list of reviewers whose reviews and ratings were consistently found to be valuable[5]), or by putting them in their block list (a list of authors whose reviews were consistently found to be offensive, inaccurate or low quality[5], thus indicating distrust). In the Epinions-reviews data set, the trust evaluations make up an Epinions WOT graph consisting of 114 222 users and 717 129 non self-referring trust relations[6]. The Epinions-products data set contains information on 49 288 users who issued or received 487 003 trust statements in total.

Note that the data sets only contain bivalent trust values, hence in our experiments $t_{a,u}$ in Definition 6.1, 6.3 and 6.6 can take on the values 0 (absence of trust) and 1 (full presence) only. This limitation leads to alterations of some of the trust-based algorithms; e.g., the choice for the threshold α in Definitions 6.1, 6.3 and 6.6 is irrelevant, and the formula in Definition 6.1 reduces to the classical average. Furthermore, in practice, for the Epinions data sets, Definitions 6.2 and 6.4 become binary propagation strategies: if a user appears directly in the web of trust of target user a, or if he can be reached from a by a trust propagation path, then trust weight $t_{a,u} = 1$ is assigned to that user.

6.2.2.1   Coverage

Coverage refers to the number of (target user,target item) pairs for which a prediction can be generated, see Definition 5.5 for its implementation in a leave-one-out experiment. For

---

[5]See www.epinions.com/help/faq/

[6]The data set also contains 15% distrust relations. In this section we focus on the trust relations; we deal with the distrust part in Sec. 6.3.

Table 6.3 Performance of trust-based recommender algorithms on the Epinions-reviews data set; MAE and RMSE $\in [0,4]$.

	ALGORITHM	Controversial items (CIs)			Randomly selected items (RIs)		
		% COV	MAE	RMSE	% COV	MAE	RMSE
(B1)	Base: score 5	100	1.45	1.96	100	0.16	0.51
(B2)	Base: average score for item	100	1.25	1.34	100	0.18	0.40
(B3)	Base: average score of user	99	1.23	1.58	100	0.36	0.50
(B4)	Base: random score	100	1.61	2.02	100	1.92	2.37
(5.2)	Collaborative filtering with R^+	94	0.96	1.13	98	0.19	0.38
(6.1)	Trust-based weighted mean	63	0.86	1.20	89	0.13	0.35
(6.3)	Trust-based collaborative filtering	63	0.87	1.16	89	0.17	0.35
(6.6)	Trust-based filtering	60	0.86	1.16	86	0.16	0.36
(6.7)	EnsembleTrustCF	94	0.94	1.11	99	0.19	0.38
(P1)	Propagated trust-based weighted mean	88	0.91	1.22	97	0.15	0.38
(P3)	Propagated trust-based CF	88	0.99	1.16	97	0.19	0.37
(P66)	Propagated trust-based filtering	84	0.94	1.13	96	0.18	0.36
(P7a)	Prop. 1 EnsembleTrustCF	96	1.00	1.16	99	0.20	0.38
(P7b)	Prop. 2 EnsembleTrustCF	94	0.96	1.12	99	0.19	0.38

Definition 5.2 we call $p_{a,i}$ computable if there is at least one user u who rated i and for whom the Pearson's correlation coefficient $w_{a,u}$ can be calculated, while for Definitions 6.1 and 6.3 a computable $p_{a,i}$ means that there is at least one user u who has rated i and for whom the (propagated and aggregated) trust estimate $t_{a,u}$ can be calculated. Finally, for Definition 6.6, predictions are possible when at least one user u is found who has rated i, and for whom both $t_{a,u}$ and $w_{a,u}$ can be computed.

Table 6.3 and 6.4 show the coverage (% COV) for controversial items and randomly selected items in the Epinions-reviews and -products data sets. The first four rows cover baseline strategies (B1)–(B4). The first baseline strategy is a system that always predicts 5/5 (B1), since this is the predominant score for items in Epinions. The second system computes the average received rating for the target item (B2), while the third one yields the average rating given by target user a (B3). The latter method will score well in a system where the users have a rating behavior with little variation. Finally, the last baseline returns a random score between 1 and 5 (B4).

In general, baselines (B1), (B2) and (B4) achieve maximal coverage for both controversial and randomly selected items: (B1) and (B4) do not rely on any additional (trust or correlation) information, and since the items in our experiments are evaluated at least 20 times, it is always possible to compute (B2). With (B3), in those cases in which the target

Table 6.4 Performance of trust-based recommender algorithms on the Epinions-products data set; MAE and RMSE $\in [0,4]$.

	ALGORITHM	Controversial items (CIs)			Randomly selected items (RIs)		
		% COV	MAE	RMSE	% COV	MAE	RMSE
(B1)	Base: score 5	100	1.94	2.46	100	1.05	1.62
(B2)	Base: average score for item	100	1.35	1.51	100	0.82	1.06
(B3)	Base: average score of user	98	1.43	1.78	99	0.95	1.22
(B4)	Base: random score	100	1.66	2.08	100	1.68	2.10
(5.2)	Collaborative filtering with R^+	81	1.34	1.58	79	0.84	1.12
(6.1)	Trust-based weighted mean	41	1.33	1.70	34	0.87	1.24
(6.3)	Trust-based collaborative filtering	40	1.32	1.65	34	0.86	1.19
(6.6)	Trust-based filtering	25	1.35	1.71	22	0.85	1.18
(6.7)	EnsembleTrustCF	84	1.32	1.57	81	0.83	1.11
(P1)	Propagated trust-based weighted mean	76	1.37	1.69	72	0.90	1.23
(P3)	Propagated trust-based CF	76	1.32	1.56	72	0.84	1.12
(P6)	Propagated trust-based filtering	57	1.36	1.64	53	0.86	1.16
(P7a)	Prop. 1 EnsembleTrustCF	90	1.32	1.55	88	0.82	1.09
(P7b)	Prop. 2 EnsembleTrustCF	84	1.32	1.57	81	0.83	1.11

user rated only one item, his average rating is lacking, so a prediction cannot be generated.

For the other algorithms in the tables, the numbers in the first column refer to the corresponding recommendation formulas and definitions. For collaborative filtering, we take into account neighbors which have a positive correlation coefficient (i.e., the users that belong to the R^+ set[7]), since this is the most often applied (and most agreed upon) approach in practice. For the trust-enhanced approaches, we distinguish between experiments that do not use propagated trust information (higher rows) and those that do (bottom rows). We only consider one-step propagation; we focus on longer paths inSec. 6.2.4. The EnsembleTrustCF algorithm and its results will be discussed in detail in Sec. 6.2.3.

Without trust propagation (and consequently also aggregation), it is clear that the coverage of the CF algorithm is superior to that of the others, and approaches the maximal value. This is due to the fact that correlation information is, in general, more readily available than direct trust information: there are normally more users for whom a positive correlation with the target user a can be computed than users in a's web of trust. On the other hand, trust-based filtering (6.6), which also uses correlation-based weights, is the most demanding strategy because it requires users in a's web of trust who have already rated two

---

[7]Results for R are discussed in Sec. 6.3.2.

other items in common with a (otherwise the Pearson's correlation coefficient can not be computed). In between these extremes, the coverage for Golbeck *et al.*'s approach (6.1) is a bit higher than that of Massa *et al.*'s (6.3) because the latter can only generate predictions for target users who have rated at least two items, otherwise the average rating for the target user cannot be computed).

This ranking of approaches in terms of coverage still applies when propagated/aggregated trust information is taken into account, but note that the difference with collaborative filtering has shrunk considerably. In particular, thanks to trust propagation, the coverage increases with about 25% (10%) for controversial (randomly selected) items in the Epinions-reviews data set, and more than 30% in the Epinions-products data set.

For the Epinions-reviews data set, the coverage results for controversial items are significantly lower than those for randomly selected items. This is due to the fact that, on average, controversial items in this data set receive less ratings than randomly selected items, which yields less leave-one-out experiments per item, but also a smaller chance that such an item was rated by a user with whom the target user a has a positive correlation, or by a user that a trusts. This also explains the lower coverage results for the nontrivial recommendation strategies. The same observations cannot be made for the Epinions-products data set : on average, the CIs receive more ratings than the RIs (21 131 vs. 12 741 vs. experiments). This explains the somewhat lower coverage performance of the algorithms for the random items.

Also remark that the coverage results for the Epinions-products data set are significantly lower in general than those for the reviews data set; the three trust-enhanced algorithms only achieve a coverage that is at least 20% worse. Users in the reviews data set rate much more items than users in the products data set, which yields less users who have rated the same items, i.e., neighbors (through trust or correlation) that are needed in the computation.

6.2.2.2 *Accuracy*

As with coverage, the accuracy of a recommender system is typically assessed by using the leave-one-out method, more in particular by determining the deviation between the hidden ratings and the predicted ratings. In particular, we use the mean absolute error (MAE) and root mean squared error (RMSE) as in Definition 5.4. Since reviews and products are rated on a scale from 1 to 5, the extreme values that MAE and RMSE can reach are 0 and 4. Even small improvements in RMSE are considered valuable in the context of recommender systems. For example, the Netflix prize competition[8] offered a $1 000 000

---

[8]See www.netflixprize.com/

reward for a reduction of the RMSE by 10%.

The MAE and RMSE reported in Table 6.3 are overall higher for the controversial items than for the randomly selected items. In other words, generating good predictions for controversial items is much harder than for randomly chosen items. This applies to all the algorithms, but most clearly to the baseline strategies (except (B4)). While in the Epinions-products data set all algorithms adjust themselves in more or less the same way, in the reviews data set (B1) and (B2) clearly experience more difficulties when generating predictions for controversial items: whereas for random items they are competitive with collaborative filtering and the trust-enhanced approaches, their MAE and RMSE on the controversial item set increase with more than 1 on the rating scale from 1 to 5.

Also note that it is more difficult to generate good recommendations in the products data set than in the reviews data set, for controversial as well as RIs. This is due to the higher inherent controversiality level of the former data set.

When focusing on the MAE of the nontrivial approaches for controversial items, we notice that, without propagation and aggregation, trust-enhanced approaches all yield better results than collaborative filtering (with one exception for trust-based filtering on the product controversial items), which is in accordance with the observations made in [38, 86]. This can be attributed to the accuracy/coverage trade-off: a coverage increase is usually at the expense of accuracy, and vice versa. It also becomes clear when taking into account trust propagation and aggregation: as the coverage of the trust-enhanced algorithms nears that of the collaborative filtering algorithm, so do the MAEs.

However, the RMSEs give us a different picture. On the controversial item sets, the RMSE of the trust-enhanced approaches is generally higher than that of collaborative filtering, which does not always occur on the random sets; recall that a higher RMSE means that more large prediction errors occur. One possible explanation for this is the fact that, for controversial items, the set R^T of trusted acquaintances that have rated the target item is too small (e.g., contains only 1 user), and in particular smaller than R^+. This hypothesis is also supported by the fact that with trust propagation (which enlarges R^T) RMSEs rise at a slower rate than the corresponding MAEs. Moreover, it is often the case that the propagated algorithms achieve lower RMSEs than their unpropagated counterparts, see e.g. the results on controversial items in the Epinions-products data set.

The experiments on both Epinions data sets, each with their own characteristics, endorse the same conclusions. For random items, intelligent strategies such as collaborative filtering and trust-based algorithms barely outperform the baselines. However, the baselines fall short in generating good recommendations for controversial items. Trust-enhanced systems perform better in this respect, although there is certainly still room for improvement; remember the higher RMSEs and the fact that trust-based approaches on product CIs yield no visible improvements over collaborative filtering. These findings call for further research on improving the algorithms and identifying specific cases where trust approaches are effective (think e.g. of Massa *et al.*'s results for cold start users).

The coverage and accuracy results show no clear winner among the three state of the art trust-enhanced strategies proposed by Golbeck *et al.*, Massa *et al.*, and O'Donovan *et al.* Trust-based collaborative filtering seems to score best on the Epinions-products data set, while trust-based weighted mean and trust-based filtering achieve the best accuracy on the Epinions-reviews data set; this trend is also confirmed by the results obtained by propagation.

6.2.3 Combining Trust- and Collaborative-Based Recommendations

It has been demonstrated that including trust in the recommendation process can significantly improve the accuracy, see for example [38, 86]; this is illustrated by the second part of Table 6.3 (only direct information, no propagation). On the other hand, the coverage of the trust-enhanced algorithms remains lower than the collaborative filtering algorithm. One way of mending this is by using trust propagation, but we have seen that then also the accuracy errors increase. Another way is to maximize the synergy between collaborative filtering and its trust-based variants; to this aim, we propose the following new algorithm. Note that it is a recommendation framework (just as Definitions 6.1, 6.3 and 6.6), and no trust metric (as Definitions 6.2 and 6.4); possible implementations for the trust metric are discussed later on in this section.

Definition 6.7 (EnsembleTrustCF). The unknown rating for target item i and target user a can be computed as

$$p_{a,i} = \overline{r_a} + \frac{\sum\limits_{u \in R^T} t_{a,u}(r_{u,i} - \overline{r_u}) + \sum\limits_{u \in R^+ \smallsetminus R^T} w_{a,u}(r_{u,i} - \overline{r_u})}{\sum\limits_{u \in R^T} t_{a,u} + \sum\limits_{u \in R^+ \smallsetminus R^T} w_{a,u}},$$

with $t_{a,u}$ and $w_{a,u}$ denoting resp. the trust and correlation between users a and u.

The rationale behind this strategy, which combines the classic and the trust-based[9] collaborative filtering approach, is that users should not necessarily be excluded from the recommendation process just because no positive correlation can be computed. They may very well have valuable information that can contribute to the recommendation; recall our discussion about similarity and trust being two different sources of useful information. To this aim, we take into account all possible ways to obtain a positive weight for a user who has rated the target item, favoring a trust relation over a correlation-based one. In particular, if a user can be reached by a direct or indirect trust relation, we use this value instead of the Pearson's correlation coefficient to obtain the user's weight. In this way, we retain the accuracy benefit by first looking at the trusted users, while on the other hand the coverage can increase by taking into account neighbors for whom no trust information is available. This new strategy is guaranteed to perform as least as well as collaborative filtering and trust-based collaborative filtering in terms of coverage, and in many cases will outperform both.

The results for EnsembleTrustCF can be found in Table 6.3 and 6.4. The middle parts contain the results for direct trust information. Of all algorithms, EnsembleTrustCF is the most flexible when it comes down to coverage, since having either some trust or a positive correlation is sufficient to make a prediction; it matches or outperforms the other algorithms, for controversial as well as random items. In particular, note that it achieves at least as much coverage as collaborative filtering, while the accuracy even increases a little bit (MAE as well as RMSE decrease); favoring trust over computed similarity has a positive effect on the quality of the recommendations, although the approaches that only take into account trust (trust-based CF and weighted mean) still perform better in the case of the reviews data set in terms of accuracy; their coverage, however, is a lot worse. Also note that the coverage of the unpropagated EnsembleTrustCF remains higher than the coverage of the propagated trust-enhanced strategies.

With respect to trust propagation and aggregation, there are several possibilities to extend EnsembleTrustCF. The first approach is to use a weighted mean-based algorithm as in Definition 6.4. Recall that for the Epinions data sets, this leads to $t_{a,u} = 1$ if u is directly or indirectly trusted. In other words, all members of the propagated WOT of a are 'boosted' in comparison to the other users for whom the correlation coefficient (normally lower than 1) is used.

---

[9] Hence, this method can also produce out of bounds results.

The second method assigns gradual propagated trust weights as in Definition 6.8. Like this, users u who cannot be reached through a direct trust relation are still rewarded for their presence in a's propagated web of trust.

Definition 6.8 (PCC-based trust propagation for bivalent settings). Let u be reachable by a trust path from a in a bivalent trust setting. The trust value from target user a in user u is estimated as $t_{a,u} = (PCC + 1)/2$.

Note that this assignment requires that the trusted user has a positive correlation with the target user, since EnsembleTrustCF only works with positive trust weights.

The results for the propagated/aggregated versions can be found in the lower part of the tables. They indicate that different data sets may require different propagation strategies: when considering accuracy, the more extreme first option is slightly better for the consumer products data set, while it is the other way round for the reviews data set. Also note that the first strategy may achieve higher coverage because of the assignment of the weights; in the second strategy no additional users are included since the ones that are newly reached by propagation must also be positively correlated with the target user (and hence are already included in the unpropagated version).

When we compare EnsembleTrustCF's results with those of the other trust-enhanced algorithms, we observe that, similarly to the unpropagated results for the reviews data set, our new algorithm is on par with the other trust-based techniques w.r.t. accuracy. EnsembleTrustCF can certainly rival with them, since it achieves the lowest RMSEs, for direct as well as propagated information, on every occasion but one (Epinions-reviews' random items). Furthermore, it is the real winner on the Epinions-products data set, as the basic and propagated versions achieve the best MAEs and RMSEs, and also the highest coverage; for unpropagated approaches it even at least doubles that of the other trust-enhanced strategies.

6.2.4 *The Impact of Propagation*

So far, we have only considered trust-enhanced recommendations by using direct trust information or trust information coming from trusted acquaintances, i.e., trust paths of length 1 and 2. In this section, we focus on the effect of including longer chains: Figure 6.4 depicts the results for the trust-based approaches for paths of up to length 1, 2, 3, and 4. In each graph, the bars represent the absolute coverage (the number of predictions that can be generated), the diamonds denote the MAE, and the circles the RMSE. The accuracy scale can be found at the left side of the graphs, and the scale for coverage on the right side. The experiments are conducted on the CI sets from the Epinions-reviews and Epinions-products data sets; similar patterns are obtained for the random items, but with lower accuracy errors (as indicated by the results for propagation paths of length 1 and 2 in Table 6.3 and 6.4). For EnsembleTrustCF, we included the best scoring trust prediction strategy w.r.t. accuracy; in other words, the binary propagation and aggregation method for the Epinions-products data set and the PCC-weighted method for the Epinions-reviews data set.

Let us first concentrate on the coverage benefit that is gained by propagating trust information more than one step. Note that the maximal coverage that can be achieved by the algorithms is 44 969 for the reviews and 21 131 for the products data set. Hence, it is clear that all algorithms achieve high overall coverage when using longer propagation chains. The profit is especially high for the transition from level 1 (direct information) to level 2, afterwards the bonuses become less high, with only marginal increases from level 3 to level 4. For the Epinions-reviews data set's controversial items, there are coverage increases up to 28% for level 4 compared to level 1, and on the products data set even till 47%; e.g., on the fourth level, trust-based filtering can generate three times as many predictions as on the first level.

Compared to the results for level 1 and 2 in Table 6.3 and 6.4, trust-based filtering continues to achieve the lowest coverage when taking into account more propagation steps, but the difference with the other trust-enhanced approaches diminishes. On the other end of the scale, EnsembleTrustCF remains the winner. Remark that the propagation algorithms on the reviews data set almost achieve the maximal coverage, while this is less so for the Epinions' products; the Epinions-products user network is less connected (compared to the reviews data set), hence more users remain outside the propagated trust network, and consequently less items can be reached, resulting in a lower coverage.

Let us now turn to the accuracy results. An investigation of the MAEs tells us that, as was the case with coverage too, the largest differences (if any) occur for the level 1-2 switch; for longer propagation the MAEs become more stable; for the product controversial items, the MAEs of all trust-enhanced methods even remain more or less the same for all path lengths (including level 1). There is one notable exception, namely the strongly increasing MAEs of trust-based collaborative filtering for the CIs in the Epinions-reviews data set.

The trust-based weighted mean only takes into account shortest paths, while trust-based CF incorporates paths with a length up to a particular horizon (in our experiments 1, 2, 3 or 4). Since the former algorithm produces smaller MAEs, this might indicate that longer

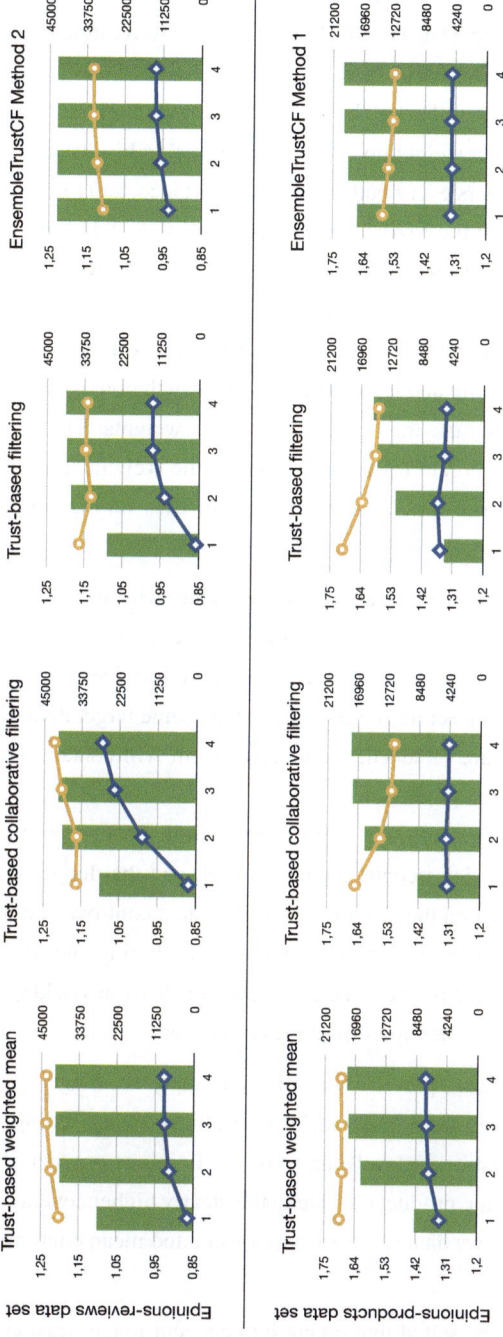

Fig. 6.4 Performance of trust-based recommender algorithms on the controversial item sets of the Epinions-reviews and -products data sets; focus on propagation lengths 1–4 (X axis) with MAE (diamonds) and RMSE (circles) ∈ [0, 4] (left Y axis), and coverage (absolute values, bars, right Y axis).

(than shortest) paths contain noisier, less accurate trust information (recall Golbeck *et al.*'s observations that lead to TidalTrust). This hypothesis is also reinforced by the results that are obtained when using binary trust assignments instead of Massa *et al.*'s horizon-based method, where every neighbor that can be reached within the horizon receives respectively a trust weight of 1, or a trust weight inversely proportional to his distance according to the horizon: the former considers every path of equal importance, and results in higher MAEs indeed: for level 2, 3 and 4 the MAEs are respectively 1.018, 1.113 and 1.139, while the RMSEs are resp. 1.189, 1.249 and 1.264. In other words, the reason for the worse results of trust-based CF can be found in the fact that it takes into account more (longer) paths, which interfere with the computation of accurate neighbor weights. The problem is less visible for trust-based filtering and EnsembleTrustCF (which both work with longer paths) because the former does not use the trust estimations as weights. The latter algorithm, on the other hand, does incorporate trust information in the weights, but also the PCC is a decisive weight factor, hence mitigating the impact of trust on the neighbor weights for users on longer paths.

The discussion in the above paragraph also explains why there is more variation in the MAEs on the review controversial items than on the products data set. Users in the Epinions-reviews data set are more connected than in the Epinions-products data set; consequently, in the former data set more trust paths to the same target item can be generated. The more (longer) paths are included, the more of them will contain noisy information, leading to less accurate item predictions.

Remark that the RMSEs follow a more or less similar pattern as the corresponding MAEs for the Epinions-reviews controversial item set, and that longer propagation paths even have a positive impact on the accuracy for the product controversial items; the RMSE decreases are most marked for trust-based collaborative filtering and trust-based filtering. In other words, less excessive prediction errors can be made by also taking into account the opinions of users that are further apart from the target user.

The conclusions from the previous sections still apply for longer propagation paths: EnsembleTrustCF achieves the lowest RMSEs in almost every setting (trust-based CF achieves slightly better results for level 3 and 4 on the Epinions-products data set), and can be seen as the winner for the product CIs due to the clearly higher coverage and low MAEs and RMSEs. On the reviews data set, trust-based weighted mean continues to achieve the lowest MAEs.

Summing up, it may be stated that taking into account longer trust chains has a positive impact on the recommendations with marked increases in coverage (with stabilization from level 3 on), whereas the accuracy is not as much affected in the opposite direction (stabilization from level 2 on).

6.3   Utility of Distrust for Recommendations

While the research on the incorporation of trust for recommendations is thriving, the investigation on the potential of distrust remains almost unexplored. Whereas in the trust modeling domain only a few attempts have been made to incorporate distrust, in the recommender domain this is even less so, especially for experimental evaluation. This is due to several reasons, the most important ones being that very few data sets containing distrust information are available, and that there is no general consensus yet about how to propagate it and to use it for recommendation purposes.

In this section, we embark upon the problem of distrust-enhanced recommendations. We discuss three strategies (Sec. 6.3.1) and provide an experimental study for controversial reviews (Sec. 6.3.2). To the best of our knowledge, the potential of utilizing distrust for memory-based recommendations has not been experimentally evaluated before (see [83] for one of the only model-based attempts).

6.3.1   *Distrust-Enhanced Recommendation Strategies*

The algorithms that we discuss in this section all use, in one way or another, direct or estimated distrust values. These distrust-enhanced algorithms can be deployed in web applications where only trust statements are available, but only fully manifest themselves in an environment where users can also explicitly indicate distrust. This brings us to the domain of trust scores which can represent both trust and distrust (see Chapter 2), and trust metrics that can compute with trust scores (see Chapters 3 and 4 for trust score propagation and aggregation operators resp.). Since we are no longer dealing with only trust values, for the remainder of this chapter, we will use the terms trust degree, distrust degree and trust score.

When considering trust score propagation for distrust-enhanced recommendations, the operators P_3 and P_4 from Definition 3.10 are ideal, since they actively incorporate distrust values into the trust estimation process. Note that the maximum effect of distrust (as a filter or debugger, see below) will be reached by using P_3. The operators P_1 and P_2 are also suitable, but their impact will be much less noticeable because the former only allows distrust in the last link on the path from the target user to the neighbor, while the latter needs environments where (explicit) ignorance can be modeled to actively infer distrust in intermediate links. Whenever trust score aggregation operators are needed, the bilattice-based, (I)OWA-based or knowledge-enhanced strategies from Chapter 4 can be used. For the combination of propagation and aggregation, we choose a central authority environment with FPTA.

The use of distrust for recommender algorithms can be explored in several ways. A first strategy is to use distrust to *filter out 'unwanted' individuals* from collaborative recommendation processes. This approach is related to the trust-based filtering algorithm from O'Donovan and Smyth (Definition 6.6), which restricts the neighbors to be trusted users.

Definition 6.9 (Distrust-based filtering). The unknown rating for target item i and target user a can be computed as

$$p_{a,i} = \overline{r_a} + \frac{\sum\limits_{u \in R^+ \setminus R^D} w_{a,u}(r_{u,i} - \overline{r_u})}{\sum\limits_{u \in R^+ \setminus R^D} w_{a,u}},$$

in which $w_{a,u}$ denotes the Pearson's Correlation Coefficient, R^+ the set of neighbors of a with a positive PCC, and R^D the set of users who evaluated i and for whom the distrust degree is greater than or equal to a given threshold β.

The algorithm in Definition 6.6 is now adapted so as to exclude distrusted users as neighbors. Remark that the algorithm does not use trust propagation to enlarge the set of neighbors, but only distrust propagation to restrict the set: users that are directly or indirectly distrusted by the target user are filtered out. In other words, no additional users are taken into account; on the contrary, less neighbors will take part in the recommendation process. A possible FPTA implementation for R^D is given in the following definition:

Definition 6.10 (Prudent distrust set determination). The set R^D of distrusted users w.r.t. target user a and target item i is defined as

$$R^D = \{u | u \text{ has rated } i \wedge (t_{a,u}, d_{a,u}) \geqslant_d (0, \beta)\},$$

with $(t_{a,u}, d_{a,u})$ the direct trust score; if this is not available, then the estimated trust score is computed as

$$(t_{a,u}, d_{a,u}) = \underset{i=1,\ldots,m}{DMAX} \left(\langle P_3 \left((t_1, d_1)_i, \ldots, (t_n, d_n)_i \right) \rangle \right),$$

in which $(t_1, d_1)_i, \ldots, (t_n, d_n)_i$ denotes the ith shortest trust score path (of length $n > 1$) from target user a to u.

Note that this is a cautious implementation of R^D w.r.t. the generated recommendations: whenever there is any trace of evidence larger than β to distrust user u, u is excluded from the recommendation process. By using P_3 as propagation operator, $(t_{a,u}, d_{a,u})$ will most often result in distrust evidence, and by choosing $DMAX$ as aggregation operator, we ensure that a user for whom at least one propagated path results in a trust score with distrust degree $> \beta$ cannot take part in the recommendation process.

In the same spirit of distrust as a filter, various researchers have suggested (but not yet evaluated) that distrust be used to *debug a web of trust* (see e.g. [50, 158]): suppose that a trusts b completely, b fully trusts x and a completely distrusts x, then the latter fact invalidates the propagated trust result (viz. a trusts x). As such, distrust-enhanced algorithms may be useful to filter out 'false positives'. This strategy leads to two new formulas, adaptations of the algorithms in Definitions 6.1 and 6.3 in which R^T is replaced by $R^T \setminus R^D$.

Definition 6.11 (Debugged trust-based weighted mean). The unknown rating for target item i and target user a can be computed as

$$p_{a,i} = \frac{\sum\limits_{u \in R^T \setminus R^D} t_{a,u} r_{u,i}}{\sum\limits_{u \in R^T \setminus R^D} t_{a,u}},$$

with R^T the set of users who evaluated i and for whom the trust value $t_{a,u}$ is greater than or equal to a given threshold α, and R^D the set of users who evaluated i and for whom the distrust degree is greater than or equal to a given threshold β.

Definition 6.12 (Debugged trust-based collaborative filtering). The unknown rating for target item i and target user a can be computed as

$$p_{a,i} = \overline{r_a} + \frac{\sum\limits_{u \in R^T \setminus R^D} t_{a,u} (r_{u,i} - \overline{r_u})}{\sum\limits_{u \in R^T \setminus R^D} t_{a,u}},$$

with R^T the set of users who evaluated i and for whom the trust value $t_{a,u}$ is greater than or equal to a given threshold α, and R^D the set of users who evaluated i and for whom the distrust degree is greater than or equal to a given threshold β.

These approaches are an extension of resp. trust-based weighted mean (6.1) and trust-based collaborative filtering (6.3), in the sense that now one needs to compute two components (R^T and R^D) instead of only one (R^T). To guarantee that the two algorithms are conservative extensions of their trust-only counterparts, R^T is implemented analogously to the strategy used in Definitions 6.1 and 6.3, i.e., if there is no direct information available, then the trust degree $t_{a,u}$ of $(t_{a,u}, d_{a,u})$ is computed as in Definitions 6.2 and 6.4 respectively. In other words, for the trust degree estimation only the trust degrees are used.

For the distrust degree estimation, we take on another approach; computing the distrust degree in a similar way as the trust degrees in TidalTrust and MoleTrust would result in unexpected and counterintuitive results: using the weighted average as aggregation strategy would mean that the opinion of a strongly distrusted user is more important than the opinion of a less distrusted agent. Instead, for the implementation of R^D in both algorithms, we use Definition 6.10. This approach will probably unjustly exclude some users, but we consider it more important that it allows to filter out the greater part of the 'false positives' in the (propagated) web of trust of the target user.

Note that we cannot use the filters in Definitions 6.11 and 6.12 in a bivalent trust setting when no propagation is involved, since then a user cannot appear in R^T and R^D at the same time.

We can also apply the above filter strategy to EnsembleTrustCF: we propose to use trust values for those users which can be reached through propagation but for whom no distrust propagation path can be found, and Pearson's correlation scores for those in $R^+ \setminus R^{TD}$ with $R^{TD} = R^T \cup R^D$, i.e., the remaining ones which have a positive correlation with a but do not belong to R^T nor R^D, i.e. neither trust nor distrust information is available about them.

Definition 6.13 (Debugged EnsembleTrustCF). The unknown rating for target item i and target user a can be computed as

$$p_{a,i} = \overline{r_a} + \frac{\displaystyle\sum_{u \in R^T \setminus R^D} t_{a,u}(r_{u,i} - \overline{r_u}) + \sum_{u \in R^+ \setminus R^{TD}} w_{a,u}(r_{u,i} - \overline{r_u})}{\displaystyle\sum_{u \in R^T \setminus R^D} t_{a,u} + \sum_{u \in R^+ \setminus R^{TD}} w_{a,u}},$$

with $R^{TD} = R^T \cup R^D$, R^T the set of users who evaluated i and for whom the trust value $t_{a,u}$ is greater than or equal to a given threshold α, and R^D the set of users who evaluated i and for whom the distrust degree is greater than or equal to a given threshold β.

To ensure a conservative extension, we use the same strategies as inSec. 6.2.3 to implement R^T; for R^D we choose Definition 6.10.

Definitions 6.9, 6.11, 6.12 and 6.13 use distrust as a debugger/filter by separately computing a set of trusted and distrusted users and then selecting the appropriate neighbors. In other words, distrust is used as a debugger/filter on the user level; after the selection, the trust degree $t_{a,u}$ is used as weight in the recommendation process. Another possibility is to perform the debug and/or filter task immediately on the weight level, as opposed to the user level in the aforementioned algorithms. Like this, the R^T and R^D sets do not have to be computed separately. As an example, consider the following modification of the trust-based weighted mean:

Definition 6.14 (Trust score-based weighted mean). The unknown rating for target item i and target user a can be computed as

$$p_{a,i} = \frac{\sum\limits_{u \in R} \max\left(0, t_{a,u} - d_{a,u}\right) \cdot r_{u,i}}{\sum\limits_{u \in R} \max\left(0, t_{a,u} - d_{a,u}\right)},$$

in which $(t_{a,u}, d_{a,u})$ denote a's trust score estimation for u.

Note that we call this new method the 'trust score'-based weighted mean: we also use the term 'weighted mean', as in Golbeck *et al.*'s approach trust-based weighted mean (6.1) and its distrust extension (6.11); we also take over another aspect of Golbeck *et al.*'s approach, namely that only shortest paths to target item i are taken into account. We use the term 'trust score-based' because, unlike Definitions 6.1 and 6.11, we do not only use trust degrees to determine the weights of the neighbors, but explicitly incorporate the distrust degree too.

In the scenario of Definition 6.14, we use the trust scores as a way to create the weights for neighbors, and at the same time also as a filter for the neighbors: the more a neighbor is trusted and the less distrusted, the higher his weight in the aggregation process. In other words, neighbors are rewarded according to their trust/distrust difference. Furthermore, users for whom there is more evidence to distrust than to trust are filtered out. Note that trust score-based weighted mean is no conservative extension of trust-based weighted mean due to the different usage of distrust as a debugger/filter.

Remark that, when no propagation is involved, trust score-based weighted mean reduces to debugged trust-based weighted mean. When propagation is involved, Definition 6.14 opens the door for new trust metrics to estimate the trust score $(t_{a,u}, d_{a,u})$, since it does not require to be a conservative extension of trust-based weighted mean. In particular, we propose the following family of trust metrics:

Definition 6.15 (Trust score metrics for distrust filter on the weight level). The trust score $(t_{a,u}, d_{a,u})$ for target user a in user u w.r.t. target item i can be computed in a FPTA setting by

$$(t_{a,u}, d_{a,u}) = \underset{i=1\cdots m}{A} \left(\langle P\left(\left(t_1, d_1\right)_i, \ldots, \left(t_n, d_n\right)_i\right)\rangle\right),$$

in which $(t_1, d_1)_i, \ldots, (t_n, d_n)_i$ denotes the ith shortest trust score path (of length $n > 1$) from a to i, A embodies a trust score aggregation operator from Chapter 4 and P a trust score propagation operator from Definition 3.10.

The remarks made in the beginning of this section w.r.t. the propagation operators apply here as well: the most distrust-intensive approach is obtained by using P_3, while P_1 produces the least effect. Since we do not require Definition 6.14 to be a proper extension of Definition 6.1, several options arise for the choice of aggregation operator; in particular the bilattice-based, (I)OWA-based and knowledge-enhanced strategies of Chapter 4. In the following section, we experiment with several of these operators.

A last distrust strategy, besides using it as a filter and/or debugger, is the direct incorporation of distrust into the recommendation process by considering distrust scores as negative weights, analogous to the use of negative correlation coefficients in the collaborative filtering approach; note the difference with their use in Definition 6.14 where they lead to weight 0. Similar to the collaborative filtering algorithm with neighbors from R (in which the PCC weights are in $[-1, 1]$), we can replace the weights so that they reflect the trust/distrust difference but are still in $[-1, 1]$. In particular, we propose Definition 6.16, which is an extended version of trust-based collaborative filtering in which distrust is regarded as an *indicator for reversing the deviation* $r_{u,i} - \overline{r_u}$. Remark that the model-based approach in [83] also uses distrust to denote dissimilar users.

Definition 6.16 (Distrust-based collaborative filtering). The unknown rating for target item i and target user a can be computed as

$$p_{a,i} = \overline{r_a} + \frac{\sum\limits_{u \in R^{TD}} (t_{a,u} - d_{a,u}) \cdot (r_{u,i} - \overline{r_u})}{\sum\limits_{u \in R^{TD}} |t_{a,u} - d_{a,u}|},$$

with $R^{TD} = R^T \cup R^D$, R^T the set of users who evaluated i and for whom the trust value $t_{a,u}$ is greater than or equal to a given threshold α, and R^D the set of users who evaluated i and for whom the distrust degree is greater than or equal to a given threshold β.

To ensure a conservative extension of trust-based collaborative filtering, we use MoleTrust to implement R^T; for R^D we choose Definition 6.10.

6.3.2 Experimental Results

Since we need data with sufficient trust statements, distrust statements, and ratings to evaluate the above algorithms, we can only use the Epinions-reviews data set. We again focus on

Table 6.5   Performance of distrust-based algorithms on the controversial items from the Epinions-reviews data set; with P_3 and $\mathcal{T} = $ min, MAE and RMSE $\in [0,4]$.

	ALGORITHM	% COV	MAE	RMSE
(5.2a)	Collaborative filtering with R^+	94	0.96	1.13
(5.2b)	Collaborative filtering with R	94	0.93	1.12
(6.16)	Distrust-based CF	67	1.00	1.32
(D9)	Distrust-based filtering	94	0.95	1.12
(D13)	Debugged EnsembleTrustCF	94	0.93	1.10
(PD11)	Propagated debugged trust-based weighted mean	86	0.91	1.23
(PD9)	Propagated debugged distrust-based filtering	91	0.96	1.18
(PD12)	Propagated debugged trust-based CF	86	0.93	1.14
(PD13)	Propagated debugged EnsembleTrustCF	92	0.95	1.17
(PD14a)	Prop. trust score-b. weighted mean - FIX	90	0.99	1.28
(PD14b)	Prop. trust score-b. weighted mean - TMAX	86	0.86	1.17
(PD14c)	Prop. trust score-b. weighted mean - KAV	86	0.85	1.17
(PD14d)	Prop. trust score-b. weighted mean - K-OWA, $\alpha = n, \beta = 8$	86	0.85	1.17
(PD14e)	Prop. trust score-b. weighted mean - K-OWA, $\alpha = 2, \beta = 8$	86	0.85	1.17

the controversial items because they receive a variety of ratings, hence enabling us to maximize the difference in performance between the approaches. Table 6.5 contains the results of our experiments; we will compare the results of the distrust-intensive approaches with their trust-only counterparts of Table 6.3. The abbreviations in the first column represent the distrust-enhanced (D) and/or propagation (P, on level 2) approaches, while the numbers refer to the formulas in Section 6.3.1. Recall that the bivalent nature of the Epinions data does not allow for a complete examination of the algorithms.

Let us first concentrate on the upper part of Table 6.5 in which we evaluate direct incorporation of distrust, i.e., distrust-based CF which regards distrust as an indicator to reverse the deviations. We also include the results for collaborative filtering with users u in R (users who have rated the target item and for whom the PCC with the target user, positive or negative, can be computed), since it is also built on the rationale of reversing deviations. For reference, we include the CF results with R^+ (only positive correlations) as well.

For distrust-based collaborative filtering, the high decrease in accuracy (increase of MAE as well as RMSE) compared to its trust-only counterpart trust-based collaborative filtering (Definition 6.3) is not compensated by a similar increase in coverage; this is also depicted in Figure 6.5. This demonstrates that distrust should not be used as a way to reverse deviations (and is also the reason why we do not consider longer propagation paths). Note that the same conclusion does not hold for R versus R^+ in CF: the former performs better

w.r.t. MAE than collaborative filtering with R^+ for the Epinions-reviews controversial item
set.

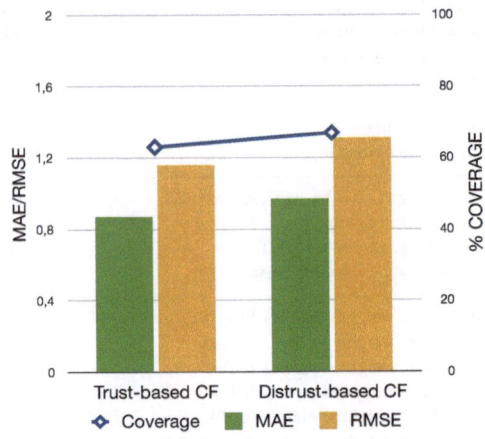

Fig. 6.5   Performance of trust-based versus distrust-based CF.

Recall that in Section 6.1 we stated that trust and similarity, and distrust and dissimilarity, do not necessarily represent the same information and may therefore be treated in
different ways: the results in the table above show us that, for the same type of algorithm
and rationale, including dissimilarity improves the recommendations while this is not the
case for the incorporation of distrust. Furthermore, we also claimed that the use of trust,
distrust, similarity and dissimilarity also depends on the application and the data, which
is illustrated by the comparison of CF with R and R^+'s results on the controversial items
in the Epinions-reviews and Epinions-products data sets. The R results for the latter data
set are worse than those for R^+, namely an MAE of 1.37 versus 1.34, and RMSE of 1.67
versus 1.58.

The second part of Table 6.5 focuses on the use of distrust to filter out 'unwanted' individuals without propagation. The results for distrust-based filtering and debugged EnsembleTrustCF show that this kind of distrust filter has little or no effect on the results of
classic collaborative filtering and EnsembleTrustCF: an item that is only rated by distrusted
users is very uncommon because of the trust/distrust ratio in the data set (only 15% of all
relations are distrust-based) and the fact that we are dealing with popular items. Hence,
the unchanged relative coverage comes as no surprise. Also note that the accuracy slightly
improves when filtering out distrusted users. Recall that we cannot use this kind of filter

for debugged trust-based weighted mean and debugged trust-based CF if no trust propagation is involved, since a user cannot put another user in his WOT and in his block list simultaneously.

In the third part of Table 6.5 we further investigate the potential of filters; we focus on the utility of distrust as a debugger for a target user's web of trust. This results in extended versions of the strategies in the lower part of Table 6.3. Recall that Definition 6.10 applied to a bivalent setting results in the set of distrusted users R^D of target user a that contains all users who are directly distrusted by a, who are distrusted by the members of a's WOT, and users in the WOT of users who are distrusted by a. In other words, 'distrust your enemies' friends, as well as your friends' enemies'.

This strategy leads to a coverage decrease of about 2%-3% for the debugged versions of trust-based weighted mean, trust-based CF, and EnsembleTrustCF, compared to their original propagated counterparts (P1), (P3) and (P7b) in Table 6.3. In other words, using distrust propagation to filter out false positives only has a marginal effect on the coverage (due to the trust/distrust ratio and the popular items). Debugging does improve the performance of trust-based CF in terms of accuracy, but for the other two algorithms no clear conclusion can be drawn: the MAEs are never worse than their trust-only counterparts, but the RMSE results show discrepant values.

Recall that Definition 6.9 does not use trust propagation to enlarge the set of neighbors, but only distrust propagation to restrict the set. This explains the decrease in coverage for (PD9) compared to the collaborative filtering method with R^+, whereas for (D9) and CF with R^+ the relative coverage remained unchanged. Note that (PD9) yields equal MAEs but increasing RMSEs.

As discussed in the previous section, another way to use distrust as filter and debugger is to integrate it on the weight level as opposed to the user level, as in the trust score-based weighted mean (Definition 6.14). In the bottom part of the table, we experiment with several implementations of Definition 6.15. In particular, we tested the trust score aggregation operators from chapter 4. As for propagation, we use the same strategy as for the other results in Table 6.5 (i.e., P_3 and $\mathscr{T} = \min$), to facilitate a fair comparison. Recall that the results for the unpropagated version are the same as the ones from Definition 6.11.

Note that KMIN, KMAX and DMAX are not included because the data set only contains bivalent trust and distrust data, and hence this type of filter will always yield weight 0 whenever there is at least 1 distrust input; as a consequence, almost no recommendations can be generated. Also recall that KAV will yield the same results as the arithmetic mean, and that the knowledge-enhanced OWA operators all coincide with K-OWA. We have included two of the best performing K-OWA implementations.

Let us compare the use of distrust as a filter on the user level (Definition 6.11) with filter on the weight level (Definition 6.14). With regard to coverage, (PD11) and the (PD14) implementations perform almost equally well: using a filter as in (PD14) may result in a smaller number of trusted neighbors, but that does not imply a drastic decrease in coverage since most target items can be reached by several trusted neighbors. The only implementation that achieves a significantly higher coverage than (PD11) is (PD14a): FIX always yields the highest number of trusted neighbors (because $\max(0, t_{a,u} - d_{a,u}) = 0.853 - 0.147 > 0$), and hence never excludes a user from the recommendation process, as opposed to (PD11) where users with (propagated and aggregated) evidence to distrust them are immediately left out, which may sooner result in items that are no longer reachable. Although the relative coverages for the other trust score-based weighted mean implementations are the same, in absolute numbers TMAX yields somewhat more recommendations (38 682 leave-one-out experiments) than KAV and the K-OWA's (resp. 38 626 and 38 553 and 38 552): TMAX results much more often in $t_{a,u} - d_{a,u} > 0$ (due to its trust maximizing behavior) than in $\leqslant 0$ (which can occur when all inputs denote full trust or ignorance; a rare scenario). On the other hand, KAV and K-OWA are much more likely to result in zero weights, especially for K-OWA with $\beta = 8$, as a higher β increases the chance for a high aggregated distrust value, and consequently a low recommendation weight, or even zero.

While the coverages remain comparable, the accuracy clearly improves when changing the filter from (PD11) to (PD14), i.e., using the weight-based filter $\max(0, t_{a,u} - d_{a,u})$ instead of the user-based filter $R^T \setminus R^D$. Moreover, whereas propagated debugged trust-based weighted mean (PD11) performed worse than propagated weighted mean (P1), propagated trust score-based weighted mean (PD14) even beats (P1). In other words, distrust can indeed play a beneficial role in the recommendation process: the filter on the weight level in combination with distrust-enhanced aggregation operators can safely be used to debug a web of trust and to accurately estimate the weights for trusted neighbors, which results in more accurate recommendations. As far as the mutual accuracy relations between the (PD14) implementations are concerned, only FIX scores visibly worse. However, this is no surprise since FIX does not produce personalized trust estimations at all.

However, Fig. 6.6 shows us that the aggregation operators do have a different impact on the accuracy of the recommendations when trust propagation is involved. More specifically, the figure focuses on the target items that cannot be reached by only taking into account web of trust members of the target user, i.e., target items that are only accessible by propagation paths of length 2.

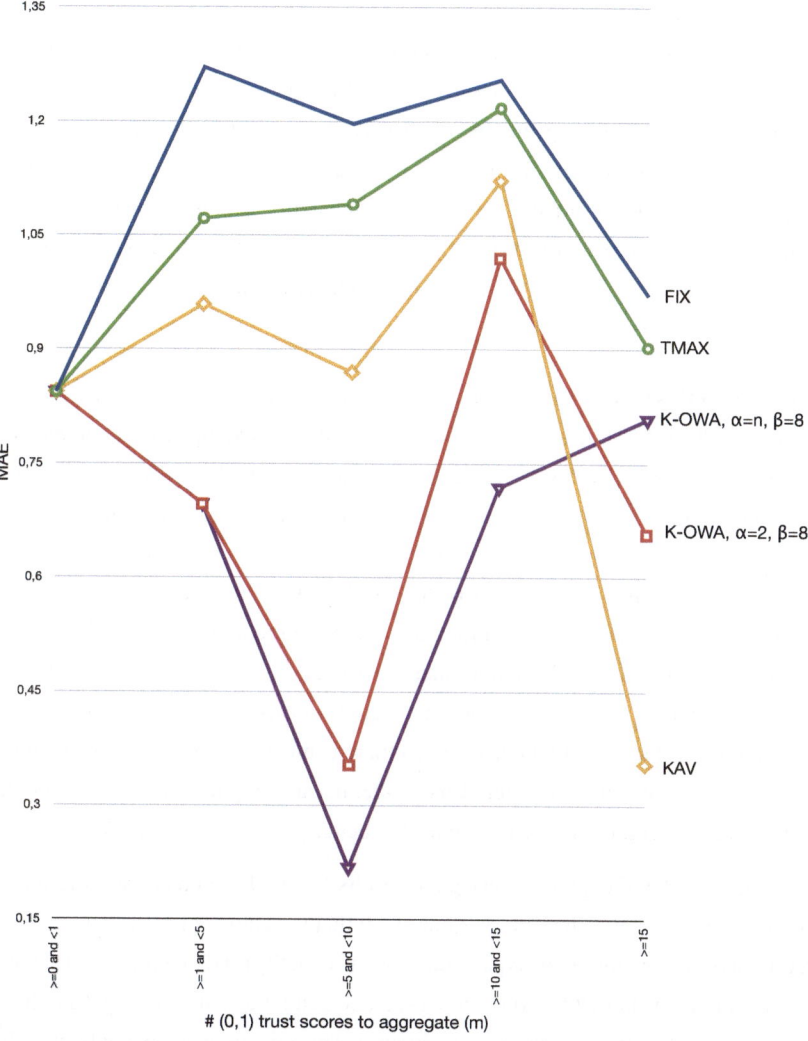

Fig. 6.6 Aggregation operators for trust score-based weighted mean on the controversial items in the Epinions-reviews data set. Split-up according to the number m of full distrust aggregates; propagation chains of length 2 with P_3 and $\mathcal{T} = \min$, MAE $\in [0,4]$, n denotes the number of aggregates (trust, distrust or ignorance).

We provide a mean absolute error analysis according to the number m of full distrust aggregates that need to be aggregated. Like this, we can better evaluate the effect of the new distrust filter $\max(0, t_{a,u} - d_{a,u})$. We did not include the RMSEs because they follow the same patterns as described below for the MAEs.

The graph tells us that the quality of the recommendations may heavily rely on the type of aggregation. The fixed values baseline performs worst on all cases, followed by TMAX, with MAEs of up to ten times the MAE of the more sophisticated operators. This means that actively computing the distrust degree matters (instead of fixing the value as FIX does, or letting it depend on the computed trust value as TMAX does). This is the strategy followed by KAV and the K-OWA implementations. Tuning the trust and distrust weights for the averaging aggregation process bears fruit: KAV (with equal weights) yields higher errors than the K-OWA's which are more adapted to the characteristics of the data set; KAV can only beat them for high m.

Remark that for this type of application and the Epinions data, distrust is easily established; only one eighth of the inputs needs to be considered. For example, as a comparison, K-OWA with $\alpha = n$, $\beta = 4$ yields MAEs of 0.84, 0.65, 0.92 and 0.85 for resp. $m = $1-5, 5-10, 10-15 and more than 15 inputs, while K-OWA with $\alpha = 2$, $\beta = 4$ results in MAEs of 0.84, 0.64, 0.89 and 0.25. This means that, in the context of distrust-enhanced recommendations, only the strongest opinions w.r.t. distrust have to be taken into account, and that the contribution of more agents introduces more noise into the recommendation process. On the other hand, w.r.t. the trust values, note that for low and intermediate m better results are achieved when taking into account only the maximum trust value ($\alpha = n$), while for high m this is no longer the case. Obviously, when there is much evidence to distrust a neighbor it is not wise to choose the maximum trust value, because higher trust values yield higher recommendation weights (this also explains the better performance of KAV for high m).

Note that TMAX did achieve very good results for the Epinions trust score prediction problem in Sec. 4.4.5, which reinforces our claim that the choice of trust score aggregation operator not only depends on the type of data, but also on the kind of application at hand. As another example, recall that for trust score prediction and the CouchSurfing data, distrust is not easily established (three quarters of all inputs). This may indicate that only little distrust evidence is needed to have an effect on the item recommendation, as discussed in the above paragraph, while establishing trust and distrust as a trust recommendation (estimation) for two unknown users in a network is a much more sensitive, personal, task which does not allow for rushed decisions.

Obviously, there is still much work to be done in the domain of distrust-enhanced recommendation (which almost received no attention so far), and distrust-based filters and
debuggers in particular. Although the results presented in this section are still preliminary,
they already indicate that regarding distrust as an indication to reverse deviations is not the
road to take. Distrust as a filter and/or debugger looks more promising, especially when
working with weight-based filters (as opposed to user-based filters).

One must bear in mind that the results depend on several factors, namely the propagation operator, the aggregation operator, the weight filter, the nature of the data, etc.,
and hence that more experiments, on other data sets with different characteristics, can help
establish a more precise conclusion.

6.4 Discussion and Future Work

One of the main problems in the trust-enhanced recommendation domain is the shortage
of suitable test data consisting of gradual trust and distrust statements and ratings. As
discussed in Sec. 5.4.1, the CouchSurfing data set contains a variety of trust and distrust
statements, but unfortunately is not suitable for our purposes since it lacks sufficient rating
information. The Epinions data do not have that particular problem, but only contain bivalent trust and distrust (only in the case of the reviews data set) data, which hinders a full
investigation of the effect and use of the propagation and aggregation operators in trust-
and distrust-enhanced recommendation algorithms. Unfortunately, there are no ideal data
sets publicly available for research.

One way to alleviate this problem is by looking for other ways to establish trust relations
when the information cannot explicitly be given by the users. Several sources of social
data can be consulted, such as online friend and business networks (think e.g. of Facebook
or LinkedIn), e-mail communication, reputation systems, etc. In the recommender system
literature, they are often lumped together and collectively referred to as trust, although they
map onto different concepts: behavioral theory clearly draws a distinction between homophily or cognitive similarity (similarity between people/tastes/etc.), social capital (reputation, opinion leadership), tie strength (in terms of relationship duration and interaction
frequency), and trust (see e.g. [92, 93]). Potentially all these social data sources could be
incorporated into a (trust-enhanced) recommender system, but so far not much research
has been conducted to find out which ones are most useful [5], and whether these sources
would provide similar results as the classical trust-based recommendation approaches dis-

cussed in this chapter. In [6], Arazy *et al.* embark upon this problem and argue that the design of social recommenders should be grounded in theory, rather than making ad hoc design choices as is often the case in current algorithms.

Another research direction of a completely different nature is related to the direction of the recommendation process; we explain the issue by the following two examples.

Example 6.3 (Forward recommendation movement). Suppose you want to see a movie i, but you do not know anything about it; hence, you have to look for opinions. To find out whether you will like or dislike the movie, you call one of your friends, say Joe. He tells you that he has no idea, but that he can give you the telephone number of a friend of his, Mariah, who has seen i. You may call her and listen to what she has to say about i ('It's a very good movie!'). According to the information you get from Joe about Mariah's trustworthiness for movie advice, and taking into account you own trust estimation of Joe, you can form an opinion on the recommendation of Mariah.

This example depicts a propagation chain with one intermediate link, viz. Joe; Mariah is the neighbor u (in the algorithms in Sec. 6.2 and 6.3). This is the approach taken by current trust-enhanced recommenders, as explained in Sec. 6.1: propagation to the source of the recommendation, followed by a combination with its rating. However, one can also argue that the movie information (rating or opinion) can be obtained in another way:

Example 6.4 (Backward recommendation movement). You phone Jack, who also has not yet seen the movie, but says that he will phone back later when he has some information about i (he is going to see some friends and there might be one who has watched the movie). An hour later, you receive his call and he tells you that it is a 'good movie'. Hence, in this situation, you do not know where the information is coming from; you can only rely upon your trust in Jack as a recommender and his (possibly derived) recommendation.

In this example, the recommendation process starts at the end of the chain. Jack (user b) hears the recommendation (the rating) of user u, reformulates u's recommendation by taking into account his trust in u, and then passes the new recommendation on to you (the target user a). Hence, the interpretation of u's recommendation by b is not necessarily the same as a's interpretation of b's recommendation: e.g., although b trusts u for movie advice, every time u waxes lyrical about a romantic movie, b weakens the recommendation because past experiences have shown him that he always liked the movie, but most of the time did not love it. If u then tells him that movie i was a 'very good' movie, he may reformulate the recommendation and tell a that it is a 'good' movie.

Figure 6.7 presents a scheme of the scenarios depicted in Examples 6.3 and 6.4. In the latter example, the process starts at the target item (the end of the chain) and moves backward to the target user by combining trust $R(b,x)$ and rating $r_{u,i}$ into a new recommendation $r_{b,i}$, the same strategy is then repeated until a is reached. This is represented by the rectangle. In this scenario, it is recommendations that are propagated in a right-to-left manner (backward movement), as opposed to the trust values in Example 6.3, which represents the classical procedure: the recommendation process starts at the target user (the beginning of the chain) and moves forward to the target item by propagating trust estimations $R(a,b)$ and $R(b,u)$ into a new trust estimation in user u (represented by the circle) and finally combining the propagated (and aggregated) $R(a,u)$ with rating $r_{u,i}$.

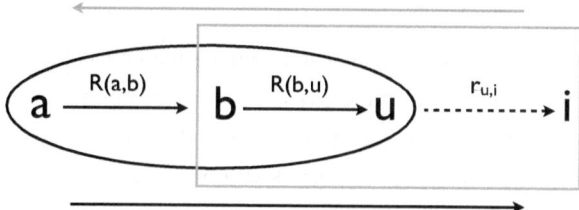

Fig. 6.7   Possible (dis)trust-enhanced recommendation directions; the circle denotes the forward movement (first trust estimation of $R(a,u)$ and final combination with the rating for target item i) and the rectangle the backward movement (reformulation of the rating).

The backward movement gives more autonomy to the users in the system and is suited for environments where privacy is an issue, because the only data that users pass on to each other are (derived) ratings, and their trust and distrust information is not exposed. The forward approach can easily be implemented in applications with a central authority. So far, there have been no theoretical or experimental studies to find out which one of the two directions delivers the best recommendations. However, related attempts to investigate the relation between the recommendation/rating strength (think of our example with the romantic movie) and the reformulation of a recommendation do exist; in the trust management domain by Abdul-Rahman and Hailes who work with the notion of semantic distance of trust opinions [1], and in the recommendation domain by Lathia *et al.* who use transposed ratings [74].

6.5   Conclusions

In this chapter, we discussed how trust and distrust information can enrich the recommendation process. We have given an overview of the state of the art in trust-enhanced recommendation research, with a focus on the approaches of Golbeck *et al.*, Massa *et al.*, and O'Donovan *et al.* Most researchers in the trust-based recommender field introduce their own algorithms and evaluate them on their own applications/data sets, without including a comparison with other trust-enhanced techniques. Therefore, we provided a head-to-head comparison of collaborative filtering and the trust-based approaches mentioned above, in terms of their coverage and accuracy of recommendations, with a focus on controversial items. Our study on two data sets with different characteristics showed that, for random items, simple baseline strategies can often produce recommendations of similar quality compared to the more intelligent strategies. However, we showed that they perform much worse for controversial items, whereas the personalized trust-enhanced algorithms continue to achieve tolerable accuracy.

We observed that there is no clear winner among the collaborative filtering and the trust-enhanced approaches, and that there is still room for improvement. To this aim, we introduced a new algorithm that combines the best of both the CF and trust world, achieving immediate high coverage while the MAE and RMSE increases remain within limits. More than that, it achieves the best RMSEs on controversial items, making it a safe option in environments where larger prediction errors are not tolerated. The same conclusions came to the fore in our experiments which concentrated on the impact of the maximum allowed propagation path length in the recommendation process. Also allowing ratings from users that are further apart from the target user in the trust network has a major positive impact on the coverage, while the accuracy of the trust-enhanced algorithms remains more or less stable.

In the second part of this chapter, we focused on the unexplored area of distrust-enhanced recommendations. We have provided the first experimental evaluation of the role of distrust as a debugger and a filter, and its relation to dissimilarity. We learned that the last option is not the road to take, but that the first two look more promising: we introduced a new distrust-enhanced strategy (trust score-based weighted mean) that uses distrust as a debugger and filter on the weight level, which achieves better results than the basic debug strategy, and even beats the standard propagated trust-only counterpart.

To our knowledge, the data set we used for our experiments is the only publicly available one that contains explicitly issued distrust statements and enough item ratings. Only 15% of all relations are distrust-based; consequently, experiments on future data sets with different characteristics may yield clearer answers to the question whether distrust can be used as a debugger and/or filter. The same remark also applies to other results in this book. For example, in data sets containing users with a more varying rating behavior, more true controversial items can be detected. It remains an open question whether distrust can play a beneficial role in recommender systems, but we believe that the reported observations and the questions raised along with them can help researchers to further examine its possibilities.

Six degrees of separation doesn't mean that everyone is linked to everyone else in just six steps. It means that a very small number of people are linked to everyone else in a few steps, and the rest of us are linked to the world through those special few.

The Tipping Point, 2000. Malcolm Gladwell

Chapter 7

Connection Guidance for Cold Start Users

In Chap. 5, we briefly discussed the most common limitations of recommender systems. In this chapter, we go more deeply into one of their main challenges, namely the user cold start problem. Due to lack of detailed user profiles and social preference data, recommenders often face extreme difficulties difficult to generate in generating adequately personalized recommendations for new users. Some systems therefore actively encourage users to rate more items. The interface of the online DVD rental service Netflix for example explicitly hides two movie recommendations, and promises to reveal these after the user rates his most recent rentals. Since it is very important for e-commerce applications to satisfy their new users (who might be on their way to become regular customers), it does not come as a surprise that the user cold start problem receives a lot of attention from the recommender system community.

One of the promising directions suggests that the incorporation of a trust network can significantly help alleviating the user cold start problem, primarily because the information included in trust statements about a recommender system's users can be propagated and aggregated, and consequently more people and products can be matched. By making a few clever connections in the trust network, newcomers can immediately gain access to a wide range of recommendations. Hence, users are highly encouraged to connect to other users to expand the network, but choosing whom to connect to is often a difficult task. Given the impact this choice has on the delivered recommendations, it is critical to guide newcomers through this early stage connection process. As research has shown that interactivity and transparency are two key factors to a better understanding and acceptance of recommenders (see e.g. [53, 133]), it is worthwhile to provide suggestions and explain the effect of making trust connections.

In the following section, we discuss possible ways to alleviate the user cold start problem and focus specifically on trust-enhanced solutions. To benefit from the trust algorithms, a new user needs to know which users are best to connect to. Therefore, in Sec. 7.2, we identify different user classes in the trust-based recommender system's network as mavens (knowledgeable users who write a lot of reviews), connectors (with a lot of connections in the trust network), and frequent raters (who rate a lot of reviews). We claim that it is more beneficial for new users to connect to one of these key figures as opposed to connecting to a random user. Verifying this claim involves investigating both the quality (i.e., accuracy) as well as the amount (i.e., coverage) of the delivered recommendations.

We deal with the problem on a local level within the trust network. The main questions to be answered are:

(1) If a cold start user a has a user b in his web of trust, how can we quantify the accuracy and the coverage impact of user b for cold start user a?
(2) What can we conclude about the impact of a particular key figure b for the cold start users in a trust-enhanced recommender system in general?

To help in answering these questions, in Sec. 7.3 we introduce new measures that have a clear foundation in social network analysis [142]. Subsequently, inSec. 7.4, we show by a number of experiments that it is more beneficial for new users to connect to key figures rather than making random connections, and discuss the impact of this type of connection guidance. To illustrate the concepts and to evaluate our proposed techniques, we use the largest of the two Epinions data sets, viz. Epinions-reviews. The results can be generalized to other trust-based recommender systems, since the key figure types can be detected in many kinds of trust-enhanced recommenders. We conclude the chapter with a discussion of future research directions.

7.1   The User Cold Start Problem

In Sec. 5.2, we explained the working of collaborative filtering systems. One of their key building blocks is the determination of the neighbors (or similar users), which is often done by computing Pearson's correlation coefficient. The effectiveness (accuracy and coverage) of collaborative filtering based recommender systems is significantly affected by the number of ratings available for each user: the more ratings are available, the more neighbors can be matched, the more items can be recommended, and the better the quality of the recommendations (as discussed e.g. in [127]); recall that adaptivity is one of the advantages of collaborative recommenders. Moreover, generating recommendations is only possible for users who have rated at least two items because Pearson's correlation coefficient requires at least two ratings per user, see Definition 5.3. Consequently, an important problem arises with cold start users: being new users, they have rarely rated a significant number of items, and since they usually constitute a sizeable portion of the recommender's user community (see e.g. [91] and Sec. 7.1.2), the user cold start problem should not be underestimated.

7.1.1 *Alleviating the Cold Start Problem*

Most of the approaches that are designed to alleviate the problem combine rating data with content data, or, in other words, include aspects from content-based systems to the recommendation process (hybrid recommenders). E.g., Middleton *et al.* [96] exploit information that is delivered by ontologies[1], while Park *et al.* [109] focus on simple filterbots (acting as pseudo-users who automatically rate items according to certain attributes). There also exist non-content based approaches, such as Ahn [3] and Huang *et al.* [58] who only use rating data: the former introduces a similarity measure which takes into account the proximity of the ratings, the rating impact and item popularity, while in the latter approach the set of neighbors is extended by exploring transitive associations between the items and users. Another recent example is Yildirim *et al.*'s random walk algorithm that is based on item rating instead of user rating similarity [150]. A different way of tackling the problem is by guiding the users throughout the initial rating stage, see e.g. the fuzzy linguistic approach in [114].

Some trust-based approaches have also explicitly focused on the use of trust for the cold start problem, see e.g. [144] in which the problem is tackled by automatic trust generation even for users who have rated only one item in common, or the algorithm in [59] that is based on random walks along the trust network and probabilistic item selection. One of the best-known and most extensive studies about trust-enhanced memory-based collaborative recommendations for cold start users was done by Massa and Avesani [88, 90]. They state that it is better to make a few connections in the trust network instead of rating a similar amount of items to bootstrap the system for cold start users.

Massa and Avesani conducted experiments on the Epinions-products data set (see Sec. 5.4.1) for their trust-based collaborative filtering system (see Definition 6.3), and showed that, for users that have only rated two items (for whom no correlation coefficient

---

[1]Formal representations of a set of concepts and the relationships between them, so that machines and applications can understand and reason with them; see e.g. [139] or www.w3.org/TR/owl-features

Table 7.1   Cold start users in the Epinions-reviews data set: users who have rated exactly one item (CS1), two items (CS2), three (CS3) or four (CS4) items.

	CS1	CS2	CS3	CS4
% of review raters	36.52	12.32	6.85	4.47
% in largest component	18.43	30.85	38.34	44.88
mean # trust relations	0.27	0.51	0.72	0.99
mean # distrust relations	0.03	0.05	0.06	0.09

can be computed in a leave-one-out experiment, and the classical collaborative filtering system cannot be evaluated), a coverage of 45% can be reached (trust propagation up to level 4). For users that have rated three (four) items, the coverage that collaborative filtering can achieve is 4% (8%), while the trust-based variant reaches 53% (59%) of all items; hence, it is clear that a recommender system can greatly benefit from the incorporation of a trust network when it comes down to generating predictions for cold start users. The fact that the users who have rated two, three or four items have on average two to three trust connections (we will show later on that in some data sets the cold start users have even less trust connections) illustrates that cold start users initially gain much more from their trust statements than from their ratings. This demonstrates the importance of drawing the newcomers' attention to the trust network, and guiding them through the connection process.

7.1.2   Case Study for the Epinions Community

In this section, we will investigate the cold start situation more thoroughly, in particular by focusing on the situation in the largest of the two Epinions data sets, i.e., the Epinions-reviews data set containing reviews and helpfulness scores. Like this, we are able to detect an extra group of key figures which are not available in the Epinions-products data set (the so-called mavens, see Sec. 7.2). We refer to Sec. 3.4.1 and 6.2.2 for a full description of the review data set.

We focus on users who have evaluated at least one item (review). In this group, 59 767 users rated only one review, 20 159 only two, 11 216 exactly three and 7 322 exactly four. These cold start users constitute about 60% of all review raters in the Epinions community. The relative numbers of users are given in Table 7.1 where the cold start users are denoted by CS1 (exactly one review), CS2 (two reviews), CS3 and CS4.

Besides evaluating reviews, users can also evaluate other users based on their quality as a reviewer; these evaluations make up the Epinions web of trust graph. About 85% of the statements are labelled as trust, which is reflected in the average number of users in a personal WOT (5.44) and in a block list (0.94). Due to the large portion of trust statements, we focus on trust information only in the remainder of this chapter, and leave the study of the impact of distrust relations for future research.

The trust graph consists of 5 866 connected components (i.e., maximal undirected connected subgraphs). The largest component contains 100 751 users, while the size of the second largest component is only 31. Hence, in order to receive more trust-enhanced recommendations, users should connect to the largest component. But as shown in Table 7.1, this cluster does not even contain half of the cold start users. This, combined with the fact that cold start users evaluate only a few users (as shown in the third and fourth row of Table 7.1), illustrates that cold start users in the classical sense are very often cold start users in the trust sense as well.

Better results can be expected when newcomers connect to a large component of the trust graph, but they may encounter difficulties in finding the most suitable people to connect to. Therefore, we define three user classes and identify them in the network.

7.2 Key Figures in a Trust-Based Recommender's Network

The first class of key figures are *mavens*, people who write a lot of reviews. This term is borrowed from Gladwell's book [36] in which mavens are defined as knowledgeable people who want to share their wisdom with others. Out of the three user classes mavens are the most visible to a new user, and hence the ones which are the easiest to evaluate: the more reviews someone writes, the better a new user can form an opinion about him and decide to put him in his personal web of trust or not.

Unlike mavens, *frequent raters* are not always so visible. They do not necessarily write a lot of reviews but evaluate a lot of them, and hence are an important supplier for a recommender system, since it is not possible to generate predictions without ratings. By including a frequent rater in a trust network, more items can be reached, which has a direct influence on a system's coverage.

While mavens and frequent raters are not necessarily bound to the trust network, *connectors* are: they connect a lot of users and occupy central positions in the trust network. Such users issue a lot of trust statements (many outlinks) and are often at the receiving end as well (many inlinks). The strength of connectors lies not in their rating capacity or visibility, but in their ability to reach a large group of users through trust propagation. When a trust-enhanced algorithm has to find a path from one user to another, a connector will be part of the propagation chain more often than a random user, and propagation chains containing connectors will on average be shorter than other chains. Shorter chains have a positive influence on the accuracy of the trust estimations and recommendations, as discussed in Chap. 6 and [38].

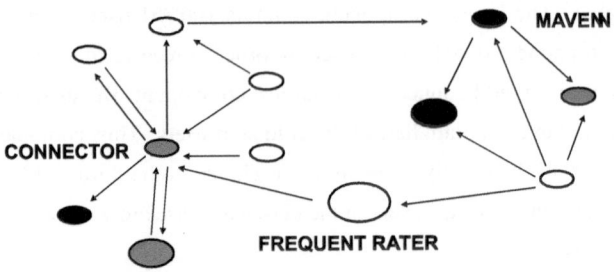

Fig. 7.1   Diagram of a trust-based recommender systems' network with examples of key figures.

Figure 7.1 shows a diagram with examples of each type: the darker the node, the more reviews the user wrote (maven). The larger the node, the more reviews the user evaluated (frequent rater). The trust network is denoted by the arrows representing trust relations; connectors are characterized by many incoming and outgoing arrows.

In the Epinions-reviews data set, we define a maven as someone who has written at least 100 reviews (M-100+), a frequent rater as someone who has evaluated at least 2500 reviews (F-2500+), and a connector as someone who has an in+out degree of at least 175 (C-175+). With these definitions[2], the community contains 1925 mavens, 1891 frequent raters and 1813 connectors. These thresholds are chosen for a number of reasons. Firstly, the characteristics of the key figures must be distinctive. For example, among all authors (i.e., users who wrote at least one review), the average number of reviews written is 4.77 while the maximum is 1496. Obviously, a user who has written merely 5 reviews cannot be regarded as a maven. Figure 7.2 shows the distribution of the number of reviews per author; there are over 300 000 authors.

The users who wrote more than 100 reviews constitute about 0.6% of all review writers, which we consider a good representation of the 'true' mavens: they certainly exhibit the desired behavior, and the size of the group is still large enough to diversify (we refer to

---

[2]Note that we cannot refine the definitions by taking into account additional information, such as the length of the review or the product type discussed in the review, because the data set does not contain any other information.

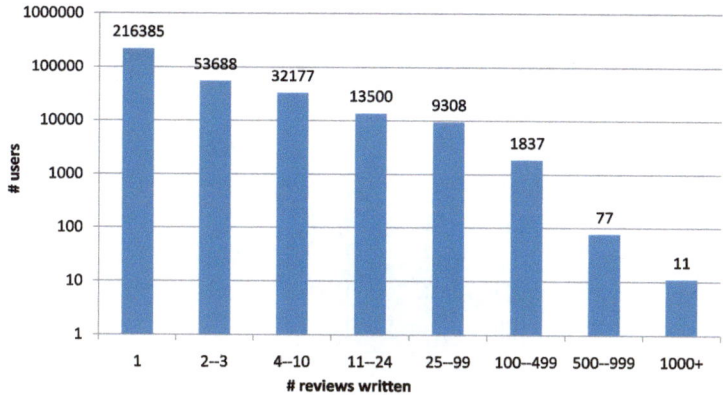

Fig. 7.2   Number of reviews written versus number of review authors in the Epinions-reviews data set.

Sec. 7.4.3 for a further discussion on this topic). The thresholds for frequent raters and con-nectors are obtained analogously, each of them representing about 1% of the corresponding user sets: the F-2500+ and C-175+ sets constitute about 1.2% of the raters and 1.4% of the trust graph members respectively. Secondly, the thresholds are also chosen such that the different key figure sets have similar sizes; this enables us to perform the analysis in the following paragraph in a fairer way. In Sec. 7.4, we experiment with other thresholds as well.

The sets of connectors and mavens share a large number of users, which is not sur-prising because mavens are visible through the reviews they write, making it more likely for others to connect to them by trust statements. This is illustrated by Fig. 7.3: the hori-zontal axis corresponds to the number of reviews a user has written; the more to the right a user is, the more of a maven he is. The vertical axis corresponds to the number of evaluations a user has received. The higher someone is on that axis, the more inlinks he receives (and the more of a connector he will be). In particular, the conditional probability $P(M\text{-}100+|C\text{-}175+)\approx 0.52$. More surprising is the relation between connectors and frequent raters, namely $P(F\text{-}2500+|C\text{-}175+)\approx 0.64$. The intersection of the maven set and the fre-quent rater set also contains many users (933), so there clearly is a strong overlap between the different groups of key figures. This indicates that users who are active on one front are often active on other fronts as well.

Note that these findings may be influenced by Epinions' 'Income Share program'

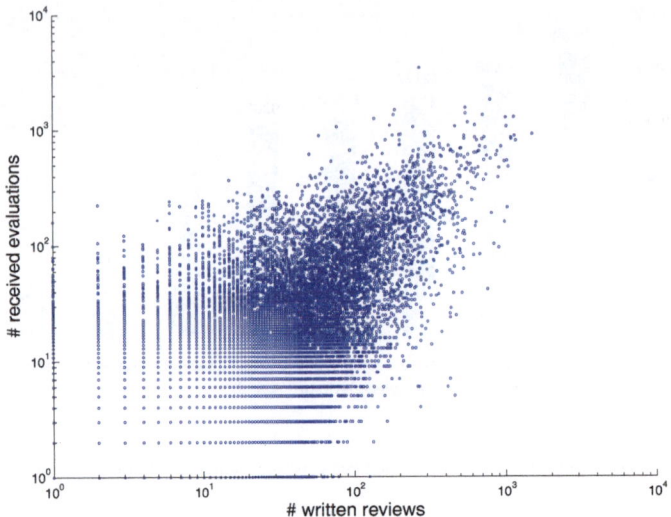

Fig. 7.3   Number of reviews written versus number of evaluations received in the Epinions-reviews data set.

(which rewards writers who contribute reviews that help other users make decisions[3]) and the benefits of being selected as a category lead, top reviewer or advisor[4]. Some of these classes are related to the key figures we defined, though our approach for identifying key figures only relies on objective data, while the selection in the Income Share program is partially subjective. Note that Epinions' interface also has an impact on the visibility and relatedness of the user classes.

Although their characteristics may be influenced by the specific situation, the three user classes can be detected in many kinds of trust-based recommendation systems, and hence the results in the remainder of this chapter can easily be generalized. In the following sections, we investigate the impact of the identified key figure types in the trust network by means of new social network analysis measures.

7.3   Measuring the Impact of Trusted Users

In this section we tackle the first question raised in the introduction: we zoom in on a user a and we inspect a user b in the web of trust of a. More in particular, we propose a way to quantify the impact of b on the coverage and the accuracy of the recommendations

---

[3]See http://www1.epinions.com/help/faq/show_~faq_earnings
[4]See www.epinions.com/help/faq/show_~faq_recognition, both accessed on March 22 2010.

generated for a through the trust network. In the remainder, we use $WOT(a)$ to denote the web of trust of a, i.e., the users that are directly trusted by a. A straightforward approach is to remove b from $WOT(a)$ and to compare the accuracy and the coverage in the resulting network with the initial situation.

A classical way to measure the accuracy of recommendations is by using the leave-one-out method and computing the MAE. The accuracy change $AC(b,a)$ is then obtained by subtracting the MAE after excluding the ratings and trust links provided by b, from the MAE when taking into account all available ratings and links (a similar formula can be obtained by using the RMSE).

Definition 7.1 (Accuracy change). Let a be a user and b a member of $WOT(a)$. We define the change in accuracy caused by user b for user a as

$$AC(b,a) = MAE(a) - MAE(a,-b),$$

in which $MAE(a)$ denotes the MAE when all WOT members of a are included, and $MAE(a,-b)$ the MAE when b is omitted from $WOT(a)$. If b is the only WOT member of a, then $AC(b,a)$ is not defined.

Consequently, a positive AC denotes higher prediction errors when taking into account the ratings and links provided by user b. The MAE formula in Definition 5.4 only takes into account items i for which a rating r_i is available. Since the problem with cold start users in the first place is that they have rated only very few items, the value of n in Definition 5.4 is typically low. Even worse: for a cold start user a who rated only one item so far, the leave-one-out method can not even be used as it hides the sole rating available for a, leaving the recommender system clueless. In Sec. 7.3.1, we therefore propose the use of a betweenness measure as a more informative way to assess the impact of user b on the accuracy for a.

The coverage for a relates to the number of items that are accessible from a, either directly or through trust propagation. The set of accessible items from a contains all items i that a has rated, or that can be reached through a trust path from a to a user x who has rated i. In the remainder, let $Acc_0(a)$ denote the set of items that are rated by a, i.e. the set of items that are accessible from a in zero propagation steps. Through propagation, more items can become accessible from a. We use $Acc_n(a)$ to denote the set of items that are accessible in n steps from a but not less, i.e., items i that have n intermediary nodes on the shortest path from a to i.

Definition 7.2 (Accessible items). We define the set of items accessible from a in $n \geqslant 0$ propagation steps, but not less, as

$$Acc_0(a) = \{i \mid \text{item } i \text{ is rated by } a\}$$
$$Acc_n(a) = \bigcup \{Acc_{n-1}(u) \mid u \in WOT(a)\} \smallsetminus \bigcup \{Acc_k(a) \mid k = 0, \ldots, n-1\}$$

Note that $|Acc_n(a)|$ is the number of new items for which a rating can be predicted in a particular trust-enhanced recommendation algorithm using n propagation steps. In a similar way we can define $Acc_n(a, -b)$.

Definition 7.3 (Accessible items after omission). Let a be a user and b a member of $WOT(a)$. We define the set of items still accessible from a in $n \geqslant 0$ propagation steps after omitting b from a's web of trust as

$$Acc_0(a, -b) = Acc_0(a)$$
$$Acc_n(a, -b) = \bigcup \{Acc_{n-1}(u) \mid u \in WOT_{-b}(a)\} \smallsetminus$$
$$\bigcup \{Acc_k(a, -b) \mid k = 0, \ldots, n-1\},$$

in which $WOT_{-b}(a) = WOT(a) \smallsetminus \{b\}$.

Note that normalizing the difference $|Acc_n(a)| - |Acc_n(a, -b)|$ by dividing it by the total amount of items available in a recommender system results in very small values as a recommender system typically contains thousands of items. Instead of looking at the number of items still accessible from a after the removal of b and relating this to the total amount of items in the recommender system, we therefore focus on the number of items that is lost when b is omitted from a's web of trust, and relate this to the total number of items accessible from a. To this end we propose in Sec. 7.3.2 an adaptation of an existing fragmentation measure[5].

7.3.1 *Betweenness*

As shorter propagation chains yield more accurate predictions (remember the results of Golbeck *et al.*'s research; see Sec. 6.2.1.1), one way of measuring the impact of users is by counting how often they are on shortest paths leading to items. To quantify this, we use the following measure which is inspired by the well known betweenness measure,

---

[5]In [141] we reflected on a first effort of measuring the coverage impact of users in a trust network. The measure we used in that paper is based on the same rationale, but the measure that we introduce in Sec. 7.3.2 has a clearer foundation in social network analysis.

commonly used to locate users who have a large influence on the flow in a network (see e.g. [29, 30, 142]).

Definition 7.4 (Betweenness). Let a be a user and b a member of $WOT(a)$. We define the betweenness of b for a on level $n \geqslant 0$ as

$$B_n(b,a) = \frac{1}{|Acc_n(a)|} \sum_{i \in Acc_n(a)} \left(\frac{\tau_{ai}(b)}{\tau_{ai}} \right),$$

in which τ_{ai} is the number of different shortest paths from user a to item i and $\tau_{ai}(b)$ is the number of those shortest paths that contain b.

Note that $B_n(b,a) \in [0,1]$. Also remark that a shortest path from a to i containing b always contains the edge from a to b as its first link.

Example 7.1. In the first scenario in Fig. 7.4, 3 items are accessible from a. b_1 is on the only shortest path from a to i_1 as well as on one of the two shortest paths from a to i_2, hence we obtain $B_1(b_1,a) = \frac{1}{3} \cdot (1 + \frac{1}{2}) = \frac{1}{2}$. Similarly, $B_1(b_2,a) = 1/2$. However, when focusing on items reached in an additional propagation step (scenario 2), the betweenness of b_1 and b_2 is no longer equal. Because b_1 connects to more users, a can reach more items through b_1 than through b_2. In other words, b_1 is more of a connector than b_2: $B_2(b_1,a) = 8/11$, while $B_2(b_2,a) = 3/11$. In scenario 2 we presuppose that all items on level 2 are different from i_1, i_2 and i_3. Note that if, e.g., i_3 were one of the two items rated by b_5, the betweenness of b_1 would decrease ($B_2(b_1,a) = 7/10$) because he is not on the shortest path to i_3.

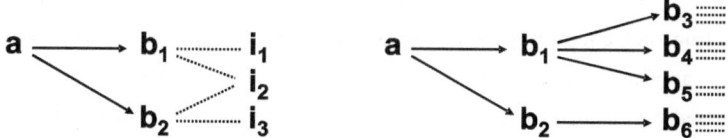

Fig. 7.4 Examples of accessible items for target user a through WOT members b_1 and b_2; scenario 1 and scenario 2.

This example illustrates that betweenness rewards connectors. If user b is the only one in a's web of trust to have rated a particular item i, then for that i the maximal value of $\tau_{ai}(b)/\tau_{ai}$ is added, namely 1. In this sense, betweenness also rewards frequent raters who contribute to the coverage.

$B_n(b,a)$ gives an indication of the absolute impact of b on the coverage of the recommendations for a, but it does not provide information on how b compares to other members of

a's web of trust. However, this is a determining factor for the real impact of b on the recommendations generated for a. A strong WOT contains strong users who rate many items and link to other strong users. Adding b to such a web of trust is less beneficial than adding b to a weak web of trust: in the latter case, a will often reach more previously unreachable items through b, whereas more items are already reachable in a strong WOT (thanks to the strong members). In other words, b will have a more significant influence when a has a weak web of trust.

We can represent the *WOT strength* by the betweenness of the best user of the web of trust besides the key figure, and compare this value to the betweenness of the key figure.

Definition 7.5 (Betweenness utility). Let a be a user and b a member of $WOT(a)$. We define the betweenness utility of user b for user a on level $n \geqslant 0$ as

$$BU_n(b,a) = B_n(b,a) - \max_{u \in WOT_{-b}(a)} B_n(u,a)$$

If b is the only WOT member of a and $n > 0$, then $BU_n(b,a) = B_n(b,a) = 1$.

Note that BU_n ranges from -1 to 1. If $n = 0$ then $B_n(b,a) = 0$. For $n > 0$, if all items are only reachable through user b, then $BU_n(b,a) = 1$; if this is the case for another WOT member, than $BU_n(b,a) = -1$.

7.3.2 *Fragmentation*

Instead of focusing on shortest paths, user b's influence can also be measured by the reduction in cohesion of the network which occurs if b is deleted from a's web of trust. User b is vital for a when he rates a lot of items and when a lot of these items are only rated by b. Deleting such a high impact user from a WOT results in a fragmented network with many items appearing in isolated fragments. For a user a we study the fragmentation in the undirected graph corresponding to the network like the one depicted in Fig. 7.4, i.e., the graph that contains as its nodes all users and items accessible from a in zero or more propagation steps, and the links that lead to them as its edges.

Example 7.2. In the first as well as in the second scenario of Fig. 7.4 all items are initially in one fragment. If we remove b_1 from $WOT(a)$ in the first scenario, two fragments arise, namely $\{i_1\}$ and $\{i_2, i_3\}$. Similarly, in the second scenario, 9 fragments (of which 8 are islands, i.e. containing only 1 item) are obtained after deleting the edge from a to b_1.

To quantify the fragmentation impact, we count the number of pairs of items that become disconnected from each other, i.e., items that are in separate fragments after removal of b.

Note that a fragment containing s items contains exactly $s \cdot (s-1)/2$ connected item pairs, since all items in the same fragment are connected to each other. The following measure, which is a modification of the traditional fragmentation measure (see e.g. [8, 14]), is based on this.

Definition 7.6 (Fragmentation). Let a be a user and b a member of $WOT(a)$. We define the fragmentation of b for a on level $n \geqslant 0$ as

$$F_n(b,a) = 1 - \frac{\sum_{j=1}^{k} s_j(s_j - 1)}{|Acc_n(a)| \cdot (|Acc_n(a)| - 1)},$$

in which k is the number of fragments of $Acc_n(a)$ after removing b from $WOT(a)$, and s_j is the number of items in the jth fragment.

The numerator describes the situation after the removal of b: there are k fragments and each jth fragment contains $s_j \cdot (s_j - 1)/2$ pairs of connected items, hence the numerator is the total number of connected item pairs after removal of b. The denominator on the other hand describes the original state of the network, i.e. before omitting b from $WOT(a)$: all $|Acc_n(a)|$ items are in the same fragment (i.e. minimal fragmentation) and this fragment contains $|Acc_n(a)| \cdot (|Acc_n(a)| - 1)/2$ connected item pairs.

A user b who has only rated items that are also reachable through other users will yield $F_n(b,a) = 0$, because the situation after deletion does not differ from the minimal fragmentation situation. In other words, the fragmentation measure rewards b's original contribution to the coverage for a: when b is removed from $WOT(a)$, items that have only been rated by b become separate fragments. The more islands, the more $F_n(b,a)$ approaches 1, the ideal situation. Note that $F_n(b,a) \in [0,1]$.

Example 7.3. In the first scenario of Fig. 7.4 it holds that

$$F_1(b_1,a) = F_1(b_2,a) = \frac{2}{3}$$

In the second scenario of Fig. 7.4, we obtain $F_2(b_1,a) = 104/110 \approx 0.95$ while $F_2(b_2,a) = 54/110 \approx 0.49$ assuming that all 11 items are in $Acc_2(a)$, which reflects that b_1 plays a more vital role than b_2 in the web of trust of a.

Much work has been done on the vulnerability of networks to disconnection. A large part of it focuses on cutpoint problems, such as the min-k-cut or the min-k-vertex sharing problem (e.g. [101]). The latter tries to minimize the number of deleted users to achieve a k-way partition. This problem is complementary to ours, as we know the number of users to be deleted: in our experiments we typically remove one user from the web of trust and study the effect.

When assessing the influence of a particular user, it is best to take into account fragmentation and betweenness together: users that have an equal fragmentation score might still be distinguished based on betweenness, and vice versa.

Example 7.4. For scenario 3 in Fig. 7.5 we obtain:

$$F_1(b_1,a) = 6/12 \; B_1(b_1,a) = 3/8$$
$$F_1(b_2,a) = 0 \qquad B_1(b_2,a) = 2/8$$
$$F_1(b_3,a) = 6/12 \; B_1(b_3,a) = 3/8$$

while in scenario 4 it holds that:

$$F_1(b_1,a) = 0 \qquad B_1(b_1,a) = 3/8$$
$$F_1(b_2,a) = 0 \qquad B_1(b_2,a) = 1/8$$
$$F_1(b_3,a) = 6/12 \; B_1(b_3,a) = 4/8$$

If we focus on fragmentation only, then the influence of b_3 is the same in both scenarios. However, it is clear that b_3 in scenario 4 is more beneficial, because he has rated more items, and more item ratings help to obtain more accurate predictions. This is reflected in the betweenness value for b_3, which is higher in scenario 4. Analogously, although b_1 has the same betweenness in both scenarios, it is clear that he is more beneficial in scenario 3, since in scenario 4 all items rated by b_1 can also be reached through other users. This is reflected by a higher fragmentation value for b_1 in scenario 3.

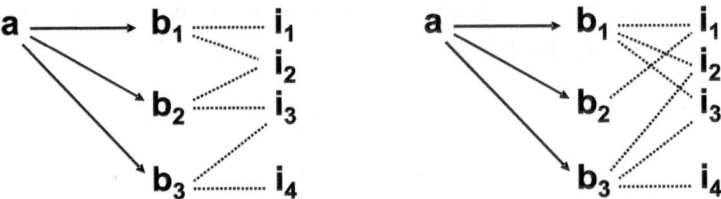

Fig. 7.5   Examples of accessible items for target user a through WOT members b_1, b_2 and b_3; scenario 3 and scenario 4.

Although in theory the fragmentation impact of b for a can range from 0 to 1, in practice its upper bound is determined by the behavior of all users in a's web of trust, more in particular by the number of items that they rated in common. While for the betweenness measure different users can score well simultaneously by occurring frequently on (different) shortest paths, for the fragmentation score they are in competition with each other. Fragmentation rewards original contributions, so the more items are rated by more than one user, the harder it is for individual users to achieve a high fragmentation score. We call the practical upper bound on $F_n(b,a)$ the *room for originality*.

Definition 7.7 (Room for originality). We define the room for originality w.r.t. a on level n as

$$F_n^{\max}(a) = 1 - \frac{|Com_n(a)| \cdot (|Com_n(a)| - 1)}{|Acc_n(a)| \cdot (|Acc_n(a)| - 1)}$$

in which $Com_n(a)$ represents the set of items in $Acc_n(a)$ that are accessible through more than one user of a's web of trust:

$$Com_n(a) = \bigcap \{Acc_n(a, -x) \mid x \in WOT(a)\}.$$

Note that $F_n^{\max}$ is the same for all users in a's web of trust. $F_n^{\max}$ is reached when a single user of $WOT(a)$ reaches all non-common items. This corresponds to the maximal fragmentation situation possible in practice.

Example 7.5. In scenario 4 of Fig. 7.5, there is only one non common item, which is reached by b_3. $Com_1(a) = \{i_1, i_2, i_3\}$, hence

$$F_1^{\max}(a) = 1 - \frac{3 \cdot 2}{4 \cdot 3} = \frac{1}{2}.$$

This value is indeed reached at $F_1(b_3, a) = 1/2$. In scenario 1 of Fig. 7.4 on the other hand, $Com_1(a) = \{i_2\}$. In this case $F_1^{\max}(a)$ is 1 which indicates that there is more room for original contribution than in scenario 4. Even though in absolute terms $F_1(b_1, a) = 2/3$ from scenario 1 is higher than $F_1(b_3, a) = 1/2$ from scenario 4, user b_3 from scenario 4 exhibits a stronger behavior as he filled the room for original contribution maximally while user b_1 from scenario 1 only managed to fill two thirds.

We take these considerations into account by normalizing the fragmentation utility w.r.t. the room for originality. Note that FU_n ranges from -1 to 1.

Definition 7.8 (Fragmentation utility). Let a be a user and b a member of $WOT(a)$. We define the fragmentation utility of user b for user a on level $n \geq 0$ as

$$FU_n(b,a) = \frac{F_n(b,a) - \max_{u \in WOT_{-b}(a)} F_n(u,a)}{F_n^{\max}(a)}$$

If $n = 0$ then $F_n(b,a) = 0$. If b is the only WOT member of a and $n > 0$, then $FU_n(b,a) = 1$.

Table 7.2   Notations used in Sec. 7.3 and 7.4

k	superscript for key figure	r	superscript for random WOT user
w	superscript for best alternative WOT user		
$AC(b,a)$	accuracy change		
AAC	average accuracy change		
$B_n(b,a)$	betweenness	$F_n(b,a)$	fragmentation
AB_n	average betweenness	AF_n	average fragmentation
$BU_n(b,a)$	betweenness utility	$FU_n(b,a)$	fragmentation utility
ABU_n	average betweenness utility	AFU_n	average fragmentation utility
$DBU(a)$	betweenness utility difference between $BU(random\ key,a)$ and $BU(random\ active,a)$	$DFU(a)$	fragmentation utility difference between $FU(random\ key,a)$ and $FU(random\ active,a)$
$ADBU$	average betweenness utility difference	$ADFU$	average fragmentation utility difference

7.4 Experimental Results

To answer the second question raised in the introduction, we performed two kinds of experiments to investigate the effect of key figures on the coverage and accuracy of cold start recommendations. In particular, the first experiment focuses on the contribution of key figures who are already in the web of trust from a cold start user, while the second experiment focuses on the impact of adding a key figure to a WOT instead of a randomly chosen user. Table 7.2 gives an overview of the measures we evaluated.

The impact of key figures in a trust-enhanced recommender network not only depends on its characteristics, but also on the recommendation algorithm that is used. We conduct our experiments for Massa and Avesani's trust-based collaborative filtering method (see Definition 6.3), since they have already shown that their algorithm can help in alleviating the cold start problem (see Sec. 7.1.1). Furthermore, trust-based filtering and EnsembleTrustCF are less suitable for this purpose because they use correlation coefficients, making it more difficult to measure the actual impact of the key figures on the trust-based recommendations.

To our knowledge, no studies have been conducted on the influence of key figures in trust-based recommenders. However, there exists some work on the impact of collaborative filtering users, in particular studies about identifying users who influence the buying behavior of other users and hence boost the sales of particular items [25, 118]. These studies link up with the broad research area of viral marketing which targets users in the network

Table 7.3   Experiment on contribution of key figures w.r.t. direct trust information; number of cold start users to be evaluated (number of cold start users that only have the key figure in their WOT).

TYPE	CS1	CS2	CS3	CS4
F-100000	79(23)	51(10)	48(10)	53(4)
F-50000	257(131)	171(59)	146(42)	131(31)
F-10000	1 124(684)	764(359)	525(315)	462(162)
F-2500	1 412(912)	925(448)	647(259)	537(178)
M-1000	124(58)	87(32)	81(22)	69(15)
M-500	466(253)	336(133)	262(78)	221(57)
M-100	2 319(1664)	1 444(816)	949(513)	781(348)
C-1000	509(264)	355(125)	275(84)	238(55)
C-500	893(508)	592(260)	439(150)	366(120)
C-175	1 948(1296)	1 230(636)	835(385)	646(250)

who have a high ability to influence others (e.g. to buy a particular item or to spread a new idea); see for example [77, 124]. However, these approaches differ from ours, as they focus on influencing the buying behavior of users, do not specifically measure the impact on the coverage and accuracy, and do not focus on cold start users. Furthermore, we use characteristics of trust-based collaborative filtering networks to define the key figures.

7.4.1   Contribution of Key Figures

In the first experiment, we analyze the role of key figures in a cold start user's web of trust and compare them with random web of trust members. To this aim, we only consider cold start users who have exactly one key figure of a specific type in their web of trust. For instance, the set of CS2 users who are connected with exactly one maven of type M-1000+. We denote such a set as U and represent a user of U by a. The corresponding key figure is denoted by k_a, and a randomly chosen member of a's web of trust by r_a, i.e., $r_a \in WOT(a) \setminus \{k_a\}$.

Table 7.3 shows how many cold start users can be evaluated. Between brackets we include the number of cold start users who only have the key figure as WOT member, i.e., the number of cold start users for whom r_a does not exist. Since we are dealing with cold start users who are also CS users in the trust sense, the latter amount will be relatively high compared to the former.

The results for the social network analysis measures in this experiment can be found in Table 7.4–7.6. A column (row) corresponds to a specific user group (key figure), e.g., a M-100 is a maven who wrote at least 100 and at most 499 reviews. We focus on the immediate impact of web of trust members, which means that, for now, we only consider direct trust information (level 1), i.e., without propagation.

Table 7.4 contains the average betweenness and fragmentation values of a key figure (AB_1^k and AF_1^k resp.), while Table 7.5 contains the average betweenness and fragmentation of a random other WOT member (AB_1^r and AF_1^r). Finally, Table 7.6 contains the results for the best alternative user, i.e., the best performing member of $WOT_{-b}(a)$ (AB_1^w and AF_1^w). Note that AB_1^w and AF_1^w represent the average WOT strength (see Definition 7.5). Also note that for the cold start users who only have the key figure in their web of trust we cannot compute AB_1^r, AF_1^r, AB_1^w and AF_1^w.

The formula for the average betweenness value of the key figures for cold start users who are connected with exactly one key figure of a certain type is given by (7.1); the other formulas are analogous.

$$AB_1^k = \frac{\sum_{a \in U} B_1(k_a, a)}{|U|} \tag{7.1}$$

A key figure is clearly very influential for a cold start user, with an average AB_1^k of 0.80 and an average AF_1^k of 0.84. As expected, the betweenness and fragmentation values for a random WOT user are significantly lower (an average AB_1^r of 0.16 and an average AF_1^r of 0.21). Frequent raters score somewhat higher than connectors and mavens, with an average AB_1^k of 0.83 and an average AF_1^k of 0.87. This is not surprising because frequent raters are the real suppliers for a recommender system; without them there would only be few ratings and consequently less recommendations. Hence, it is more difficult for members of such a WOT (containing a frequent rater) to obtain a high betweenness and fragmentation value, than for members of another web of trust. This explains why AB_1^w and AF_1^w are generally lower for CS users connected to a frequent rater. For instance, AB_1^w is on average 0.15 for frequent raters, as opposed to 0.18 and 0.19 for connectors and mavens, respectively. More surprising is the fact that mavens score very well too. This is especially useful for new users because it is much easier to decide whether to trust the (more visible) mavens.

Figure 7.6 depicts the course of the average betweenness and fragmentation utility of the different key figure types (average over all key figures for a particular cold start group). Recall that the utility compares the impact of the key figure (B_1^k and F_1^k) to that of the best alternative user in the WOT (B_1^w and F_1^w). For the fragmentation utility values, also another contextual factor is taken into account, namely the room for originality $F_1^{\max}$.

The figure clearly shows that the use of having a key figure in a web of trust decreases as the new user becomes more active. Indeed, as is illustrated in Table 7.1, more active

Table 7.4 Experiment on contribution of key figures w.r.t. direct trust information; evaluation for frequent raters (F), mavens (M) and connectors (C) on level 1: average betweenness and fragmentation for the key figure, AB_1^k and AF_1^k in $[0, 1]$, σ^B and σ^F denote the standard deviation for the betweenness and fragmentation averages.

TYPE (#)	AB_1^k (σ^B)				AF_1^k (σ^F)			
	CS1	CS2	CS3	CS4	CS1	CS2	CS3	CS4
F-100000 (2)	0.90 (0.20)	0.86 (0.25)	0.85 (0.27)	0.85 (0.24)	0.94 (0.20)	0.88 (0.26)	0.88 (0.28)	0.90 (0.21)
F-50000 (36)	0.85 (0.26)	0.83 (0.25)	0.80 (0.26)	0.80 (0.29)	0.89 (0.25)	0.88 (0.24)	0.87 (0.25)	0.85 (0.28)
F-10000 (459)	0.89 (0.26)	0.85 (0.28)	0.84 (0.28)	0.83 (0.28)	0.92 (0.24)	0.89 (0.26)	0.89 (0.26)	0.89 (0.26)
F-2500 (1394)	0.85 (0.31)	0.80 (0.34)	0.73 (0.39)	0.71 (0.38)	0.88 (0.29)	0.84 (0.32)	0.77 (0.37)	0.76 (0.36)
M-1000 (11)	0.75 (0.34)	0.75 (0.31)	0.69 (0.36)	0.72 (0.35)	0.80 (0.33)	0.82 (0.28)	0.75 (0.35)	0.77 (0.35)
M-500 (77)	0.80 (0.33)	0.73 (0.37)	0.68 (0.38)	0.70 (0.36)	0.84 (0.31)	0.78 (0.35)	0.74 (0.36)	0.75 (0.35)
M-100 (1837)	0.91 (0.24)	0.85 (0.30)	0.83 (0.32)	0.81 (0.33)	0.93 (0.22)	0.89 (0.27)	0.87 (0.30)	0.85 (0.30)
C-1000 (47)	0.88 (0.24)	0.82 (0.28)	0.79 (0.30)	0.79 (0.31)	0.92 (0.22)	0.88 (0.23)	0.85 (0.28)	0.85 (0.28)
C-500 (253)	0.81 (0.33)	0.78 (0.34)	0.72 (0.36)	0.74 (0.34)	0.84 (0.31)	0.83 (0.32)	0.78 (0.34)	0.81 (0.31)
C-175 (1513)	0.86 (0.30)	0.80 (0.35)	0.77 (0.36)	0.72 (0.38)	0.89 (0.27)	0.83 (0.33)	0.82 (0.33)	0.77 (0.36)

Table 7.5 Experiment on contribution of key figures w.r.t. direct trust information; evaluation for frequent raters, mavens and connectors on level 1: average betweenness and fragmentation for a random WOT member, AB_1^r and AF_1^r in $[0,1]$, σ^B and σ^F denote the standard deviation for the betweenness and fragmentation averages.

TYPE (#)	AB_1^r (σ^B)				AF_1^r (σ^F)			
	CS1	CS2	CS3	CS4	CS1	CS2	CS3	CS4
F-100000 (2)	0.07 (0.19)	0.01 (0.02)	0.05 (0.15)	0.04 (0.15)	0.09 (0.20)	0.06 (0.16)	0.09 (0.22)	0.03 (0.08)
F-50000 (36)	0.14 (0.26)	0.08 (0.15)	0.11 (0.20)	0.13 (0.25)	0.19 (0.27)	0.14 (0.22)	0.14 (0.24)	0.16 (0.26)
F-10000 (459)	0.17 (0.30)	0.16 (0.29)	0.13 (0.24)	0.12 (0.23)	0.21 (0.33)	0.18 (0.28)	0.16 (0.27)	0.17 (0.28)
F-2500 (1394)	0.21 (0.33)	0.23 (0.34)	0.23 (0.34)	0.21 (0.32)	0.27 (0.37)	0.27 (0.37)	0.30 (0.39)	0.24 (0.35)
M-1000 (11)	0.21 (0.33)	0.15 (0.22)	0.17 (0.28)	0.16 (0.28)	0.24 (0.33)	0.21 (0.27)	0.22 (0.32)	0.18 (0.29)
M-500 (77)	0.19 (0.30)	0.20 (0.30)	0.18 (0.29)	0.15 (0.26)	0.26 (0.35)	0.26 (0.33)	0.22 (0.33)	0.20 (0.30)
M-100 (1837)	0.21 (0.33)	0.20 (0.32)	0.23 (0.34)	0.19 (0.32)	0.26 (0.36)	0.26 (0.36)	0.28 (0.38)	0.25 (0.36)
C-1000 (47)	0.13 (0.24)	0.12 (0.21)	0.11 (0.21)	0.14 (0.26)	0.14 (0.25)	0.15 (0.25)	0.14 (0.23)	0.14 (0.25)
C-500 (253)	0.22 (0.33)	0.20 (0.31)	0.17 (0.28)	0.15 (0.24)	0.28 (0.36)	0.26 (0.35)	0.23 (0.32)	0.21 (0.31)
C-175 (1513)	0.25 (0.34)	0.24 (0.35)	0.25 (0.35)	0.25 (0.35)	0.30 (0.39)	0.31 (0.38)	0.29 (0.39)	0.31 (0.39)

Table 7.6 Experiment on contribution of key figures w.r.t. direct trust information; evaluation for frequent raters, mavens and connectors on level 1: average betweenness and fragmentation for the best alternative WOT member, AB_1^w and AF_1^w in $[0,1]$, σ^B and σ^F denote the standard deviation for the betweenness and fragmentation averages.

TYPE (#)	AB_1^w (σ^B)				AF_1^w (σ^F)			
	CS1	CS2	CS3	CS4	CS1	CS2	CS3	CS4
F-100000 (2)	0.10 (0.20)	0.08 (0.16)	0.12 (0.22)	0.11 (0.18)	0.11 (0.20)	0.09 (0.17)	0.13 (0.24)	0.10 (0.15)
F-50000 (36)	0.13 (0.24)	0.14 (0.20)	0.16 (0.23)	0.18 (0.27)	0.15 (0.26)	0.18 (0.24)	0.21 (0.25)	0.22 (0.29)
F-10000 (459)	0.10 (0.25)	0.14 (0.27)	0.14 (0.26)	0.15 (0.26)	0.13 (0.28)	0.18 (0.30)	0.18 (0.30)	0.20 (0.30)
F-2500 (1394)	0.13 (0.28)	0.18 (0.32)	0.24 (0.35)	0.26 (0.35)	0.16 (0.32)	0.22 (0.36)	0.29 (0.40)	0.32 (0.39)
M-1000 (11)	0.20 (0.29)	0.20 (0.25)	0.24 (0.30)	0.22 (0.29)	0.24 (0.33)	0.28 (0.32)	0.30 (0.34)	0.26 (0.31)
M-500 (77)	0.17 (0.30)	0.23 (0.32)	0.27 (0.33)	0.24 (0.29)	0.21 (0.34)	0.28 (0.36)	0.33 (0.37)	0.31 (0.35)
M-100 (1837)	0.09 (0.23)	0.14 (0.29)	0.16 (0.30)	0.18 (0.31)	0.11 (0.27)	0.17 (0.32)	0.19 (0.34)	0.22 (0.36)
C-1000 (47)	0.09 (0.20)	0.15 (0.24)	0.17 (0.24)	0.18 (0.27)	0.12 (0.24)	0.19 (0.28)	0.22 (0.29)	0.22 (0.31)
C-500 (253)	0.17 (0.30)	0.19 (0.30)	0.24 (0.32)	0.22 (0.30)	0.21 (0.34)	0.24 (0.35)	0.30 (0.36)	0.29 (0.36)
C-175 (1513)	0.13 (0.28)	0.19 (0.33)	0.21 (0.33)	0.26 (0.36)	0.16 (0.32)	0.22 (0.37)	0.25 (0.38)	0.31 (0.40)

cold start users rate more items and issue more trust statements; consequently, the web of trust sizes become larger. This means that there is a higher chance that one of the WOT members is a stronger user, yielding higher values for B_1^w and F_1^w, and lower values for the key figures.

On the one hand, the figure gives us a good overview of the evolution of the utility for different classes of cold start users, but on the other hand it also presents a distorted image of the real impact of the key figure classes due to the aggregated information: there is no breakdown for the types within the same key figure class. The actual impact of each individual key figure type is depicted in Fig. 7.7. We can make several observations.

Firstly, whereas Fig. 7.6 suggests that mavens result in higher AFU_1's, Figure 7.7 shows that, overall, frequent raters do achieve the highest fragmentation utility values, which is in accordance with the results in the previous tables: leaving aside the least active frequent raters group, mavens and connectors score less in all but one occasion, namely the group of cold start users with exactly one M-100 maven in their WOT. This particular maven group also contains a high number of frequent raters (more than 500 F-2500 and over 300 F-10000+ frequent raters), yielding an immediate impact on the coverage. This explains e.g. the higher results compared to the F-2500 group (which only contains key figures that have rated less than 10 000 items).

According to Fig. 7.6 it appears that connectors perform significantly worse than mavens and frequent raters w.r.t. fragmentation utility, but Fig. 7.7 demonstrates that this is mainly due to the M-100 group; apart from these key figures, connectors also achieve good results, and score well compared to mavens. Note that the mutual relations between the key figure types are preserved for the betweenness utility. connectors do not necessarily rate many items, while mavens who write a lot of reviews may often also rate a lot reviews from other users (including other visible mavens). Moreover, whereas the frequent raters achieve the highest betweenness and fragmentation values, their overall utility is somewhat lower than for mavens. As Figure 7.7 shows, this is mainly due to the very good performance of the M-100 group (containing one of two F-100000 and several F-50000 frequent raters).

As discussed in Sec. 7.3, the fragmentation measures reflect the impact of users on the coverage of a recommender. Example 7.1 illustrated that the betweenness measures also partially reflect the coverage effect when only taking into account direct trust information. However, as mentioned earlier, an increase in coverage is beneficial only to the extent that the accuracy does not drop significantly. In Sec. 7.3, we proposed to use the accuracy change (Definition 7.1) to measure the accuracy impact of users, but also explained that

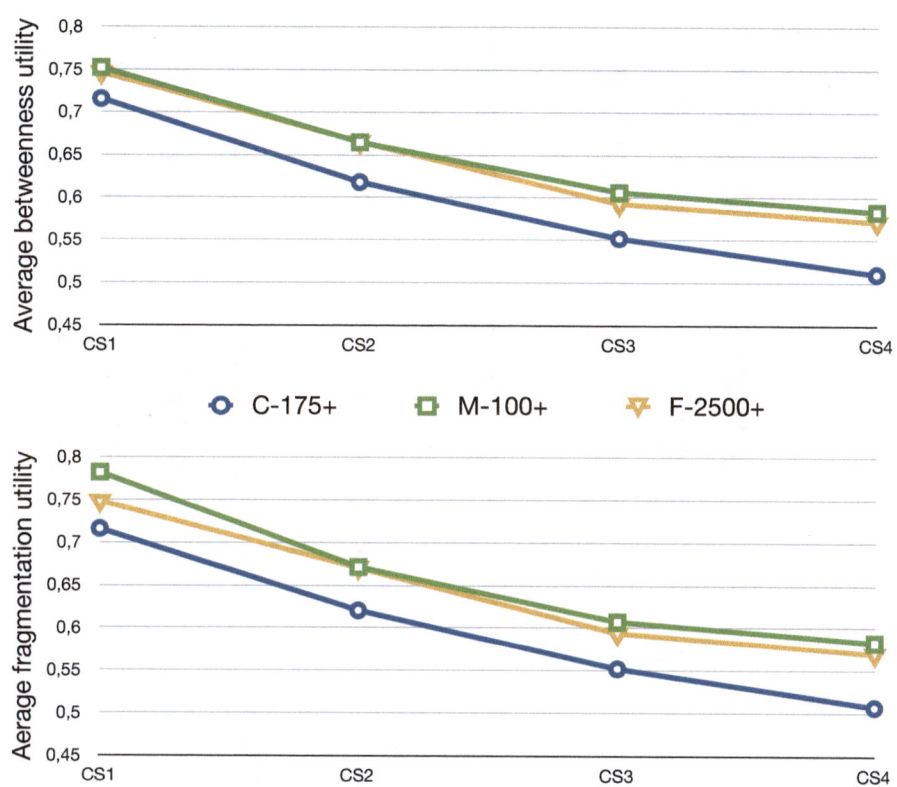

Fig. 7.6 Experiment on contribution of key figures; average betweenness and fragmentation utility (ABU_1, AFU_1 in $[-1,1]$) of all key figures for CS users.

applying the betweenness measures should give us a more informed opinion, especially when not only direct information is taken into account, but also propagation paths.

In the remainder of this section, we focus on the accuracy of the recommendations. We first illustrate that the accuracy change can only give us a hint of a key figure's impact on the accuracy of the recommendations for cold start users, and then proceed by focusing on the betweenness utility results on level 2, i.e., for propagated trust information.

We computed the average AC values (AAC) as in Eq. (7.2). The results are shown in Table 7.7.

$$AAC = \frac{\sum_{a \in U} AC(k_a, a)}{|U|} \tag{7.2}$$

Note that no results are generated for the CS1 group: Definition 6.3 uses the mean of a user's ratings, but the leave-one-out method already hides the sole rating of a CS1 user.

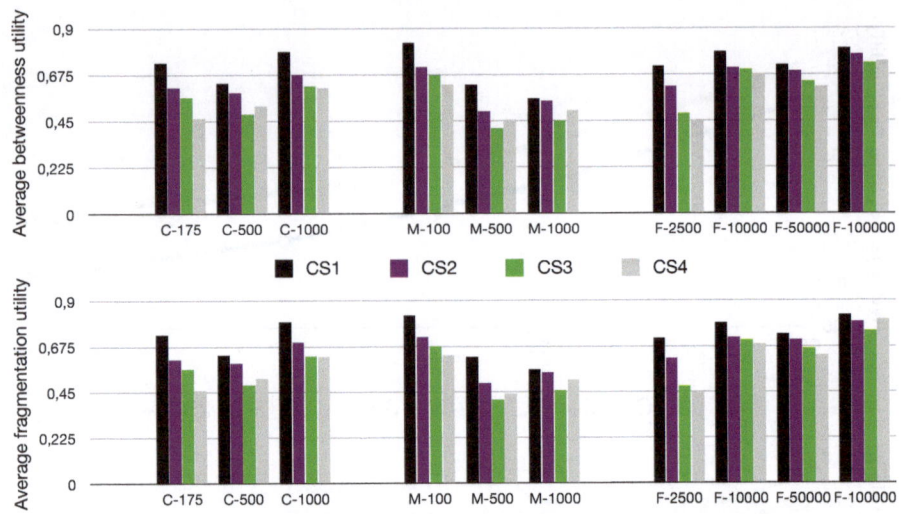

Fig. 7.7   Experiment on contribution of key figures; average betweenness and fragmentation utility (ABU_1, AFU_1 in $[-1, 1]$) of key figure groups for CS users.

Also note that for a CSm user (with $m > 1$), exactly m leave-one-out experiments can be performed.

Since items are rated on a scale from 1 to 5, the extreme values of AC and AAC are -4 and 4. Because we use the leave-one-out method, we can only take into account items that are rated by the cold start user a, i.e., items of $Acc_0(a)$. On level 1, AAC measures the average accuracy change for items that are immediately accessible through users u of $WOT(a)$, i.e., items that are in $Acc_0(u)$. In other words, for a particular cold start user a, the leave-one-out experiment can be applied on the items of $Acc_0(a) \cap \bigcup_{u \in WOT(a)} Acc_0(u)$.

On level 2, we consider items that become accessible through trust propagation (items in $Acc_0(a)$ and in $\bigcup_{u \in WOT(a)} Acc_1(u)$); the values are obtained by subtracting the MAE of the predictions generated by information reached through trusted third parties (TTPs) other than the key figure, from the MAE of the predictions based on all TTPs (including the key figure). In other words, positive accuracy changes denote higher prediction errors when taking into account the key figure.

The results for direct trust information demonstrate that the absence or presence of a key figure in a web of trust does not significantly affect the accuracy. In other words, the key figures have a positive effect on the coverage (as has been shown in the preceding experiment), while maintaining sufficient accuracy. The results for propagated information

Table 7.7 Experiment on contribution of key figures; average accuracy change (in $[-4,4]$) of all key figures for cold start users.

| TYPE | direct information only | | | propagation length 2 | | |
	CS2	CS3	CS4	CS2	CS3	CS4
F-100000	−0.23	0.04	0.08	0.00	0.04	0.01
F-50000	−0.04	−0.09	0.05	0.04	0.00	0.08
F-10000	0.16	−0.02	0.00	0.03	0.01	0.02
F-2500	−0.06	0.03	−0.03	−0.05	0.01	0.00
M-1000	0.05	−0.14	−0.12	0.09	0.05	0.13
M-500	0.02	−0.01	0.04	0.05	0.00	0.01
M-100	0.16	0.08	0.04	0.01	0.00	0.01
C-1000	0.01	0.04	0.02	0.07	0.03	0.05
C-500	0.06	−0.05	0.05	−0.01	0.00	0.02
C-175	0.01	0.03	−0.04	−0.01	0.00	−0.04

(items on level 2 but not on level 1) lead to the same conclusion. However, we should note that these results can only serve as a very cautious indication of the accuracy impact. Firstly, since we are dealing with cold start users, only few leave-one-out experiments can be conducted. For a CS2 user for example, maximum 2 ratings can be predicted, but for the CS2 users in the level 1 experiment in Table 7.7, on average merely 1.2 items can be reached. For CS3 and CS4 this is respectively 1.5 and 1.8 on a maximum of 3 and 4. There are more reachable items on level 2 (1.7 for a CS2 user, 2.2 for a CS3 and 2.9 for a CS4 user), but still it remains a fact that one needs more predictions to come to a preciser conclusion. Furthermore, for CS1 users, no accuracy change at all can be computed.

The betweenness utility is based on how many times the key figure appears on shortest paths leading to the items (see Sec. 7.3.1). Since it has been shown that shorter trust paths lead to more accurate predictions (see Chap. 6), the betweenness utility can be used as a more informative measure of the accuracy impact. This is especially true for cold start users for whom it is not possible to compute meaningful accuracy change values. Another argument to focus on the betweenness utility values instead of the accuracy change is that the former also enables us to investigate the accuracy advantage of key figures for CS1 users.

Figure 7.8 depicts the evolution of the betweenness utility when using direct trust information only, or by allowing trust propagation. The dark bars represent the same information (but in a different presentation) as in the upper part of Fig. 7.7, i.e, ABU_1. The light bars represent ABU_2. The graphs show that also on level 2 the utility of key figures decreases as the cold start users become more active.

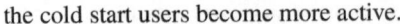

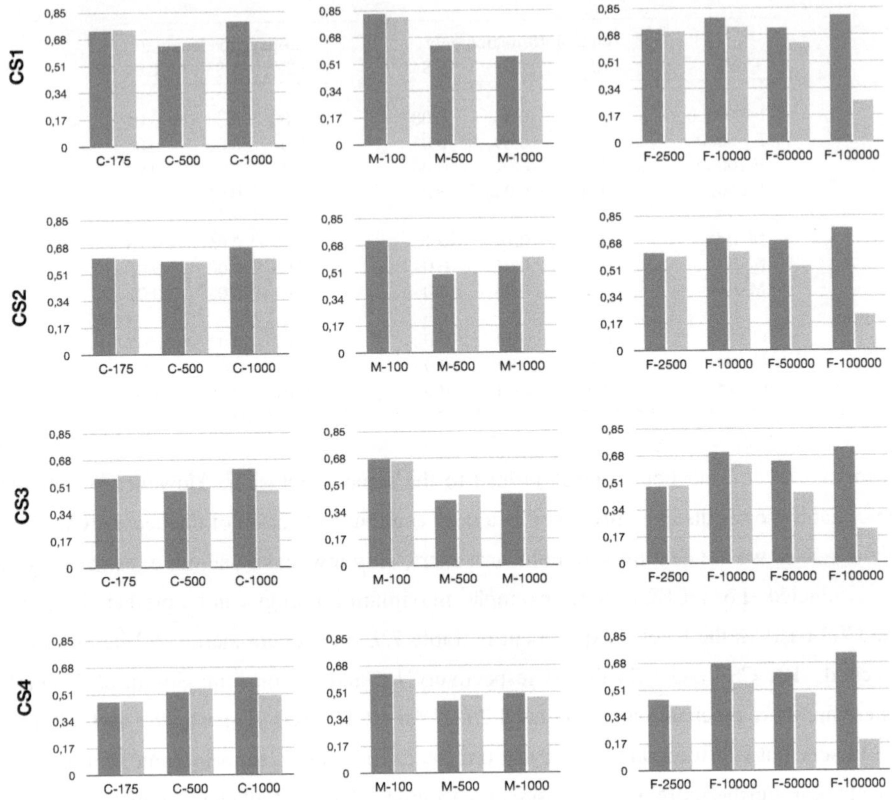

Fig. 7.8   Experiment on contribution of key figures; average betweenness utility (in $[-1, 1]$) of key figures groups for cold start users, focus on direct information (dark bars) and propagation paths of length 2 (light bars).

Recall that the frequent raters achieved in almost every scenario the highest ABU_1's. However, this is no longer the case for ABU_2. In fact, of the three key figure types it is the only one which always results in utility decreases going from level 1 (direct information) to level 2 (propagation). Indeed, the strength of frequent raters lies in their immediate impact on coverage, and not in centrality (the latter leading to higher occurrence on shortest paths, resulting in better accuracy). For example, take a look at the drastic decreases going from F-50000 to F-100000.

Connectors are supposed to be more central in the network, and hence one expects high betweenness utility increases. This starts to reveal itself in the betweenness utility evolution for level 2. However, the increases are small, and in some cases even connectors result in utility decreases. This phenomenon can be explained by the fact that the items on level 2 can be reached through more WOT members of the cold start users than the items on level 1, and that this has an impact on the betweenness values. In Definition 7.4, if a key figure b is the only member of $WOT(a)$ through which item i can be reached, then $\tau_{ai}(b)/\tau_{ai} = 1$, which results in high betweenness values. However, the more WOT members other than the key figure contribute to i, the lower $\tau_{ai}(b)/\tau_{ai}$ will be, yielding lower betweenness values too. This explains the small utility difference w.r.t. level 1 and 2 in Fig. 7.8.

The above argumentation is also confirmed by an inspection of the room for originality values $F_1^{\max}$ and $F_2^{\max}$ (see Definition 7.7). Recall that they measure the 'popularity' of the items in $Acc(a)$, in the sense that they reflect the number of users who have rated them and the number of paths leading to them. The more WOT members who can contribute to an item i, the lower the $F^{\max}$ values will be. Indeed, for Fig. 7.8, the $F_2^{\max}$ values are lower than their level 1 counterparts. As an example, for the CS3 user group, all $F_1^{\max}$ values approach 1, whereas for C-175, C-500 and C-1000, the $F_2^{\max}$ values amount to 0.77, 0.67 and 0.60 respectively, which explains why the C-175 group achieves the highest ABU_2 values.

Note that mavens continue to perform very well: they do not only achieve good fragmentation scores, but can also compete with connectors on several occasions, for direct as well as propagated information. Also note that the level 2 graphs in Fig. 7.8 confirm our finding that key figures are active on several fronts: the good results for mavens reflect the fact that they also exhibit the connector characteristic.

7.4.2 Benefit over Random Users

The number of users in the previous experiments is fairly small compared to the total number of cold start users; for example, 84.36% of the CS4 users have no F-2500 in their WOT, as opposed to 7.34% whose web of trust contains exactly one. To take into account a larger group of users, we also conducted an experiment with groups of CS users who have no key figure of a particular type in their WOT. We denote such a group by U. The number of users in each group can be found in Table 7.8; note the difference in order of magnitude with the numbers in Table 7.3.

The goal of the experiment is then to investigate the effect of adding a key figure to such a cold start user's web of trust. For instance, we connect a M-100, M-500 or M-1000 to each

Table 7.8   Experiment on benefit over random users;
number of cold start users to be evaluated.

TYPE	CS1	CS2	CS3	CS4
F-2500+	56 601	18 273	9 875	6 177
M-100+	56 601	18 099	9 742	6 101
C-175+	56 431	17 986	9 673	6 065

CS2 user whose WOT does not contain a maven.

In particular, for one experiment, we calculate for each user a in a given group U the difference $DFU(a)$ between the fragmentation utilities $FU_1(k,a)$ and $FU_1(r,a)$, in which k represents a randomly chosen key figure of a given type and r a randomly chosen member of the set of all active users. Active users are those who rated at least one user or one item, hence this set contains key figures as well. DBU is defined analogously for betweenness. In other words, DFU and DBU measure the extra gain when adding a key figure to the WOT instead of a random user.

Figure 7.9 and 7.10 depict the average utility differences $ADFU$ and $ADBU$ for each user group when a specific key figure is added to the WOT. The formula for $ADFU \in [-2,2]$ is given by (7.3), the formula for the average betweenness utility difference is analogous.

$$ADFU = \frac{\sum_{a \in U} DFU(a)}{|U|} = \frac{\sum_{a \in U} (FU_1(k,a) - FU_1(r,a))}{|U|} \qquad (7.3)$$

Clearly, adding a key figure to a web of trust is more beneficial than adding a random user. For example, the fragmentation utility of an added key figure increases on average with 0.41 compared to the utility of the randomly added user.

The figures also show that, in general, the more active the key figure is, the more advantageous it is to have such a user in a WOT. E.g., users who are connected with a F-10000+ have a larger DFU and DBU than users connected with a F-2500. This phenomenon also occurs with mavens and connectors, which confirms once again that users who are active on one front (being a maven or connector) are often active on other fronts as well (being a frequent rater, i.e., boosting the number of accessible items).

Note that the differences become larger for more active CS users. As Table 7.9 illustrates, this is because the utility of randomly added users decreases more rapidly than the utility of key figures when the cold start user rates more items. Note that the table contains three lines for random users, for each cold start user class, i.e., the CS users who are

Table 7.9 Experiment on benefit over random users; average fragmentation and betweenness utility of key figures and random users for cold start users.

TYPE	AFU_1				ABU_1			
	CS1	CS2	CS3	CS4	CS1	CS2	CS3	CS4
F-100000	0.9997	0.9993	0.9992	0.9990	0.9998	0.9997	0.9995	0.9994
F-50000	0.9991	0.9982	0.9978	0.9973	0.9995	0.9990	0.9988	0.9985
F-10000	0.9964	0.9928	0.9909	0.9894	0.9981	0.9962	0.9951	0.9940
F-2500	0.9883	0.9772	0.9716	0.9654	0.9940	0.9878	0.9846	0.9817
Random	0.7298	0.5516	0.4432	0.3209	0.9076	0.8350	0.7892	0.7408
M-1000	0.9917	0.9849	0.9798	0.9794	0.9960	0.9917	0.9908	0.9891
M-500	0.9794	0.9595	0.9500	0.9398	0.9898	0.9801	0.9738	0.9700
M-100	0.9574	0.9210	0.9059	0.8739	0.9783	0.9591	0.9501	0.9363
Random	0.7402	0.5640	0.4459	0.3451	0.9106	0.8403	0.7976	0.7489
C-1000	0.9876	0.9975	0.9703	0.9136	0.9934	0.9880	0.9842	0.9812
C-500	0.9832	0.9677	0.9615	0.9524	0.9912	0.9837	0.9808	0.9723
C-175	0.9705	0.9490	09329	0.9598	0.9855	0.9732	0.9653	0.9573
Random	0.7463	0.5772	0.4650	0.3453	0.9132	0.8470	0.8035	0.7558

not connected to any frequent rater, the CS users who have no maven in their WOT, or no connector.

7.4.3 Discussion

For new users, choosing the right web of trust members can come as an overwhelming task. Therefore, the recommender system can guide and interact with such cold start users by proposing a list of members which are worth exploring because they have an immediate and positive impact on the generated recommendations. Such 'suggestion lists' are a common technique in social networking sites. For example, in FilmTrust[6], Golbeck encourages users to expand their network by showing two lists of users which people can connect to: a set of random users and a set of random people with no friends in the network. LinkedIn[7] and Live QnA[7] provide similar services with their 'Just joined LinkedIn' and 'Meet a QnA superstar' lists respectively.

The results in the previous sections indicate that trust-enhanced recommender systems can be improved by including a new building block for alleviating connection guidance issues. In particular, we propose to suggest key figures (mavens, connectors, frequent raters) as possible connections for cold start users. Such assisting systems can be further refined. Because not every user has the same likes and dislikes, the system

---

[6]See trust.mindswap.org/FilmTrust

[7]See www.linkedin.com and qna.live.com

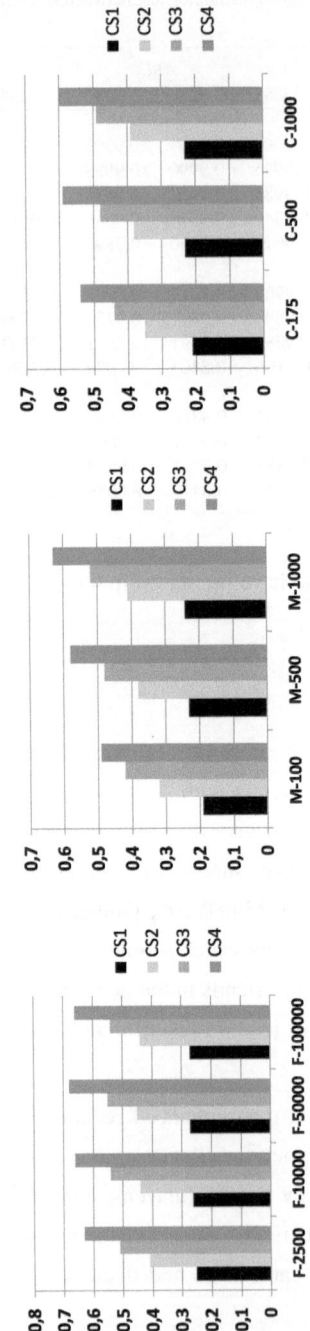

Fig. 7.9   Experiment on benefit over random users; average fragmentation difference between key figures and random users for cold start users, $ADFU \in [-2, 2]$.

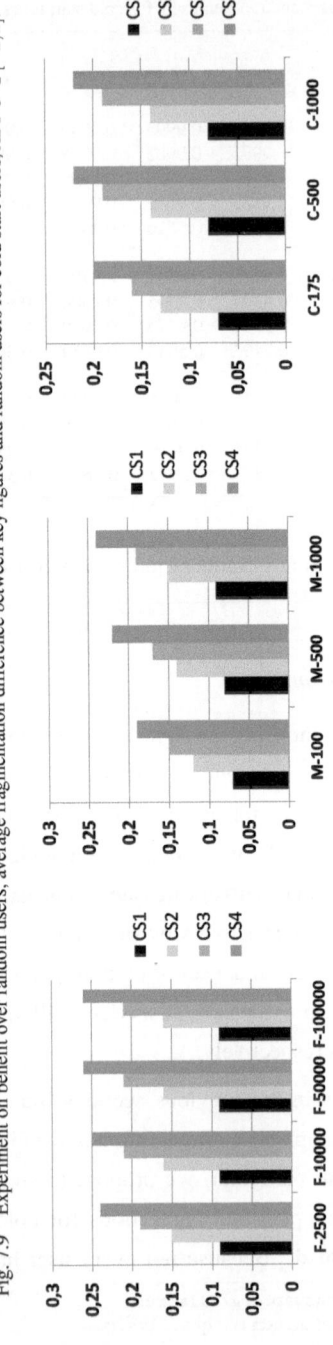

Fig. 7.10   Experiment on benefit over random users; average betweenness difference between key figures and random users for cold start users, $ADBU \in [-2, 2]$.

can propose several types of users, think for instance of a 'mainstream' key figure who rates a lot of popular items, or one with more distinct preferences. Furthermore, the system could narrow down the selection and present more 'tailor-made' key figures if the user has indicated that he is only interested in some specific item categories. Of course, the key figures only appear as suggestions; a new user can (and must) always check whether the candidates are worth to be included in his web of trust.

A possible consequence of our technique is that mavens and frequent raters eventually become connectors too, since the more people connect to key figures, the higher the number of inlinks they will have and hence the more of a connector they will be. Note that we showed in Section 7.2 that this phenomenon already occurs in a moderate form in the original dataset.

A related side effect is the appearance of clusters around established users in the trust network. If this clustering is undesirable, it can be restricted by choosing appropriate thresholds for the key figure selection. If one chooses high thresholds, a small number of 'true' key figures are obtained, which might lead to a small number of star-like clusters. This can be avoided by low thresholds, yielding many key figures. By generating random suggestion lists of these key figures, the network can remain more equally connected. In other words, the occurence of strong clusters diminishes, but along with it also the power of the selected key figures, because we have shown that less active key figures yield lower betweenness and fragmentation values. Hence, it is clear that the thresholds must be chosen carefully in agreement with the characteristics of the recommender system's network, and that a trade-off should be made between the desired performance and network topology.

7.5   Conclusions and Future Work

The user cold start problem is one of the main challenges for classical recommender systems. It has been shown that including a trust network among the users can alleviate the problem, but this requires that newcomers make clever connections in the trust network. Unfortunately, cold start users in the classical sense are very often cold start users in the trust sense as well, meaning that they have very few users in their personal web of trust. In this chapter, we proposed to tackle this problem by guiding the new users throughout the trust connection phase. More specifically, we proposed to suggest newcomers to add identified key figures to their web of trust instead of randomly chosen users, as the former lead to much more beneficial cold start recommendations.

To prove the advantages of this approach, we first need suitable measures to assess the influence of WOT members on the amount (coverage) and the quality (accuracy) of the generated cold start recommendations. However, we explained that the traditional coverage and accuracy measures are not very useful in cold start situations. Therefore, we introduced a new set of techniques that are more informative and that have a clear foundation in social network analysis. Each measure reflects a different aspect of the influence on the newcomers' recommendations: the betweenness-based measure focuses on a user's ability to reach items via short propagation chains (measuring the impact on the accuracy), while the fragmentation-based measure focuses on a user's capacity for delivering new items (measuring the impact on the coverage). Since these measures only reflect the impact of a single WOT member, without taking into account environmental factors such as the strength of the other WOT users, we also introduced two utility measures which reflect the actual advantage of adding a particular user to a newcomer's web of trust.

Secondly, we need techniques to identify advantageous users in the trust-based recommender network. of a system in which users can write reviews, evaluate them, and are connected by trust statements, We proposed to classify users according to the number of reviews they write, the numbers of items they rate and the amount of trust connections they have. This led to three key figure classes: mavens who share their knowledge by writing a lot of reviews, frequent raters who provide a lot of ratings, and connectors who are central in the trust network because they trust, and are trusted by, many users.

The final step to prove our claim involved a series of experiments on the review data set from Epinions. Our first experiments illustrated that all three key figure types are very influential in a cold start user's web of trust. The second set of experiments clearly demonstrated that generated recommendations for new users are indeed much more beneficial (w.r.t. coverage and accuracy) if they add an identified frequent rater, connector or maven to their web of trust instead of a randomly chosen user.

Every key figure type has its pros and cons: frequent raters immediately boost the number of generated recommendations (positive impact on coverage), but have little power in connecting the newcomers to other users in the system. The latter is exactly the strength of connectors, who occupy central positions in the trust network and hence will appear much more often on shortest paths to items (positive impact on the accuracy). The last class of key figures, the mavens, have the advantage of being visible through the reviews they write, which greatly facilitates the process of deciding whom to trust. Newcomers may safely be encouraged to connect to mavens, because the experiments show that they are often active on other fronts (connecting and rating) as well, which leads to an immediate positive effect on the generated recommendations.

Hence, the incorporation of a new assistance component that computes connection suggestions (identified mavens, connectors and frequent raters) for newcomers in a trust-based recommender system can greatly enhance the recommendation experience. Furthermore, aside from interaction and personalization, another benefit of our connection guidance technique is the ability to better explain the effect of WOT members on coverage and accuracy of the system, which is a new step in the development of more transparent recommender systems. For these reasons, we think that our technique might be a good asset for existing and future trust-enhanced recommender systems.

There are several interesting paths for further research on connection guidance. For instance, by refining the connector type (think of 'outconnectors' with many outlinks) one may gain an insight into the impact of connectors when taking into account propagation. Furthermore, besides an in-depth study of connector types, the applicability of the proposed techniques for other trust-enhanced recommendation types, and an investigation of the potential and impact of distrust relations on the key figure identification process, one can also investigate the power of other key figures like hubs and authorities. These can for example be identified by using well-known evaluation measures such as HITS [67] and PageRank [107].

Remark that the connection guidance issue that we have discussed in this chapter links up with the broader problem of trust bootstrapping, i.e., the problem of how to establish initial trust relations in the network. O'Donovan, too, addresses this problem, but in a very different way: he introduces PeerChooser, a new procedure to visualize a trust-based collaborative filtering recommender system [103]. the traditional correlation coefficient, and information coming from the underlying trust-space generated fom the rating data (remember the profile- and item-level trust of Section 6.2.1.2). One of the main features of the system is its possiblity to extract trust information on the fly, directly from the user at recommendation time. This is done by moving specific icons (representing users in the system) on an interactive interface. In this way, the user can indicate his mood and preferences, thereby actively providing real-time trust information.

We believe that the problems of connection guidance and trust bootstrapping deserve the attention of the research community, especially since they can greatly contribute to a better acceptance of trust-enhanced recommenders.

*I may not have gone where I intended to go, but I think I have
ended up where I needed to be.*

The Long Dark Tea-Time of the Soul, 1988. Douglas Adams

Chapter 8

Conclusions

With the advent of e-commerce applications and the ever growing popularity of social networking tools, a novel kind of recommender systems has been born; the so-called trust-enhanced recommenders which infer trust information from the social network between their users, and incorporate this knowledge into the recommendation process to obtain more personalized recommendations. Since the pioneering work of Jennifer Golbeck and Paolo Massa, research on trust-based recommendations is thriving and attracts and inspires an increasing number of scientists around the world. In this book, we contributed to some of the most recent and exciting developments in this still nascent domain, namely the potential of distrust, recommendations for controversial items, and connection guidance for cold start users.

Trust metrics and recommendation algorithms are the two key building blocks in every trust-enhanced recommender system. For the first pillar, our novel contributions are particularly in the modeling and computation of distrust. In our quest for a lightweight (dis)trust model that can be used in many intelligent web applications, we reviewed the current approaches and came to the conclusion that they cannot cope with knowledge defects such as (partial) ignorance and conflicting information, although these issues can have a significant impact on the (ranking of) trust estimations and recommendations. Therefore, we proposed to model trust and distrust as two distinct but related concepts, and introduced a bilattice-based model that resolves the problems w.r.t. representation of ignorance and inconsistency (chapter 2). Furthermore, the new model enables us to preserve a large part of the available trust provenance information; information which can play a vital role in

189

the trust computation process (propagation and aggregation), especially when also distrust is involved.

While the concepts of trust propagation and trust aggregation take hold, the study of their counterparts for distrust is scarcely out of the egg. Our main contributions in the field of trust metrics are in this challenging, yet largely unexplored domain. We contributed to a better understanding of the matter by investigating the propagation and aggregation problem on a theoretical basis but also from a practical point of view. In particular, we introduced new families of trust score propagation operators on the basis of fuzzy logic concepts, so that they can be used to model different kinds of distrust behavior. We showed on two large real-world social data sets from the e-commerce and opinions site Epinions and the travellers network CouchSurfing that the distrust-oriented propagation operators perform better than the standard trust-only operators (chapter 3). The same data sets were used to study the trust score aggregation problem. We investigated how standard aggregation properties and methods can be extended for use in a bilattice setting, and focused on the potential of ordered weighted averaging strategies and the incorporation of knowledge defects. We demonstrated that the latter two approaches can produce significantly more accurate trust estimations than the classic operators for bilattice elements (chapter 4).

Although the results in this first part of the book shed more light on the problem of propagation and aggregation, the study of computational trust and distrust is still a work in progress. For example, besides the further exploration and implementation of propagation methods, aggregation strategies, and their combination, another interesting research path that we have not tackled so far is the update of trust and distrust information: as relationships can evolve over time, it is certainly worthwhile to investigate the effect of changes in the trust network on the generated trust estimations.

The second part of the book deals with the application of trust networks to the field of recommender systems. In this part, too, we paid special attention to distrust. We provided the first experimental study on its potential in memory-based collaborative recommendation processes; we demonstrated through experiments on a review data set from Epinions that distrust cannot be used as an indication to reverse opinions, but that its role as debugger of trust predictions, or as a filter of neighbors is more promising: we showed that a weight filter in combination with the trust score aggregation operators from chapter 4 can produce more accurate recommendations without loosing in terms of coverage, compared to Golbeck's trust-based weighted mean which only uses (propagated) trust information (chapter 6).

W.r.t. trust, we gave a comprehensive overview of the domain of trust-enhanced recommendation algorithms and focused specifically on their performance for controversial items, since these are very challenging for a recommender system to accurately recommend. To this aim, we introduced a new detection measure which is more suited for the evaluation of the different recommendation approaches for controversial items (chapter 5). We conducted a head-to-head comparison of collaborative filtering and state of the art trust-enhanced algorithms, and demonstrated that for random items simple baseline strategies prove to be equally effective. However, we also showed that the more sophisticated algorithms outperform the basic approaches when it comes down to controversial items, but that there is still room for improvement. Therefore, we introduced a new algorithm that combines the best of both the trust world and the collaborative world, resulting in immediate high coverage while the accuracy of the delivered recommendations remains adequate (chapter 6).

Our last contribution in the domain of trust-enhanced recommendations, besides our focus on distrust and controversial items, is related to the user cold start problem, a major issue that is high on the agenda because generating satisfying recommendations for newcomers can greatly contribute to a better acceptance of (trust-based) recommender systems (chapter 7). We tackled the problem on the user level, as opposed to the algorithm level for the controversial item problem. We provided a set of social network analysis techniques based on the classic betweenness and fragmentation measures to quantify the impact of several classes of useful key figures in a trust-enhanced recommender's network, in the sense that they have an immediate positive impact on the accuracy and coverage of the system for cold start users. Experiments on a large data set from Epinions clearly showed that the generated recommendations for new users are more beneficial if they connect to an identified key figure compared to a randomly chosen user, which illustrates that guiding new users throughout the early stage trust connection process certainly bears fruit.

Research on trust-based recommender systems is broad and diverse, so naturally not all its aspects are covered in this book. One interesting direction for future work is the investigation of the potential of trust and distrust as mechanisms to detect and prevent abuses and malicious users. Others include e.g. live user experiments to get a better idea on the performance, benefits and disadvantages (think of transparency, participation, novelty, etc.) of trust-enhanced recommendation algorithms.

Bibliography

[1] Abdul-Rahman, A. and Hailes, S. (2000). Supporting trust in virtual communities, in *Proceedings of the 33rd Hawaii International Conference on System Sciences*, pp. 1769–1777.

[2] Adomavicius, G. and Tuzhilin, A. (2005). Toward the next generation of recommender systems: a survey of the state-of-the-art and possible extensions, *IEEE Transactions on Knowledge and Data Engineering* , pp. 734–749.

[3] Ahn, H. (2008). A new similarity measure for collaborative filtering to alleviate the new user cold-starting problem, *Information Sciences* **178**, pp. 37–51.

[4] Almenárez, F., Marín, A., Campo, C. and García, C. (2004). PTM: A pervasive trust management model for dynamic open environments, in *Proceedings of the First Workshop on Pervasive Security, Privacy and Trust, in conjunction with Mobiquitous.*

[5] Arazy, O., Elsane, I., Shapira, B. and Kumar, N. (2007). Social relationships in recommender systems, in *Proceedings of the 17th Workshop on Information Technologies & Systems*, pp. 146–151.

[6] Arazy, O., Kumar, N. and Shapira, B. (2009). Improving social recommender systems, *IT Professional* **11**, pp. 38–44.

[7] Artz, D. and Gil, Y. (2007). A survey of trust in computer science and the semantic web, *Journal of Web Semantics* **5**, pp. 58–71.

[8] Arulselvan, A., Commander, C., Elefteriadou, L. and Pardalos, P. (2009). Detecting critical nodes in sparse graphs, *Computers and Operations Research* **36**, pp. 2193–2200.

[9] Atanassov, K. (1986). Intuitionistic fuzzy sets, *Fuzzy Sets and Systems* **20**, pp. 87–96.

[10] Belnap, N. (1977a). *How a computer should think*, Ryle, G. (ed.) Contemporary Aspects of Philosophy, pp. 30–56.

[11] Belnap, N. (1977b). *A useful four-valued logic*, Epstein, G., and Dunn, J. (eds.) Modern Uses of Multiple-Valued Logics, pp. 7–37.

[12] Berners-Lee, T., Hendler, J. and Lassila, O. (2001). The semantic web, *Scientific American* **284**, pp. 35–43.

[13] Blabanović, M. and Shoham, Y. (1997). Fab: content-based, collaborative recommendation, *Communications of the ACM* **40**, pp. 66–72.

[14] Borgatti, S. (2006). Identifying sets of key players in social networks, *Computational and Mathematical Organizational Theory* **12**, pp. 21–34.

[15] Burke, R. (2002). Hybrid recommender systems: survey and experiments, *User Modeling and User-Adapted Interaction* **12**, pp. 331–370.

[16] Cacioppo, J. and Berntson, G. (1994). Relationship between attitudes and evaluative space: a critical review, with emphasis on the separability of positive and negative substrates, *Psychological Bulletin* **115**, pp. 401–423.

[17] Castelfranchi, C. and Falcone, R. (2001). *Social trust: a cognitive approach*, Castelfranchi, C

and Tan, Y (eds.) Trust and Deception in Virtual Societies, pp. 55–90.

[18] Chocquet, G. (1953). Theory of capacities, *Annales de l'Institut Fourier* **5**, pp. 131–295.

[19] Cofta, P. (2006). Distrust, in *Proceedings of the Eighth International Conference on Electronic Commerce*, pp. 250–258.

[20] Constantinople, A. (1969). An eriksonian measure of personality development in college students, *Development Psychology* **1**, pp. 357–372.

[21] Cornelis, C., Lu, J., Guo, X. and Zhang, G. (2007). One-and-only item recommendation with fuzzy logic techniques, *Information Sciences* **177**, pp. 4906–4921.

[22] Crandall, D., Cosley, D., Huttenlocher, D., Kleinberg, J. and Suri, S. (2008). Feedback effects between similarity and social influence in online communities, in *Proceedings of the 14th ACM SIGKDD International Conference on Knowledge Discovery and Data Mining*, pp. 160–168.

[23] De Cock, M. and Pinheiro da Silva, P. (2006). A many-valued representation and propagation of trust and distrust, *Lecture Notes in Computer Science* **3849**, pp. 108–113.

[24] Detyniecki, M. (2001). Numerical aggregation operators: state of the art, in *Proceedings of the First International Summer School on Aggregation Operators and their Applications*.

[25] Domingos, P. and Richardson, M. (2001). Mining the network value of customers, in *Proceedings of the seventh ACM SIGKDD Conference on Knowledge Discovery and Data Mining*, pp. 57–66.

[26] Falcone, R., Pezzulo, G. and Castelfranchi, C. (2003). A fuzzy approach to a belief-based trust computation, *Lecture Notes in Artificial Intelligence* **2631**, pp. 73–86.

[27] Finin, T., Kagal, L. and Olmedilla, D. (eds.) (2006). *Proceedings of the Models of Trust for the Web Workshop*.

[28] Fitting, M. (1991). Bilattices and the semantics of logic programming, *Journal of Logic Programming* **11**, pp. 91–116.

[29] Freeman, L. (1977). A set of measures of centrality based on betweenness, *Sociometry* **40**, pp. 35–41.

[30] Freeman, L. (1979). Centrality in social networks I: Conceptual clarification, *Social Networks* **1**, pp. 215–239.

[31] Gambetta, D. (1988). *Can we trust Trust?*, Gambetta, D (ed.) Trust: Making and Breaking Cooperative Relations, pp. 213–237.

[32] Gans, G., Jarke, M., Kethers, S. and Lakemeyer, G. (2001). Modeling the impact of trust and distrust in agent networks, in *Proceedings of the Third Workshop on Agent-oriented Information Systems*, pp. 45–58.

[33] Gargov, G. (1999). Knowledge, uncertainty and ignorance in logic: bilattices and beyond, *Journal of Applied Non-Classical Logics* **9**, pp. 195–283.

[34] Ghose, A. and Ipeirotis, P. (2007). Designing novel review ranking systems: predicting the usefulness and impact of reviews, in *Proceedings of the Ninth International Conference on Electronic Commerce*, pp. 303–310.

[35] Ginsberg, M. (1988). Multi-valued logics: A uniform approach to reasoning in artificial intelligence, *Computational Intelligence* **4**, pp. 265–316.

[36] Gladwell, M. (2000). *The Tipping Point: How Little Things Can Make a Big Difference* (Little Brown).

[37] Goffman, C. (1969). And what is your Erdös number? *The American Mathematical Monthly* **76**, p. 791.

[38] Golbeck, J. (2005). *Computing and applying trust in web-based social networks*, Ph.D. thesis.

[39] Golbeck, J. (2006). Generating predictive movie ratings from trust in social networks, *Lecture Notes in Computer Science* **3986**, pp. 93–104.

[40] Golbeck, J. (ed.) (2009). *Computing with Social Trust* (Springer London).

[41] Golbeck, J. and Hendler, J. (2006). Filmtrust: movie recommendations using trust in web-

based social networks, in *Proceedings of the 3rd IEEE Consumer Communications and Networking Conference*, pp. 282–286.

[42] Golbeck, J., Parsia, B. and Hendler, J. (2003). Trust networks on the semantic web, *Lecture Notes in Artificial Intelligence* **2782**, pp. 238–249.

[43] Gómez, D. and Montero, J. (2004). A discussion on aggregation operators, *Kybernetika* **40**, pp. 107–120.

[44] Grabisch, M., Orlovski, S. and Yager, R. (1998). *Fuzzy aggregation of numerical preferences*, Slowinski, R (ed.) Fuzzy Sets in Decision Analysis, Operations Research and Statistics, pp. 31–68.

[45] Gray, E., Seigneur, J., Chen, Y. and Jensen, C. (2004). Trust propagation in small worlds, *Lecture Notes in Computer Science* **2692**, pp. 239–254.

[46] Grossman, L. (2009). Time's person of the year: You, Time, http://www.time.com/time/ magazine/article/0,9171,1569514,00.html, retrieved Dec 8, 2009.

[47] Gruhl, D., Guha, R., Liben-Nowell, D. and Tomkins, A. (2004). Information diffusion through blogspace, in *Proceedings of the 13th International World Wide Web Conference*, pp. 491–501.

[48] Guare, J. (1990). *Six Degrees of Separation: a Play* (Vintage Books).

[49] Guha, R. (2003). Open rating systems, Tech. rep., Stanford Knowledge Systems Laboratory.

[50] Guha, R., Kumar, R., Raghavan, P. and Tomkins, A. (2004). Propagation of trust and distrust, in *Proceedings of the 13th International World Wide Web Conference*, pp. 403–412.

[51] Guttman, R., Moukas, A. and Maes, P. (1998). Agent-mediated electronic commerce: a survey, *The Knowledge Engineering Review* **13**, pp. 147–159.

[52] Hasan, O., Brunie, L. and Pierson, J. (2009). Evaluation of the iterative multiplication strategy for trust propagation in pervasive environments, in *Proceedings of the International Conference on Pervasive Services*, pp. 49–54.

[53] Herlocker, J., Konstan, J. and Riedl, J. (2000). Explaining collaborative filtering recommendations, in *Proceedings of the 2000 ACM conference on Computer supported cooperative work*, pp. 241–250.

[54] Herlocker, J., Konstan, J., Terveen, L. and Riedl, J. (2004). Evaluating collaborative filtering recommender systems, *ACM Transactions on Information Systems* **22**, pp. 5–53.

[55] Hess, C. and Schiedler, C. (2008). Trust-based recommendations for documents, *AI Communications* **21**, pp. 145–153.

[56] Hogg, T., Wilkinson, D., Szabo, G. and Brzozowski, M. (2008). Multiple relationship types in online communities and social networks, in *Proceedings of the 2008 AAAI Spring Symposium on Social Information Processing*, pp. 30–35.

[57] Hu, J. and Wellman, M. (1998). Online learning about other agents in a dynamic multiagent system, in *Proceedings of the second international conference on Autonomous Agents*, pp. 239–246.

[58] Huang, Z., Chen, H. and Zeng, D. (2004). Applying associative retrieval techniques to alleviate the sparsity problem in collaborative filtering, *ACM Transactions on Information Systems* **22**, pp. 116–142.

[59] Jamali, M. and Ester, M. (2009). TrustWalker: a random walk model for combining trust-based and item-based recommendation, in *Proceedings of the 15th ACM SIGKDD International Conference on Knowledge Discovery and Data Mining*, pp. 397–406.

[60] Jøsang, A. (2001). A logic for uncertain probabilities, *International Journal of Uncertainty, Fuzziness and Knowledge-Based Systems* **9**, pp. 279–311.

[61] Jøsang, A., Gray, E. and Kinateder, M. (2006a). Simplification and analysis of transitive trust networks, *Web Intelligence and Agent Systems* **4**, pp. 139–161.

[62] Jøsang, A. and Knapskog, S. (1998). A metric for trusted systems, in *Proceedings of the 21st National Computer Security Conference*, pp. 16–29.

[63] Jøsang, A. and Lo Presti, S. (2004). Analysing the relationship between risk and trust, *Lecture Notes in Computer Science* **2995**, pp. 120–134.

[64] Jøsang, A., Marsh, S. and Pope, S. (2006b). Exploring different types of trust propagation, *Lecture Notes in Computer Science* **3986**, pp. 179–192.

[65] Kahanda, I. and Neville, J. (2009). Using transactional information to predict link strength in online social networks, in *Proceedings of Third International AAAI Conference on Weblogs and Social Media*, pp. 74–81.

[66] Kamvar, S., Schlosser, M. and Garcia-Molina, H. (2003). The Eigentrust algorithm for reputation management in P2P networks, in *Proceedings of the 12th International World Wide Web Conference*, pp. 640–651.

[67] Kleinberg, J. (1999). Authoritative sources in a hyperlinked environment, *Journal of the ACM* **46**, pp. 604–632.

[68] Klement, E., Mesiar, R. and Pap, E. (2000). *Triangular Norms* (Kluwer Academic).

[69] Klir, G. and B, Y. (1995). *Fuzzy Sets and Fuzzy Logic: Theory and Applications* (Prentice Hall PTR).

[70] Kunegis, J., Lommatzsch, A. and Bauckhage, C. (2009). The Slashdot Zoo: mining a social network with negative edges, in *Proceedings of the 18th International World Wide Web Conference*, pp. 741–750.

[71] Lam, S. and Riedl, J. (2004). Shilling recommender systems for fun and profit, in *Proceedings of the 13th International Conference on World Wide Web*, pp. 393–402.

[72] Lamere, P. and Celma, O. (2007). Music recommendation tutorial at ISMIR, .

[73] Lange, D. and Oshima, M. (1999). Seven good reasons for mobile agents, *Communications of the ACM* **42**, pp. 88–89.

[74] Lathia, N., Hailes, S. and Capra, L. (2008). Trust-based collaborative filtering, *IFIP International Federation for Information Processing* **263**, pp. 119–134.

[75] Lekakos, G. and Caravelas, P. (2008). A hybrid approach for movie recommendation, *Multimedia Tools and Applications* **36**, pp. 55–70.

[76] Lesani, M. and Bagheri, S. (2006). *Applying and inferring fuzzy trust in semantic web social networks*, Kodé, M.T., Lemire, D. (eds.) Semantic Web and Beyond 2, pp. 23–43.

[77] Leskovec, J., Adamic, L. and Huberman, B. (2007). The dynamics of viral marketing, *ACM Transactions on the Web* **1**, 5.

[78] Levien, R. (2009). *Attack-resistant trust metrics*, Golbeck, J. (ed.) Computing With Social Trust, pp. 121–132.

[79] Lewicki, R., McAllister, D. and Bies, R. (1998). Trust and distrust: new relationships and realities, *Academy of Management Review* **23**, pp. 438–458.

[80] Li, X. and Gui, X. (2009). A comprehensive and adaptive trust model for large-scale P2P networks, *Journal of Computer Science and Technology* **24**, pp. 868–882.

[81] Liu, Y., Huang, X., An, A. and Yu, X. (2008). Modeling and predicting the helpfulness of online reviews, in *Proceedings of 8th IEEE International Conference on Data Mining*, pp. 443–452.

[82] Luo, J., Liu, X. and Fan, M. (2009). A trust model based on fuzzy recommendation for mobile ad-hoc networks, *Computer Networks* **53**, pp. 2396–2407.

[83] Ma, H., Lyu, M. and King, I. (2009). Learning to recommend with trust and distrust relationships, in *Proceedings of the third ACM conference on Recommender systems*, pp. 189–196.

[84] Manning, D., Raghavan, P. and Schütze, H. (2008). *Scoring, term weighting and the vector space model*, Introduction to Information Retrieval, pp. 109–133.

[85] Marsh, S. and Briggs, P. (2009). *Examining trust, forgiveness and regret as computational concepts*, Golbeck, J. (ed.) Computing With Social Trust, pp. 9–43.

[86] Massa, P. and Avesani, A. (2007a). Trust-aware recommender systems, in *Proceedings of the*

First ACM Recommender Systems Conference, pp. 17–24.

[87] Massa, P., Avesani, A. and Tiella, R. (2005). A trust-enhanced recommender system application: Moleskiing, in *Proceedings of the 20th ACM Symposium on Applied Computing*, pp. 1589–1593.

[88] Massa, P. and Avesani, P. (2004). Trust-aware collaborative filtering for recommender systems, *Lecture Notes in Computer Science* **3290**, pp. 492–508.

[89] Massa, P. and Avesani, P. (2007b). Trust metrics on controversial users: balancing between tyranny of the majority and echo chambers, *International Journal on Semantic Web and Information Systems* **3**, pp. 39–64.

[90] Massa, P. and Avesani, P. (2009). *Trust metrics in recommender systems*, Golbeck, J. (ed.) Computing with Social Trust, pp. 259–285.

[91] Massa, P. and Bhattacharjee, B. (2004). Using trust in recommender systems: an experimental analysis, *Lecture Notes in Computer Science* **2995**, pp. 221–235.

[92] Mayer, R., Davis, J. and Schoorman, D. (1995). An integrative model of organizational trust, *The Academy of Management Review* **20**, pp. 709–734.

[93] McAllister, D. (1995). Affect- and cognition-based trust as foundations for interpersonal cooperation in organizations, *The Academy of Management Journal* **38**, pp. 24–59.

[94] McKnight, D. and Chervany, L. (2000). Trust and distrust definitions: one bite at a time, *Lecture Notes in Computer Science* **2246**, pp. 27–54.

[95] McPherson, M., Smith-Lovin, L. and Cook, J. (2001). Birds of a feather: homophily in social networks, *Annual Review of Sociology* **27**, pp. 415–444.

[96] Middleton, S., Alani, H., Shadbolt, N. and De Roure, D. (2002). Exploiting synergy between ontologies and recommender systems, in *Proceedings of the WWW2002 Semantic Web Workshop*.

[97] Milgram, S. (1967). The small-world problem, *Psychology Today* **1**, pp. 61–67.

[98] Mooney, R. and Roy, L. (2000). Content-based book recommending using learning for text categorization, in *Proceedings of the Fifth ACM Conference on Digital Libraries*, pp. 195–204.

[99] Mui, L., Mohtashemi, M. and Halberstadt, A. (2002). A computational model of trust and reputation, in *Proceedings of the 35th Hawaii International Conference on System Sciences*, pp. 2431–2439.

[100] Mulder, G., Puls, D. and Woltring, M. (2003). *Van Dale Groot Woordenboek Spaans-Nederlands* (Van Dale Uitgevers).

[101] Narayan, H., Roy, S. and Patkar, S. (1996). Approximation algorithms for min-k-overlap problems using the principal lattice of partitions appproach, *Journal of algorithms* **21**, pp. 306–330.

[102] Noh, S. (2007). Calculating trust using aggregation rules in social networks, *Lecture Notes in Computer Science* **4610**, pp. 361–371.

[103] O'Donovan, J. (2009). *Capturing trust in social web applications*, Golbeck, J. (ed.) Computing With Social Trust, pp. 213–257.

[104] O'Donovan, J. and Smyth, B. (2005). Trust in recommender systems, in *Proceedings of the 2005 International Conference on Intelligent User Interfaces*, pp. 167–174.

[105] O'Donovan, J. and Smyth, B. (2006). Mining trust values from recommendation errors, *International Journal on Artificial Intelligence Tools* **15**, pp. 945–962.

[106] O'Mahony, M., Hurley, N., Kushmerick, N. and Silvestre, G. (2003). Collaborative recommendation: a robustness analysis, *ACM Transactions on Internet Technology* **4**, p. 2004.

[107] Page, L., Brin, S., Motwani, R. and Winograd, T. (1998). The pagerank citation ranking: bringing order to the web, Tech. rep., Stanford Digital Library Technologies Project.

[108] Papagelis, M., Plexousakis, D. and Kutsuras, T. (2005). Alleviating the sparsity problem of collaborative filtering using trust inferences, *Lecture Notes in Computer Science* **3477**,

pp. 224–239.

[109] Park, S., Pennock, D., Madani, O., Good, N. and De Coste, D. (2006). Naïve filterbots for robust cold-start recommendations, in *Proceedings of the 12th ACM SIGKDD international conference on Knowledge discovery and data mining*, pp. 699–705.

[110] Pazzani, M. (1999). A framework for collaborative, content-based and demographic filtering, *Artificial Intelligence Review* **13**, pp. 393–408.

[111] Pazzani, M. and Billsus, D. (2007). Content-based recommendation systems, *Lecture Notes in Computer Science* **4321**, pp. 325–341.

[112] Petty, R., Wegener, D. and Fabrigar, L. (1997). Attitudes and attitude change, *Annual Review of Psychology* **48**, pp. 609–647.

[113] Pitsilis, G. and Marshall, L. (2006). A trust-enabled P2P recommender system, in *Proceedings of the 15th IEEE International Workshops on Enabling Technologies: Infrastructure for Collaborative Enterprises*, pp. 59–64.

[114] Porcel, C. and Herrera-Viedma, E. (2010). Dealing with incomplete information in a fuzzy linguistic recommender system to disseminate information in university digital libraries, *Knowledge-Based Systems* **23**, pp. 32–39.

[115] Prade, H. (2007). A qualitative bipolar argumentative view of trust, *Lecture Notes in Artificial Intelligence* **4772**, pp. 268–276.

[116] Priester, J. and Petty, R. (1996). The gradual threshold model of ambivalence: relating the positive and negative bases of attitudes to subjective ambivalence, *Journal of Personality and Social Psychology* **71**, pp. 431–449.

[117] Ramchurn, D., Huynh, D. and Jennings, N. (2004). Trust in multi-agent systems, *The Knowledge Engineering Review* **19**, pp. 1–25.

[118] Rashid, A., Karypis, G. and Riedl, J. (2005). Influence in ratings-based recommender systems: an algorithm-independent approach, in *Proceedings of the 2005 SIAM International Conference on Data Mining*.

[119] Rehák, M., Foltýn, L., Pěchouček, M. and Benda, P. (2005). Trust model for open ubiquitous agent systems, in *Proceedings of the 2005 IEEE International Conference on Intelligent Agent Technology*, pp. 536–542.

[120] Resnick, P., Iacovou, N., Suchak, M., Bergstorm, P. and Riedl, J. (1994). Grouplens: An open architecture for collaborative filtering of netnews, in *Proceedings of the 1994 ACM conference on Computer Supported Cooperative Work*, pp. 175–186.

[121] Resnick, P. and Varian, H. (1997). Recommender systems, *Communications of the ACM* **40**, pp. 56–58.

[122] Rich, E. (1979). User modeling via stereotypes, *Cognitive Science* **3**, pp. 329–354.

[123] Richardson, M., Agrawal, R. and Domingos, P. (2003). Trust management for the semantic web, in *Proceedings of the Second International Semantic Web Conference*, pp. 351–368.

[124] Richardson, M. and Domingos, P. (2002). Mining knowledge-sharing sites for viral marketing, in *Proceedings of the eighth ACM SIGKDD International Conference on Knowledge Discovery and Data Mining*, pp. 61–70.

[125] Schafer, B., Konstan, J. and Riedl, J. (1999). Recommender systems in e-commerce, in *Proceedings of the first ACM conference on Electronic commerce*, pp. 158–166.

[126] Schweizer, B. and Sklar, A. (1961). Associative functions and statistical triangle inequalities, *Publicationes Mathematicae Debrecen* **8**, pp. 169–186.

[127] Shardanand, U. and Maes, P. (1995). Social information filtering: algorithms for automating "word of mouth", in *Proceedings of the 1995 CHI conference on Human Factors in Computing Systems*, pp. 210–217.

[128] Sinha, R. and Swearingen, K. (2001). Comparing recommendations made by online systems and friends, in *Proceedings of the DELOS-NSF Workshop on Personalisation and Rec-

ommender Systems in Digital Libraries.

[129] Stølen, K., Winsborough, W., Martinelli, F. and Massacci, F. (eds.) (2006). *Lecture Notes in Computer Science*, Vol. 3986 (Springer Berlin Heidelberg).

[130] Strang, D. and Soule, S. (1998). Diffusion in organizations and social movements: from hybrid corn to poison pills, *Annual Review of Sociology* **24**, pp. 265–290.

[131] Sugeno, M. (1974). *Theory of fuzzy integrals and its applications*, Ph.D. thesis.

[132] Sun, E., Rosenn, I., Marlow, C. and Lento, T. (2009). Gesundheit! Modeling contagion through Facebook news feed, in *Proceedings of Third International AAAI Conference on Weblogs and Social Media*, pp. 146–153.

[133] Swearingen, K. and Sinha, R. (2001). Beyond algorithms: an HCI perspective on recommender systems, in *Proceedings of the SIGIR 2001 Workshop on Recommender Systems*.

[134] Tang, W., Ma, Y. and Chen, Z. (2005). Managing trust in peer-to-peer networks, *Journal of Digital Information Management* **3**, pp. 58–63.

[135] Time (2002). *Time Person of the Year : 75th Anniversary Celebration* (Time Inc. Home Entertainment).

[136] Torra, V. (1996). The weighted OWA operator, *International Journal of Intelligent Systems* **12**, pp. 153–166.

[137] Travers, J. and Milgram, S. (1969). An experimental study of the small world problem, *Sociometry* **32**, pp. 425–443.

[138] Uchyigit, G. and Ma, M. (eds.) (2008). *Personalization Techniques and Recommender Systems* (World Scientific Publishing).

[139] Uschold, M. and Grüninger, M. (1996). Ontologies: principles, methods and applications, *Knowledge Engineering Review* **11**, pp. 93–136.

[140] Verbiest, N., Cornelis, C., Victor, P. and Herrera-Viedma, E. (2010). Strategies for incorporating knowledge defects and path length in trust aggregation, in *Proceedings of the 23rd International Conference on Industrial, Engineering & Other Applications of Applied Intelligent Systems, to appear.*

[141] Victor, P., Cornelis, C., Teredesai, A. and De Cock, M. (2008). Whom should I trust? The impact of key figures on cold start recommendations, in *Proceedings of the 23rd Annual ACM Symposium on Applied Computing*, pp. 2014–2018.

[142] Wasserman, S. and Faust, K. (1994). *Social Network Analysis: Methods and Applications* (Cambridge University Press).

[143] Watts, D. and Strogatz, S. (1998). Collective dynamics of 'small-world' networks, *Nature* **393**, pp. 440–442.

[144] Weng, J., Miao, C. and Gohl, A. (2006). Improving collaborative filtering with trust-based metrics, in *Proceedings of the 2006 ACM Symposium on Applied Computing*, pp. 1860–1864.

[145] Yager, R. (1988). On ordered weighted averaging aggregation operators in multicriteria decision making, *IEEE Transactions on Systems, Man, and Cybernetics* **18**, pp. 183–190.

[146] Yager, R. (1993). Families of OWA operators, *Fuzzy Sets and Systems* **59**, pp. 125–148.

[147] Yager, R. (2003). Fuzzy logic methods in recommender systems, *Fuzzy Sets and Systems* **136**, pp. 133–149.

[148] Yager, R. and Filev, D. (1999). Induced ordered weighted averaging operators, *IEEE Transactions on Systems, Man, and Cybernetics* **29**, pp. 141–150.

[149] Yager, R. and Kacprzyk, J. (eds.) (1997). *The Ordered Weighted Averaging Operators: Theory and Applications* (Kluwer Academic).

[150] Yildirim, H. and Krishnamoorthy, M. (2008). A random walk method for alleviating the sparsity problem in collaborative filtering, in *Proceedings of the 3rd ACM conference on Recommender systems*, pp. 131–138.

[151] Yuan, W., Guan, D., Lee, Y., Lee, S. and Hur, S. (2010). Improved trust-aware recommender system using small-worldness of trust networks, *Knowledge-Based Systems, in press: doi: 10. 1016/j. knosys. 2009. 12. 004*.

[152] Zadeh, L. (1965). Fuzzy sets, *Information and Control* **8**, pp. 338–353.

[153] Zaihrayeu, I., Pinheiro da Silva, P. and McGuinness, D. (2005). IWTrust: Improving user trust in answers from the web, in *Proceedings of the Third International Conference On Trust Management*, pp. 384–392.

[154] Zhang, S., Ouyang, Y., Ford, J. and Makedon, F. (2006). Analysis of a low-dimensional linear model under recommendation attacks, in *Proceedings of the 29th Annual International ACM SIGIR Conference on Research and Development in Information Retrieval*, pp. 517–524.

[155] Zhang, Y., Wu, Z., Chen, H., Sheng, H. and Ma, J. (2008). Mining target marketing groups from users' web of trust on Epinions, in *Proceedings of the 2008 AAAI Spring Symposium*, pp. 116–121.

[156] Ziegler, C. (2009). *On propagating interpersonal trust in social networks*, Golbeck, J. (ed.) Computing With Social Trust, pp. 133–168.

[157] Ziegler, C. and Golbeck, J. (2007). Investigating correlations of trust and interest similarity - Do birds of a feather really flock together? *Decision Support Systems* **43**, pp. 460–475.

[158] Ziegler, C.-N. and Lausen, G. (2005). Propagation models for trust and distrust in social networks, *Information Systems Frontiers* **7**, pp. 337–358.

[159] Ziegler, N., McNee, S., Konstan, J. and Lausen, G. (2005). Improving recommendation lists through topic diversifications, in *Proceedings of the 14th International World Wide Web Conference*, pp. 22–32.

Subject Index